Made Simple   THE

This new instructive series
has been created
primarily for self-education
but can equally well
be used as
an aid to group study.
However complex the subject,
the reader is taken
step by step,
clearly and methodically,
through the course. Each volume
has been prepared by
experts,
using throughout the
Made Simple technique of teaching.
Consequently the gaining
of knowledge now becomes
an experience to be enjoyed.

Accounting	German
Advanced Algebra & Calculus	Intermediate Algebra & Analytic Geometry
Anthropology	Italian
Art Appreciation	Latin
Art of Speaking	Law
Biology	Management
Book-keeping	Mathematics
Chemistry	New Mathematics
Commerce	Organic Chemistry
Economics	Philosophy
Electricity	Physics
Electronic Computers	Psychology
Electronics	Russian
English	Spanish
French	Statistics
Geology	Typing

THE ART OF SPEAKING
Made Simple

William R. Gondin, Ph.D.
Edward W. Mammen, Ph.D.

Advisory editor
James Dodding

Made Simple Books
W. H. ALLEN   London

© 1967 by Doubleday & Company, Inc., and completely reset
and revised 1970 by W. H. Allen & Company Ltd.

Made and printed in Great Britain
by Butler & Tanner Ltd, Frome and London
for the publishers W. H. Allen & Company Ltd,
Essex Street, London W.C.2

ISBN 0 491 00365 X Casebound
ISBN 0 491 00619 5 Paperbound

Foreword

Speech is the most important means of communication people have with one another and it is essential to be able to use it fluently, effectively and with confidence. It is equally essential, both professionally and socially, to know what is appropriate to the occasion—what to say, when to say it and how to say it.

Spoken English is now an important subject of the curriculum of most schools and colleges, and there are various voice, speech and public speaking examinations held by a number of established organizations such as the English Speaking Board and the Associated Board, of the Royal Schools of Music. This book contains material on all the subjects covered by such examinations and will be a valuable help to teacher and pupil alike.

The book is particularly suitable for the student working alone. He will find the questions and exercises especially useful for checking knowledge and putting new techniques into practice. The list of suggested further reading gives full guidance on more detailed study of all topics discussed.

Each chapter is complete in itself and does not depend on prior reading, although cross-references are given. Whatever the vocal problem, need or interest, the reader will find *The Art of Speaking Made Simple* of immediate help as a practical guide and reference book. There are sections on conversation, interviews, speaking in public, discussion techniques, parliamentary procedure, as well as material for the actor and the verse speaker. The final chapter is designed especially for the reader from overseas who aims to improve the standard of his English pronunciation.

JAMES DODDING

Table of Contents

FOREWORD   v

1 CONVERSATION   1
   (1) What is Conversation?   1
   (2) Conversational Weak Spots and Strong Points   2
   (3) Topics for Conversation   3
       Common Misconceptions   3
       What to Talk About   3
       What Not to Talk About   4
       Discovering and Developing Topics   5
       Is It Topic Trouble?   6
   (4) Adjusting to the Other Fellow   6
       Adjusting to Strangers   7
       Special Problems: The Old   8
       Children   8
       V.I.P.s   9
       The Other Sex   9
       When You Dislike Someone   9
   (5) Attitudes   9
       Good Attitudes   10
       Faulty Attitudes   11
   (6) Getting Conversation Started   12
       Introductions   12
       Starting the Conversation   13
       After the Introduction   14
   (7) Keeping the Conversation Going   15
       Listening   15
       Your Contributions   15
       Transitions   16
       Trouble   17
       End of Conversation   17
   (8) On the Telephone   17
   (9) Faults   18
       Pet Words   18
       Superfluous Words and Phrases   19
       Fad Words   19
       Too Much Slang   19
       Affectations   19
       Exaggeration   19
       Telling Personal Experiences Awkwardly   20
       Forgetting Names   20
   (10) Practice   21

2 INTERVIEWS   22
   (1) Applying for a Position   22
       General Preparation   23
       Special Preparation   25
   (2) The Interview Itself   26
   (3) Interviewing the Applicant   28
       Preparation for the Interview   28
   (4) The Sales Interview   31
       Steps in Selling   32
       Common Faults in Selling   34

3 SPEAKING IN PUBLIC   36
   (1) Feeling at Ease   36
   (2) Basic Concepts   38
   (3) Beginners' Faults   40
   (4) Visual Factors   41
   (5) Types of Delivery   44
   (6) Choosing a Subject   47
   (7) Deciding on the Response You Want   50
       The General Purpose   50
       The Specific Purpose   51
   (8) Analysing the Audience   52
   (9) Toasts   54
   (10) Using a Microphone   57
   (11) Talking on the Radio   57
   (12) Talking on Television   59

4 COMPOSING A SPEECH   60
   (1) The Body of the Speech   61
   (2) The Introduction   64
   (3) The Conclusion   68
   (4) Narration   69
   (5) Exposition   74
   (6) Argument   78
   (7) Composition as a Feeling for Form   84

5 FORMAL SPEAKING PROCEDURE   86
   (1) Rules of Order   87
   (2) The Chair   87
   (3) Rising to be Recognized   89
   (4) Having the Floor   90
   (5) Making and Seconding Motions   90
   (6) The Order of Business   91
       The Call to Order   92
       The Minutes   92
       Reports   93
       General Orders   94
       Unfinished Business   94
       New Business   95
       Adjournment   96

(7) Explanation of the Table of Motions   97
    Precedence   97
    Authority to Interrupt   97
    Need for a Seconder   98
    Debatability   98
    Amendability   98
    Required Votes   98
    Renewability   99
    Special Notes   99
    Page References   99
(8) Table of Motions   100–101
(9) Subsidiary Motions   102
    Motions Regulating Debate   204
    Motions Postponing Consideration   105
(10) Privileged Motions   107
(11) 'Incidental' Motions   110
(12) Main Motions   117
(13) Review Motions   118

6 DISCUSSION TECHNIQUES   121
    (1) Formal and Informal Procedure   121
    (2) Parliamentary Strategy   123
    (3) Organizing an Action Group   125
    (4) Constitutions, By-laws and Rules   131
    (5) Platform Debates   133
    (6) Platform Discussions   136
    (7) Forums   136
    (8) Informal Group Discussion   137
    (9) Discussion as Group Thinking   138
    (10) Requirements for Co-operative Discussion 139
    (11) Pointers on Agenda   141
        Clarification of the Question   142
        Surveying the Facts of the Problem   142
        Diagnosing Possible Causes, Suggesting Possible Solutions 143
        Evaluation   144
        Summarizing   145

7 DEVELOPING THE VOICE   147
    (1) Principles of Practice   147
    (2) Ear Training   148
    (3) Analysing Your Voice   149
    (4) Basic Concepts in Developing the Voice   150
        Free the Voice   150
        Concentrate on Meaning   151
        Let Emotion Help You   151
    (5) The Voice Mechanism   152
        The Vocal Cords and Phonation   153
        The Breath   154
        Resonance   154

(6) Phonation—The Production of the Basic Tone 154
    Achieving Relaxation 156
    Toning Sluggish, Lax Muscles 156
    Faulty Phonation 157
(7) Controlled Breathing 160
    Possible Methods of Breath Control 160
(8) Pitch 162
    To Find Your Habitual Pitch Level 163
    To Find Your Optimum Pitch Level 163
    Varied Pitch Levels 164
    Intonation 165
    Inflexions 166
(9) Volume 168
    To Strengthen a Weak Voice 168
(10) Quality 170
    To Focus the Tone 170
    To Develop Nasal Resonance 171
    Faulty Nasal Resonance 171
    To Develop Oral Resonance 172
    To Develop Throat Resonance 173
(11) Rate 174
    Phrasing 175

8 PRONUNCIATION 177
(1) Acceptable English Pronunciation 177
(2) The Dictionary 177
(3) How to Use a Dictionary 178
(4) Pronunciation Key 179
    Vowels 179
    Consonants 180
    Syllables 180
    Accent 180
(5) Common Mistakes in Pronunciation 181
    Spelling Pronunciations 181
    Reversing the Order of Sounds 183
    Added Sounds 183
    Sounds Left Out 183
    Substitution of One Sound for Another 184
    Confusing Words with Similar Spelling 185
    Accenting the Wrong Syllable 185
    Affectations 186
(6) Aids to Better Pronunciation 188
    Influence of Part of Speech on Pronunciation 188
    Words We Read but Seldom Say 189
    Choice of Pronunciation 189
(7) Foreign Words and Phrases 190
    Latin Words and Phrases 190
    French Words and Phrases 192
    German Words and Phrases 194
    Italian Words 194

(8) Names of Persons and Places   195
  Names of Persons   195
  British Place Names   196
  Foreign Place Names   197

9 ARTICULATION   199
  (1) How Articulation Can Be Improved   199
  (2) The Organs of Speech   201
  (3) The Importance of Listening   202
  (4) Vowels and Diphthongs   203
    The Special Role of Vowels in Speech   204
  (5) Vowel Production   205
    The Extreme Vowels   205
    The Front Vowels   210
    The Low Vowels   211
    The Back Vowels   212
    The Central Vowels   213
    Distortions   216
  (6) The Consonants   218
    The Alveolars   218
    The Linguo-Dentals   226
    The 'R' Sound   227
  (7) General Articulation Faults   228
    Omissions   228
    Additions   229
    Over-Articulation   230
    Foreign Influence   231

10 FOREIGN ACCENT   232
  (1) Stress   232
    Stress in Speech   234
    Strong and Weak Forms   234
  (2) Linking Words and Syllables   235
  (3) Falling and Rising Inflexions   236
  (4) Vowels and Diphthongs   238
    Production of Vowels   238
    Production of Diphthongs   238
    Length of Vowels and Diphthongs   239
  (5) Consonants   240
    The Alveolars   240
    The Linguo-Dentals   240
    The 'R' Sound   240
    The 'W' and 'V' Sounds   241
    The 'Y' and 'J' Sounds   241
  (6) Cognate Confusion   242
    The P, T, K, B, D and G Sounds   244
    Words ending in -d and -ed   245
    Words ending in -s and -es   245

(7) 'NG' Clicks and Confusion 245
 Correcting the Substitution of N for NG 246
 Correcting the NG Click 247
(8) Consonant Combinations 249

ANSWERS 250

SUGGESTED FURTHER READING 252

INDEX 255

CHAPTER ONE

CONVERSATION

Good conversation is fun. It can make an evening pass pleasantly and creatively, even excitingly.

Conversation also has more serious values. It links people together—family, business associates, friends. It is perhaps the most important single factor in establishing or improving human relations.

Good conversation aids us in that much criticized drive to 'get ahead'; but it also helps us to achieve that relaxation, that freedom from worry and care, that peace of mind and soul which we all desire.

Yet many of us, when we plan a party, spend much time preparing food and games but do not give conversation a thought. Although it is bound to be an important part of the evening in any case, we seldom plan for it. We invite guests without considering whether they will have mutual interests to talk about. In introducing those who are meeting each other for the first time we often fail to mention things they have in common that can set them off on a pleasurable conversation.

We may also fail to prepare ourselves to take the lead, if necessary, with a topic we can count on everybody being interested in.

Even in business interviews we may prepare for everything except the very core of the matter. We may come with shoes shined, trousers pressed, fingernails manicured—but vague about what we are going to say.

Many of us are not merely unprepared—we dread conversation itself.

Some of us are shy about meeting strangers; some of us shun working on committees; some of us avoid *any* conversational situation.

Where conversation is avoided it is probably because we feel inadequate in talking to others. We are afraid of repeating the mistakes we made at our first dinner party, or at our first job interview.

Those who find themselves shying from conversation must first examine this feeling of inadequacy, then do something to remedy it.

The two most important first steps are: (*a*) understanding what conversation is, and (*b*) analysing our own conversation to decide what our specific weaknesses are.

(1) What is Conversation?

Conversation, in part, is self-expression. It provides us with opportunities for asserting our individuality, telling the world just how we feel, or 'letting off steam'. Talk of this sort is pleasurable and valuable.

It is like the therapy of gardening, breeding tropical fish, painting, novel-writing or any other form of recreational activity you enjoy. It serves as a sort of safety-valve and can come easily to almost everybody.

However, when a person monopolizes a conversation merely to 'get something off his chest', it makes very bad conversation. It is too one-sided. No number of monologues ever adds up to *real conversation*. When everyone wants to score a goal, the ball doesn't get passed around enough for a good game.

At its best, conversation means the pooling of information, the sharing of interests, the bringing together of ideas.

Conversation is a two-way thing, involving give and take, action and reaction. Indeed it is a many-way thing—the communication of many ideas among many people.

(2) Conversational Weak Spots and Strong Points

If you find yourself shying away from conversation, analyse your experiences in recent conversational situations. Ask yourself such questions as:

Did I find it difficult to pick a *topic* for conversation? Did I cause embarrassment by talking on some tabooed topic, or on some subject that bored other people?

Was adjusting to persons my problem? Did I get tongue-tied in the presence of certain individuals, or of certain *types* of individuals? Did I fail to give proper deference to older or more distinguished persons?

Was my general **attitude** at fault in dealing with people? Was I dogmatic, condescending, argumentative? Did I *adjust* well to the attitudes of others? To their changes in attitude?

Did I have trouble *starting* a conversation? Getting *others* to start? Did I fail to keep a conversation *going*? Did I let it peter out? Could I have moved more smoothly from one topic to another? Was I clumsy in ending a conversation?

Was it some *mechanical* fault that made me ill at ease? Was it mis-pronunciation, forgetting names, over-use of slang?

On the basis of your analysis, give special study to sections of this chapter which most apply to you. Take up one area at a time and follow the suggestions for practice given at the end of the chapter.

Prepare carefully for the more formal conversational situation. If you are to go into a business conference or an interview, become as well informed as you can about its subject. If you are to meet some new people, try to learn as much as you can about them. Even in casual meetings you can do *some* planning—you can *think before you speak*.

But do not prepare and rehearse phrases to use on a specific occasion, for this is futile. You can never anticipate the exact turn a conversation will take. In using this chapter, moreover, you must not expect it to ease you over your very next conversational hurdle and all hurdles thereafter. No chapter, or book for that matter, can tell you what to say when your Aunt Matilda, aged seventy-five, arrives unexpectedly with her pet canary one gloomy Sunday and announces that she plans to spend three weeks with you. But armed with some principles, and some previous practice of these, you ought to be able to greet her or turn her away with more poise than apoplexy.

EXERCISE No. 1

During the coming week take careful note of your conversations and their characteristics. What were your weak spots, your strong point? At the end of the week, decide what you need most to improve upon.

Each successive week, for a month or two, sit down at approximately the same time and repeat the process. Pick a time when your schedule isn't likely to be broken or interrupted.

(3) Topics for Conversation

Common Misconceptions

If your difficulty seems to be finding suitable topics, the real problem may be that you are thinking about topics in the wrong way. You may have some misconceptions concerning the things people talk about.

One common misconception is that only the very unusual event is worth talking about. You ransack your mind for some preposterous coincidence, some tremendous achievement, some shattering experience, some hilarious situation.

Vastly exciting and amusing events do occur in this world, of course, and people enjoy hearing and telling about them. But they are the highlights of good conversation, not its main substance. Many an agreeable evening has been spent in small talk about the ordinary happenings and problems of everyday living—getting the children off to school, whether tomato plants should be staked or not, good places to spend the week-end.

So if you have never had quintuplets nor explored the upper Amazon, nor been forced at the point of a gun to prepare breakfast for four bank robbers, you need not remain silent. However simple the life you lead, it provides plenty of material for conversation.

Another misconception is that a topic must be literary, or abstruse, or very learned.

People do talk about the special theory of relativity, gambits in chess, and atomic fission, but more often they talk about life and love, and food and drink, and the weather. So do not feel that only topics you have studied for months are suitable for conversation.

What to Talk About

As a matter of fact, almost any topic is suitable for conversation.

You can talk about basketball or badminton, knitting or crocheting, truth or beauty, tea or sympathy, hitch-hiking or door-to-door selling, the Stock Exchange or the supermarket, or shoes, or ships, or sealing-wax, or cabbages, or kings.

You can discuss books, plays, films, television programmes, current affairs, national policies, or local politics.

You can swap stories, anecdotes, observations, opinions. You can recall some idea from a magazine article, a newspaper column, a sermon.

Your reaction to the idea may be more important to the conversation than the topic itself, for one purpose of conversation is to enable other people to compare their thoughts with yours. They hope you will prove enthusiastic about the same things as they are; they find minor differences of opinion intriguing.

Conversation is a friendly art with a double pleasure—the warmth of sharing similar beliefs, and the stimulation of discovering differences.

So don't hesitate to express agreement, for fear of being thought unoriginal; and don't hesitate to express disagreement, for fear of being considered contrary.

If you were unimpressed by some film the others are raving about, don't think you must stay silent about it. If you think reporters are a nuisance at international conferences, say so. But remember to voice your dissent in such a friendly way that the conversation can continue. If you force your opinion as if you had a mission to convert others, you will not be contributing to the conversation, but stopping it.

Air your prejudices, too, if you want, provided you show by words or your tone that you know them to be prejudices; and provided, of course, that they are not offensive. If you can't stand calorie-counting, or amateur psychoanalysis, don't hold back. On the other hand, avoid becoming known as a person who is 'anti' everything, or who 'can't stand' things. It matters very little to anyone that you 'can't stand roses'. And not at all to the rose.

Some persons like to make challenging statements. To an admirer of Toscanini, they will say: 'Don't you think he took everything too fast?' Such remarks may provoke stimulating discussion; they may also provoke discord. The challenge must be carefully handled, and perhaps you had better leave it till you are very sure of yourself and your company.

Before offering a topic, be sure you know something about it. This doesn't mean your knowledge must be encyclopaedic. But be sure you are familiar with it. If you have had only a week-end of skiing, you had better not tell how to execute a stem-Christy (there may be an expert present); you will be much safer describing your first reactions to skiing, your first fall.

What Not to Talk About

The wide variety of topics available to you is proved by the small number of topics to be avoided.

Parading your private life before strangers is taboo. So also is shaming other people by describing their faults to a general company. Unless you aim to be untouchable, you had better not tell the plots of books, films or plays to those who haven't yet enjoyed them. Your chances of being invited again are slight if upon being introduced you promptly launch into a shady story.

Having only *one* topic for conversation is as bad as having none, or violating a taboo. We have all suffered from the bore who could only 'talk shop', or who would never let anyone forget his aches and pains, or who chattered incessantly about the brilliance of his children.

If you think the variety of your topics is limited, set about finding some new ones.

Discovering and Developing Topics

You read newspapers daily, probably a magazine or two; you listen to radio programmes or watch television; you hear stories from friends; maybe you go to church and hear sermons; maybe you attend the theatre; you have a multitude of interesting experiences with customers, salespeople, colleagues, your family.

These are fruitful sources of topics for conversation. But are you neglecting them? Do you use reading simply as a time-filler? Is the newspaper only something to look at while you travel from home to work and back? Do you listen without really paying much attention? Do you say, 'That was a good talk,' and promptly forget it? Do you hurry so busily and thoughtlessly from moment to moment that you never let your experiences sink in and become significant?

If so, begin to make use of these sources.

When you come across a likely item in the newspaper, make a mental note of it. Circle it in pencil. Better still, tear it out.

Fix in mind any assertions you find in a magazine, if you think they are worth repeating: for example, 'The Victorians were perfectionists. They had a naïve faith that there was a best way of doing things, and they kept on trying until they found it.'

Remember the pungent phrase from the speech or sermon: 'Every man is an unrepeatable experiment.'

Out of such materials, build your own storehouse of topics. If your memory is not good enough to store such bits, keep a notebook or a card-file.

Develop this material, moreover, while it is still fresh in mind. Talk an idea over with family and friends. It may seem quite a different, certainly a fuller one when you have examined and explored its possibilities.

Read up on topics that particularly interest you. The *British Humanities Index*, which should be available in your local library, will help you to find articles on the subject. Make this reading active. Moreover, for every hour you spend reading, set aside some time afterwards for thinking about what you've read.

If you keep on discovering and developing topics in these ways, you will never be at a loss for conversation.

Is It Topic Trouble?

One possibility remains—that you haven't really got topic trouble at all. There may have been topics you could discuss competently, but you were too shy to speak up when they were mentioned.

You may have set your sights too high. You may have talked very well without realizing it.

Or you may have wrong goals. You may have been comparing yourself with someone who is a good conversationalist, but in a style not suited to you.

If that is the case, start afresh. Next time the opportunity arises, sit in, but only as a listener. Use your silence. Listen carefully. Practise listening. Be able to report afterwards, to yourself, or to others, what topics were covered and how.

Compare the participants, their successes and failures. Evaluate their techniques.

At another time, though still making no direct contributions, ask questions. Try to draw people out. And evaluate what you hear.

At still another time use only single-statement contributions and questions. Evaluate the performances of others. Evaluate your own.

On the next occasion let yourself go. See how you do.

You may be very proud of the result.

EXERCISE NO. 2

Jot down a list of possible topics from your past reading and listening. Make a separate list of topics you have heard discussed in groups you were with during the week.

Do any topics occur on both lists?

Could you have used any other of the topics from the first list?

If so, why didn't you?

(4) Adjusting to the Other Fellow

One may be able to talk at considerable length on some topic, or a great many topics, and yet not be adept at conversation. One may tell some very good stories connected with the topic and yet provoke groans and boredom instead of laughter and interest.

For good conversation involves *two, three, or more persons*, not just one. It demands recognition of the knowledge and interests of the *other fellow*, of the *group*.

The good conversationalist tries to find topics the others *also* are interested in and *also* know something about.

The good conversationalist, as far as he can, avoids the wrong topics —those that will have little appeal for the others or that may embarrass them.

The good conversationalist *slants* his contributions to his listeners, much as a magazine slants its stories and articles to the particular group of readers it seeks to serve.

If you meet a designer who has worked on the 'Whirlfast' mixer which you have recently purchased, you can tell him so, you can praise the appliance, or ask him about problems in designing it. But you must not begin with a recital of defects you have found in it or with your notions of how he should have designed it.

Try to *stimulate* talking. Like Falstaff, be not only witty in yourself, 'but the cause that wit is in other men'. Try not to hinder the interchange of ideas. Try to keep the conversation moving. Try to keep it pleasant.

With old friends, this is no problem. We know their likes and dislikes. We enjoy talking about the same things. We feel at ease with them, even during long silences. If we didn't, we wouldn't be old friends.

But with strangers, difficulties arise. Discovering their interests may take effort and time. We may even have grown shy of meeting and talking with strangers generally.

Are those your problems? If so, let us see what you can do to make meeting and talking with strangers easier and more pleasurable.

Adjusting to Strangers

When you know that you are going to meet strangers at some function, try to find out something about them from mutual friends. Inquire about their occupations and interests.

When you go into a strange home, be observant. Look for clues that will help you to know the people who live there a bit better. What pictures, books, magazines do they live with? Do they read *The Times* and *The Observer*? Or do they enjoy *Reveille* and *The People*? If you don't like their taste in bric-à-brac or lampshades, cross those topics off your list. Look for things you can praise or that suggest a mutual interest.

At a large party, survey the several groups before you join one. Try to spot a likely-looking one, one whose members at least *look* as if they might have something in common with you.

When you join a group, listen for a while for hints about the speakers' personalities before making contributions yourself. It is better to hold back a bit than to blunder. (If what you hear doesn't interest you, wander off to another group and listen there for a while before joining in.)

Pay attention to the remarks made by the host or hostess in introducing you to the stranger. For example, with 'Mr. Carr has just returned from the Middle East,' as a lead, you can comment that the Arab countries are much in the news these days; or you can ask him about his mission, or his opinion on recent events there. Or you can merely express pleasure at the opportunity of learning about the Middle East at first hand. In a few moments you will probably know considerably more about him.

Volunteer information about yourself. Mention what you do, or happen to have been doing just before you met him. This will probably lead him to tell you something about himself.

Ask *personal*, but *not too personal*, questions. Obviously, one doesn't ask a person's salary. But if one's host is with Unilever, you can certainly ask of a guest, 'Are you with Unilever too?' If he is, you can express interest or go on to further questions. If he isn't, he'll probably say what his work really is, and you can go on from there.

The stranger's first few remarks should give you clues to his interest. If he says, 'This rain is certainly good for crops,' you know that his interests are different from one who says, 'If we have any more rain, the shops may as well close down.'

The other fellow may be more ill at ease than you. Help him out. Talk about small matters to put him at ease.

Be on the alert for changes in mood and be ready to shift with them. Notice the other fellow's facial expressions, his hand movements, his stance. When does he perk up? When does he look vague or uninterested?

With strangers, especially, shun the argumentative approach, the challenging statement. Avoid politics and religion. You probably won't get far with such topics, and your host will certainly not thank you.

Special Problems: The Old

The elderly are a special group. They deserve deference, of course, and particular consideration. They sometimes show peculiar quirks of memory. The immediate past sometimes fades from their minds and they may show interest only in their own present concerns and the distant past. Encourage them to talk about their hobbies, or get them to reminisce. You may be rewarded with some interesting stories of the old days.

Some elderly people keep alert and take an active interest in news of the day, so be ready to talk of national and international events. If they are semi-invalids, they may be glad to have someone to talk to. But let *them* do most of the talking.

Children

The *young* are a problem too. Avoid the question approach. 'How's my little man?' or 'How's school?' will, at best, draw a monosyllable in answer. Better, tell them some interesting experience of yours. Almost any sort of animal story will do for the toddlers, horses and dogs for the seven-to-twelves, sports and hobbies for the teens.

Some will be shy. Remember that you are strange to them and formidably old and big. Don't rush at them with endearments; don't make them the centre of interest. Hold back, show a polite interest in them, but no more than in the others present. Let them size you up and get used to you.

Some will be forward or unruly. If you are kicked in the shins or are asked about your bald spot, be as good-natured as you can.

Above all, don't talk *down* to them. They aren't adults of a smaller and inferior breed, and they resent being treated as such. They are *children*, with their own interests and view of life, and very conscious of their own individuality. Talk straight and simply to them, and your reward will be an interesting conversation.

V.I.P.s

Having to talk to one's *superiors* is a problem we all encounter. In business and social life, we feel an added tension on meeting persons far above us in prestige, authority, skill, or knowledge.

Don't kowtow to them. Don't be so overawed that all you can do is simper and fawn. On the other hand, don't try to impress them by showing off, nor seek to impress others by attempting to show them up.

Keep your own individuality. Show the celebrity respect without sacrificing self-respect. Ask his judgement on matters in his field, but don't be afraid to give your own point of view.

Remember, too, the celebrity is as human as you are. He probably likes to talk about his children, or even about good food or the weather.

The very important person may prove to be a bore. If he's a bridge-builder who knows only how much better his bridges are than anyone else's, treat him as you would other bores. Listen politely for as long as you think necessary, then excuse yourself and move on.

The Other Sex

The other sex is an eternal problem, and not only in conversation. So the advice here will be kept simple. Unless you have serious designs, stay away from sex as a topic. Find something to praise in the other person, find some topic not exclusively male or female.

A woman might comment on the aroma of cigars but hardly on their taste or draw. For a man, similarly, comment on coiffures might do; but not opinions on curlers and cosmetics.

When You Dislike Someone

Occasionally you must talk to a person you *dislike*. Here the advice is also simple. Keep your talk polite, very polite; and keep it impersonal.

(5) Attitudes

A group of students, asked what bothered them most in conversation, answered that it wasn't the topic, or the people as such, but rather the *attitudes* of people. They found it easy to talk with the *friendly* person, difficult to talk with the *dogmatic* person.

Are you uncertain about your own attitude? Is your worry, not *what* you say, but *how* you say it? Do you think you might improve your attitudes, but don't know quite what to aim at?

Below are two lists, one of attitudes generally considered good in conversation, one of faulty attitudes. If you think you have some of the good attitudes, strengthen and develop them. If you're afraid you have some of the faulty attitudes, change them.

Good Attitudes

Be interested. Be interested in what's going on, in what's being talked about: in the other fellow, and in what he's doing.

Be interested, not just in the one person you know very well, but in **all** the persons in the group. Let your gaze move from eye to eye. Pick out the person who hasn't said much, who looks ill at ease, and make a special point of talking to *him*.

Be friendly. Conversation withers if you are critical of the persons present, or are caustic about their contributions, or show, by your expression, that you don't think much of them.

Don't be misled into copying the type of insulting banter that goes on between professional comedians. Their feuds are carefully concocted by their script-writers, and have no counterpart in genuine conversation.

Be cheerful. Smile. Make it an interested, friendly smile. Show your good humour in the way you say things.

Leave your tragic mask at home. Don't try to get people to gather round by exhibiting what a hurt, misunderstood soul you are.

Be animated, and yet relaxed. You're alive, so let your face and gestures show it. Time enough for immobility when rigor mortis sets in. If you are lively and enthusiastic, other people will pick it up and respond in the same way.

But good conversation also has a certain calmness, a feeling of relaxation about it. It isn't hard work: it is a refreshing *rest* from work.

Be flexible. Topics change, and people, and moods. The good conversationalist changes with them. Tenacity is a quality we admire in a bulldog, and rigidity in a ramrod. But neither of these qualities has a place in conversation.

Be tactful. Follow that old adage, think *before* you speak. Think *first*, not *afterwards*. That is the essence of tactfulness.

If your neighbour's son has been expelled from school, keep off the topics of juvenile delinquency and progressive education.

We can't help wounding people at times because we do not know all their sensitive spots. But we should try not to wound through mere thoughtlessness.

Be courteous. One could make a presentable case for the idea that good conversation is good manners. This does not mean merely remembering to say 'Please' when asking for something, or thanking one's host for a pleasant evening. It does mean having a general attitude of consideration for others.

Dr. Johnson was notorious for his colossal rudeness, but he was much more a monologist than a conversationalist. People swallowed his insults for the sake of his enthralling discourses.

Quote Dr. Johnson's definition of 'oats', if you want to—'food for horses in England, for people in Scotland'—but only if there are no Scots present.

Faulty Attitudes

Don't be dogmatic. Avoid the sweeping generalizations, such as 'All politicans are corrupt.' Lord Acton took care to say, 'All power *tends* to corrupt.'

Moderate your statements. Avoid *all* and *always,* Use *some, sometimes, a few, many, a great many, occasionally, infrequently,* whichever you think is warranted. Be careful, too, not to say *golfers* when you really mean *those golfers I happen to have met during my three-day stay at Pitlochry.*

Learn the face-saving and argument-avoiding uses of: *perhaps; do you think; last week I heard someone say that; maybe I'm wrong, but.*

More important, avoid using a dogmatic *tone.* Some people manage to say, 'It looks like snow,' as if they were professional meteorologists and infallible to boot. Conversely, you can get away with outrageous exaggerations if you say them lightly and with a twinkle.

Don't be condescending. An attitude of being superior to everything and everybody will soon leave you in splendid isolation. There are better amusements than sitting alone looking down one's nose.

Don't be argumentative. Almost everybody likes a good fight—in the prize ring or the political arena—but no one is overjoyed to discover a battle in the living room.

Save your strength for fighting the good fight where it will do some good—in the courts or at the polls.

Take the chip off your shoulder when you're going into company. The company will have a better time, and so will you. Do not argue for argument's sake. When you disagree, be, in Robert Louis Stevenson's phrase, an 'amicable adversary'.

Don't be lifeless. The other fellow expects to get some response from you to his witticism. Don't let him carry the entire burden of the talking. And *look* interested—even if you're not. This will at least encourage him to keep the conversation going until you can think of a way of turning it.

Moreover, make your responses something more than monosyllables.

Conversation is a game which requires at least two players, and no game is fun if one player is half-hearted about it.

Don't be insincere. Praise people, but don't overpraise them. Don't gush, don't be fulsome. And praise the right thing. If your hostess serves excellent food on acceptable but undistinguished china, praise the food, not the plates.

Don't be egocentric. Express your opinions and state your reactions without giving the impression that you think the universe revolves about you. Don't talk in such a way that your topics can be described as 'the Pyrenees and me', 'inflation and me', 'the Taj Mahal and me', 'the High Court and me', 'the decimal point and me', etc.

Don't aim to be 'the life and soul of the party'. We admire the wonderful story-teller, the brilliant wit, the character whose infectious humour keeps the party convulsed with laughter. But we shouldn't let our admiration lead us into thinking that our every remark must be a joke, that the chief goal of conversation is laughter. Good humour is as important as humour, and good conversation can be serious as well as gay.

Telling a good story is an act which improves with practice. You can gather humorous phrases to embellish your anecdotes by reading magazines such as *Punch*, or authors such as Oscar Wilde—but be careful to avoid using overworked or hackneyed expressions.

Try to find your own strengths in conversation. You may discover that the person who is regarded as the best conversationalist in your group is the one who *listens* better than anyone else.

Don't be a mumbler. Speak clearly. Speak up. Before a remark can be understood, before a question can be answered, before a joke can be laughed at, it must be heard, and it must be intelligible.

(6) Getting Conversation Started

Some people get off to a bad start in conversation by becoming confused during introductions. These are often the same people who don't help their guests much in introducing them. Others sail briskly through the introduction stage, and then come to a dead halt.

Let us examine these two phases of beginning a conversation:

Introductions

The principles underlying introductions are not difficult. Always introduce the man to the woman (defined here as a female of at least eighteen): 'Mrs. Smith, may I introduce Mr. Jones?' (The only exceptions are that a woman is introduced to a member of the Royal Family, a member of the aristocracy, an older man distinguished by his country, the Prime Minister, or a church dignitary.)

Girls under eighteen are introduced to the other person, whether man or woman: 'Mr. Thomas, my daughter Jane.'

In general, in introducing people of the same sex, the younger person is introduced to the older, and the less to the more distinguished person.

The wording of the introduction may take any one of several forms.

The most formal is: 'May I introduce——'

The most typical is the mere saying of the two names: 'Mrs. Clark, Mrs. Brown', the first name spoken with a rising inflection, the second with a falling inflexion. In introducing a man to a woman, the woman's name is said first: 'Mrs. Clark, Mr. Grant.'

Other forms include: 'Mr. Black, may I introduce you to Mrs. Cary?' or 'Mr. Black, I should like to introduce you to Mrs. Cary.'

'Mrs. Blane, this is——'

'Mrs. Clements, do you know Mrs. Fisher?'

'Mrs. Clements, you know Mrs. Fisher, don't you?'

'Mr. Huggard, have you met Miss Jebb?' (But not, 'Miss Jebb, have you met Mr. Huggard?')

In introducing the members of one's family socially, omit such titles as *Mr.* and *Mrs.* 'Mr. Tarr, this is my wife.'

A woman introduces her husband to friends as 'Harry'; to acquaintances as 'my husband.'

Introduce your son's wife to friends as 'Jack's wife'; to acquaintances as 'my daughter-in-law'. For other in-laws, use: 'This is my father-in-law', 'This is my wife's brother', 'This is my sister Ellen's husband'.

Young people generally introduce each other without titles: 'Harold Thorp, Peg Ortley'.

To introduce yourself, say: 'I am Fred Nash', 'I am Ethel Robinson'.

In introducing one person to a group, introduce him to all at a small party; if the party is large, to one or two people and rely on these to make him acquainted with others.

In replying to an introduction, simply smile, or say, 'How do you do?' or 'How do you do, Miss Swift?'

Exercise No. 3

The Smiths have just settled down in Bromley. The family consists of: Mr. Smith, his wife, their married son, Richard, their daughter Ellen, 20, their other daughter Ruth, 16, and Richard's wife, Helen.

The day after they've moved in, there arrive in quick succession three callers: Mrs. Brown a church-worker; Mrs. Early, a neighbour; and Colonel Black, a friend of Mr. Smith's from his school days, but not known to the rest of the Smith family.

Assume you are one of the Smiths, that you answered the door for the first of the callers, and that you must introduce the rest of the family and also the other callers. Get friends or members of your own family to take various roles.

Starting the Conversation

We have discussed the general forms of introduction. But the host, or whoever does the introducing, should also mention some fact, tell something about either or both the persons introduced, that will help to start them off in conversation. Say: 'Mrs. Green is Secretary of our 'Women's Institute', or 'Mrs. Green grows the best roses in this part of the world', or 'Mr. Fitch is with the B.B.C.', or 'Mr. Fitch does a great deal of sailing'.

There is a story that a very successful and well-known stage collaboration began when an author and producer were introduced by their host with the remark: 'You two ought to have something in common because you both have red hair and you both look discouraged.'

Even at a large party, the attentive host will try to remain a few minutes with newly-introduced guests to see that they get into conversation.

After the Introduction

If you're uncertain about the other person's name, be sure to get it straight. This is insurance against the arrival of a friend to whom you will have to introduce the new acquaintance.

If the name is unusual, you may comment cautiously on this, or ask about the spelling, for some people are very proud of their names. But Osbert Thwistletick has probably suffered enough from his name already, without your comment. In that case, try, discreetly to check up on his name with your host or hostess. If you really *have* forgotten his name when someone else arrives to be introduced, you simply have to be honest about it. Apologize and ask him his name again.

If you cannot think of any original remark with which to start the conversation, you can always fall back on the standard 'It's a lovely party, isn't it?' or some pleasant comment about the house or the other guests.

Keep to light, casual topics for a while: the party, the house, the guests, the occasion, the weather, the food, the difficulty of managing the egg nog, the hors-d'œuvres, the napkin. . . .

Let more serious topics develop later.

Keep the *tone* light at the beginning. An industrialist and an economist, on being introduced, adopted a bantering tone. 'You're one of those fellows who tell us how to run a business.' 'Well, you seem to like it. You're always stealing our best brains to work for you.' Several more smiling interchanges, and they settled down to serious talk.

Asking the other fellow about himself and his work or interests, or volunteering information about yourself, are, as has been suggested, excellent starters. 'Do you come from this part of the country?' 'Have you lived here long?' Or, if the host has mentioned his being an engineer, you can well ask whether he is a civil, electrical or chemical engineer. But don't be too personal.

In volunteering information, be sure merely to mention what you do or what you're interested in. Don't launch into a five-minute description of your entire working-day routine.

Finding a mutually satisfactory topic to talk about, and the right tone, may take time and effort.

Sometimes two people 'click' immediately. Almost as soon as they are introduced, they are immersed in exchanging hints on the cultivation of mushrooms or where to stay in Venice.

But sometimes half a dozen or more topics will be attempted and none will strike a spark. If this happens, don't give up. Keep trying. Bearing in mind what you know of the other fellow or the group, keep throwing out the best ideas you can. All of a sudden, there it will be —the thing that two of you, or all of you, can have a very good time talking about.

(7) Keeping the Conversation Going

There are many factors involved in keeping a conversation going, not the least being that the participants are willing to go on talking. Here are a few suggestions to help you.

Listening

Listen to what is being said. Don't let the talk flow over and past you like water over a stone. Focus on the ideas, focus sharply.

Listen actively. Let yourself react to what is said. Think about it. Feel about it. Show your reaction. Nod, smile. Don't be a jelly fish, floating passively with the tide.

Try to listen so well that you will be able to tell afterwards fairly accurately what was said. Concentrate on the topic or the aspect of it that is being discussed *now*. Don't think ahead to what may be said two minutes from now. This may help you endure a boring speech. But conversation requires alertness. You don't want to come to, suddenly, to find everyone waiting for you to answer a question you haven't heard. That's stopping the conversation, not keeping it going.

Don't interrupt. Listen politely to the other fellow. Give him his say. Don't be so anxious to cut in with your idea that you disconcert the person talking. Learn to listen so well that you can tell when he *is* coming to the end of his contribution, so that you can come in with yours as a fellow contributor, not an intruder. Then you can have your say, and you will have been a pleasant companion too.

Your Contributions

Your contributions may be of almost any sort: forthright statements of fact, questions, expressions of opinion, mild disagreement, comments refining what has already been said to something that you think is closer to the truth.

But make sure that in your contribution, as in your listening, you are 'on the ball'. Don't hark back to sports cars, when the group has left that topic ten minutes ago and is now discussing income tax. And don't spend your time planning what to say when they get round to skin-diving. The planned bright remark usually sounds dragged in.

Try to make your contributions more than monosyllables. *Yes, no, perhaps,* are not stimulating. Give your fellow-talkers something to work on. On the other hand, don't deliver orations, long discourses. Be crisp. Let your remark have a beginning and an end. You may have a lot to say on the topic. But the other fellow may have a few worth-while ideas too. Give him a chance.

Remember the point made at the beginning of this chapter: conversation means give-and-take. The long contribution may stifle talk. The too-short one does little to help.

Transitions

The time comes when the best of topics seems to be exhausted. Interest wanes, contributions lag. That's the time to turn to a *new* topic.

One way to make the transition is to let the old topic die. Miss Frost says the last word on central-heating. Silence. Then, out of nowhere, 'I met an interesting character last week. He breeds worms.' And you're off to interesting characters, worms or odd occupations.

Another way is to pick up the last bit of talk on the old topic and shift by one or more steps to something new. When no one has anything to add on different types of mortgages, you may remark: 'Mortgages don't come into plays much any more, do they? In the old days no self-respecting drama could do without one. The suspense was terrific, everybody wondering whether Sir Jasper was going to be paid off or not in the last act. But nowadays it's bigamy, and psychoneurotics . . . .' So there you are, right in the middle of modern drama. Or bigamy. Or psychoanalysis.

A third way is to shift suddenly and sharply, making no pretence that you're doing anything else. 'Well, we've about finished Hemingway, haven't we? If nobody minds I'd like to ask about that picture over there. It's bothered me ever since I came . . .' Or more simply, 'To change the subject . . .'

Try not to change the subject unwittingly. If the topic is wonder drugs, and someone is telling how her Aunt Martha was cured, don't latch onto the *Aunt* part and give your Aunt Emma's recipe for elder-berry wine. If you must talk about aunts, restrict yourself to those who have swallowed aureomycin and lived.

Don't change the subject too soon. While the topic still seems to interest the others, don't let your waning interest lead you into pushing them around. Make a polite comment or two, or sit silent and try to look interested. A certain amount of patience is the price that has to be paid for the delight of good conversation.

Trouble

Sooner or later we all make a *faux pas*. In the excitement of talking, we momentarily forget the tragedy that has happened to some member of the group. Before we know it we have blundered and said something that hurts.

The way out depends on the individual situation. If you've blundered badly, and know the people well, perhaps you'd better say, 'I'm sorry, Jane,' and move on to another topic. But if you've only veered close to danger, then do your best to veer swiftly away. Do not make a scene by profuse apologies, and try not to become flustered. By staying poised yourself, you help the other person do the same.

When it's the other person who has blundered, do your bit to help. Become interested in the safe topic which she happens to think of, and talk about that. If she becomes flustered, supply one of your own.

End of Conversation

There are times when conversation is out of place. The game of bridge doesn't require conversation, and some players prefer silence during the play, except for the bidding. We go to the theatre to hear the play, not a neighbour's comments. (A converse suggests itself here: if you have friends in for the evening, ask if they'd like to see a particular television programme before you condemn them to a watch-night of silence.)

The best of conversations must end. Start to go before the other fellow takes out his watch, don't dawdle over the coats and avoid starting new conversations at the door. Pay your respects briefly, and go.

Ending a conversation is also a way of keeping one going—the next one, the one you hope you'll be invited for.

(8) On the Telephone

To the caller at the other end, a telephone conversation conveys the same friendly interest that a guest in your home feels as you give him your smiling, warm attention. Don't let the impersonality of the instrument betray you into dead-pan talking. Use a pleasant and friendly conversational tone.

Speak clearly, precisely, and energetically on the phone. Open the mouth for the vowels, produce the consonants firmly (see Chapter Nine). The telephone is not a high-fidelity instrument, and *Smith* may sound like *Fish* if you slur or mumble.

Talk unhurriedly. If you talk too fast, you will only have to repeat.

Speak directly into the phone, your lips half an inch away from the mouthpiece.

To introduce yourself on the phone, simply say, 'This is John Brown' or 'Good morning, Mr. Jones. John Brown calling.' If the one who answers is not the person you want, say 'May I speak to Mr. Jones, please? This is John Brown.' If you're calling on a business matter and don't want any particular person, begin with your business: 'Furniture department, please,' or 'Will you please take an order for——?' If you think you've got the wrong number, don't ask sharply, 'Who is that?' or 'What number is that?' Say courteously, 'I beg your pardon, but is that Waterloo 0109?'

In answering a call at your office, give your name, or your department and name, or the name of your firm and your name, whichever is most suitable. At home, answer with your name, your number or 'Hello', letting your caller introduce himself. Avoid 'This is John Brown's residence', for it sounds as if you were acting the part of a butler. If you are asked to answer the phone in the house of a friend, it is best to say the number clearly.

Finally, answer calls promptly and let your conversation be as brief as the situation permits. The telephone allows only two to talk at a time. By humouring a long-winded acquaintance you may be discourteous to a friend who is trying to call you. For good telephone conversation, remember the motto: 'Phone as you would be phoned to'.

(9) Faults

The major faults in our conversation are, of course, the violation of any of its underlying principles, such as talking on topics which are taboo, or conversing without regard for other people.

But there are also several mechanical faults which we should avoid. These result from carelessness, allowing ourselves to slip into a conversational rut, not thinking seriously about conversational techniques, not criticizing our own conversational efforts.

Do you have any of the faults below? If so, try to eliminate them by adopting the suggestions for correction.

Pet Words

A common fault is to have pet words and to use them whether they are suitable or not.

Some people call all things they like or want to praise *super*, or *great*, or *fabulous*. They describe all things they dislike or consider unsatisfactory as *ghastly*, or *poisonous*, or *grim*, or *putrid*. Sometimes an overheard conversation seems to consist largely of *too awful* and *terrific*.

Obviously, a mountain is not *super*; and there are many words other than *ghastly* for describing people, places and books.

The correction lies in learning to use those other words. Eliminate the pet words from your conversation for a while. Try to use terms which fit what you are describing. Refine your evaluations. Praise and blame with discrimination. Think first: is it *excellent, good, fair, poor, completely lacking in merit*? Learn to use *admirable, deficient, awesome, spurious*. Build your vocabulary. Then, if you wish, return to *fabulous* and *ghastly*, but use them properly.

Superfluous Words and Phrases

Some people, add *naturally*, or *really*, or *actually*, or *literally* to most of their remarks: 'Naturally, I told him to go, and naturally, he——' Other overused phrases are: *frankly, to tell the truth, so to speak, you see, you know, if you see what I mean, do you get the point?*
Eliminate such unnecessary words and phrases.

Fad Words

Still other persons load their talk with the fashionable words and phrases of the moment. They do not *dislike* things, they are *allergic* to them. At present *overall picture, contact, dynamic, process, basic, in terms of*, could well be used less often. These words and phrases are over-used and abused, when not misused.

Too Much Slang

There's nothing wrong with slang itself. Even university professors use it—though perhaps confined to old forms now considered 'acceptable'.
But much newly-coined slang hardly lasts the year out.
Avoid too much slang. Use it occasionally and sparingly when you think it will lend vigour and colour to your conversation.

Affectations

Occasionally a person, after studying French for perhaps two years, wants people to know how well she has been educated. She sprinkles her conversation with *bête noire, accouchement, fin de siècle, amour*, etc. Don't join her ranks. Avoid using too many foreign words and phrases.
Also occasionally, we meet affectation with a reverse twist. The well-educated person decides to be 'one of the boys'. He slips crude or 'with it' expressions into otherwise very grammatical sentences. Such an attempt is as futile as the result is ludicrous.
In conversation, don't feel that the addition of a few too-well-chosen words will make you something different from what you are.

Exaggeration

You must have heard a would-be wit proclaim his story beforehand as 'the funniest story I ever heard', only to look crestfallen when the company didn't laugh quite as hard as he expected. Or you've heard an enthusiast describe the wonders of a gadget, and then have to back down when some more objective user listed its limitations.
Avoid embarrassment by avoiding exaggeration or a too-big build-up.
Your story may go over better if you introduce it with 'I heard a funny story about that the other night.'

Telling Personal Experiences Awkwardly

An interesting personal experience can be ruined by too much dialogue, and by too much 'So he said', 'So I said', 'And she said', 'And they said'. There's more apparatus here than story.

An interesting personal experience can also be ruined by too much detail: 'I went into this tobacconist's—I was in a bit of a hurry as I wanted to catch the 3.30 train, it's the only decent one in the afternoon —you probably know the one I mean, it's the little one almost next door to Barclay's—there used to be a ladies' hairdresser above it, but I think that closed down a few months ago—at any rate I had run out of cigarettes so I went into this little tobacconist's—I had a dark blue suit on——' It's going to be a long while before anything happens in this story.

Good stories can be ruined by vagueness of detail: 'Well, it seems there was this man and he went into this shop and he asked for one of those, those what-d'ye-call-'ems. . . .' This man doesn't seem to know what 'this' story is about.

Make up your mind what the point of your personal experience is. Give names or not as you please. Mention only the details that count, but be specific about those. Use dialogue sparingly, to advance the story or to reveal character.

Listen to good story-tellers to improve your technique. And read stories for the help they can give. There's a very good one which begins: 'Once upon a time there were three bears, a father bear, a mother bear, and a baby bear.' A wonderful opening, for with fewer than twenty words, you're right into the story.

Forgetting Names

People like to have their egos bolstered. To remember the other person's name is to please him, to praise him by showing him that he's worth remembering. Knowing the names of his constituents is the politician's stock-in-trade.

By forgetting the other person's name you hurt him. You are acknowledging that you have forgotten an essential portion of his identity. Such forgetfulness is, therefore, a conversational fault which should be remedied.

If you forget names, it is probably because you *do* nothing about remembering them. Or perhaps you are so excited and confused during introductions that you never consciously hear a name to remember.

To help yourself overcome this handicap you should say to yourself, before attending a function where you know that you will meet strangers, that this time you're going to remember names. During introductions, fix the idea of remembering names in your mind. Help yourself by repeating the name, 'How do you do, Miss Finch.' If you are uncertain about the name, ask to have it repeated. During the conversation, use the name once or twice. In such ways you can fix the name in your memory.

There are several systems for remembering names. You can try associating the name in some way with the person. Pick an outstanding characteristic of the person: red hair—Mrs. Carroll; explorer—Mr. Stark. Or select some group of personal characteristics: small woman with large, blue eyes—Miss Janes. Another system is to use the name itself as a link. For Mr. Cuff, say 'link', silently to yourself; for Mr. Church, add a silent 'hill'. Some people use numbering systems, 1—Clark, 2—Firestone. Others try to find a key word beginning with the same letter as the name: Bergenthal—berry.

Try out these systems, and select the one you find most helpful. Or combine two systems; or develop one of your own. The possible weaknesses of the association systems are that you may remember the key better than the name, or, worse, that you may not remember the key.

However, *using* names and *concentrating* on remembering them are probably as efficient as any system. And you can strengthen your memory by reviewing names after you have met three or four persons.

(10) Practice

There are very few practice *exercises* for conversation. One can rehearse the telling of a story. One can practise introductions.

The best *practice* for conversation is conversation itself.

Practise at home with your family. If you feel your weakness is topics, talk about the play you have all seen (or the film, or the television programme). Try to keep the conversation going for a long time. Build conversations out of the events of the day as given in your evening newspaper. Bring half a dozen possible topics to the dinner table.

Practise with your friends. Invite a few over for the evening. In planning the evening don't let it be all bridge or some other game. Reserve part of the evening for conversation. If you feel that an innate friendliness is one of your strengths, and want to develop it, concentrate on an attitude of friendly interest in the talk of the others for that evening.

Practise with strangers. Try to put the principles you have been reading about here into practice. Be on the alert for hints that will help you. Adjust to the other person. Try to talk. Be an alive, interested listener and talker.

Most important of all, seek out conversation. Look for the situations in which conversations will develop. Cultivate a healthy, positive attitude towards meeting friends and strangers. Each opportunity to talk will provide practice. And as you improve, you will know more and more the stimulation and relaxation that good conversation offers.

B

CHAPTER TWO

INTERVIEWS

The interview is a business or business-like conversation, which has some characteristics in common with social converation. It, too, is a give-and-take situation. The participants should know what they are talking about, should adjust to the others present, should be interested, friendly, and tactful, and should avoid such faults as 'pet' words, exaggeration, or excessive slang.

But the interview differs from social conversation in several important respects:

The interview is a serious conversation with a specific purpose. One participant tries to persuade or motivate the other, to learn facts from him, or to give him information. We do not request an interview for the mere pleasure of talking. We seek out the other person because we want a job, need help on some problem, or want to sell him something.

The interview usually looks towards a decision. We get the job or make the sale, or we do not. Information is given to induce a decision, or at least to serve a specific use.

In an interview, one participant is always in a superior position. Dependent upon the laws of supply and demand, the employer or the applicant, the buyer or the seller, may be in that superior position. But he should not abuse his privilege, for market conditions may change. In any case, an interview stands a better chance of success if each participant has a strong sense of his responsibilities to the other.

Other points about the interview are that it is initiated by one of the participants, that a time and place are set and that it usually has a time limit.

Finally, the interview has much less flexibility than the social conversation. The participants may talk about things other than the purpose of their meeting, of course, but they should not wander too long or too far. They must get down to the *business* of their conversation.

This chapter covers the two types of interview most likely to interest the general reader—the employment interview and the sales interview.

(1) Applying for a Position

When applying for a position, you are engaging in what is essentially a sales interview. The goods you are selling are you, your skills and abilities.

Though the thought in your mind may be, 'Am *I* going to get the job?' you will probably be more successful if you try to show the employer what you can do for *him*.

Keep this in mind while preparing for the employment interview, and during the interview itself.

General Preparation

First analyse the company or companies that might possibly employ you, and the jobs you might possibly obtain. Having decided on the position or positions you would like to obtain and the companies to which you would like to apply, prepare a personal-data sheet and a list of your qualifications. Find out, if possible, with whom you will have the interview and what form the interview is likely to take.

Analysing the Company. A company analysis will enable you to eliminate jobs where you think you would not fit in or be happy. It should also help during your interview, if you are asked the almost inevitable question, 'Why do you want to work for *us*?'

Try to include in your analysis as much as you can of the following data about the company:

Present Status. How old is it? How large? Is it financially stable, expanding or declining? What are its business policies? What distinguishes it from other companies in its field?

Organization. How is it organized? Where are its plant, office(s), sub-divisions? Who are its executives?

Products and Services. What products and/or services does it offer? What is the prestige of these products or services? What competition do these products have? How are these products or services regarded by users?

Personnel. How many people does it employ? Does it offer any kind of training scheme? What are its policies on salaries, promotion, benefits?

Most of the above information can be obtained from booklets, brochures and annual reports issued by the company. Additional information can be obtained from trade journals and business magazines, *Who's Who*, business directories, registers, guides and catalogues available in your library. (The *Bankers' Almanac and Yearbook* and the *Times Issuing House Yearbook* are particularly useful.)

You may be able to get valuable help from friends—especially if they work for the company or know someone who does. An inspection of the plant may also be possible.

Analysing the Job. The employer may think you better fitted for a position other than the one you apply for. Also, if there are no openings in your special field, he may ask you to take another job temporarily.

Prepare a job analysis which answers the following questions:

(*a*) What education and/or special training is required?

(*b*) What experience is necessary or helpful?

(*c*) What personality traits are essential? Does one work mostly with things, with people, or about equally with both?

(*d*) What are the duties of the position? What skills, abilities and aptitudes does it call for? What disadvantages does it have? Does it promise a career? Is it a dead-end?

Personal Data. Prepare a personal data sheet, a summary of factual material about yourself, and have it handy for reference. Keep it up to date. Some modification of this could be sent along with your letter of application. The sheet will also be useful to refer to when filling in application forms. Re-read it before an interview and refresh your memory of names and dates. The following items are suggested by questions most commonly asked on application forms:

Name, address, telephone number.

Age, date of birth, place of birth, nationality.

Marital status: name of wife or husband; number, relationship and age of dependants.

Immediate next of kin: full Christian name and surname, address and relationship to you.

Education and training: name and type of school(s) from the age of eleven, giving dates. Main subjects studied; diplomas or certificates gained. University or Technical College (full time), giving dates. Main subjects studied; degrees, diplomas or certificates gained. Part-time education, giving dates. Main subjects studied; degrees, diplomas or certificates gained.

Membership of technical or professional associations.

Territorial or reserve commitments.

Details of present and previous employment, including service in H.M. Forces. Addresses of previous employers, dates of employment, positions held, description of duties, salaries, reasons for leaving.

Special skills: business, technical, artistic, knowledge of foreign languages.

Details of any serious illness or disabilility.

If you are a disabled person, give your registration number and the expiry date of your certificate.

References: names, addresses and telephone numbers of at least two people, not relatives, who know you socially or in business; their occupations and the number of years they have known you.

Hobbies and interests.

Also, work out an inventory of your assets (and liabilities). Answer honestly the questions below. This will help you to decide between jobs as well as preparing you for the interview:

What sort of work do I find most interesting? What kind of work do I dislike? e.g. contacting people, working with my hands, working on ideas, writing, experimental work, outdoor work, talking to groups of people, giving orders, following instructions.

What special skills or aptitudes have I?

What is the most outstanding accomplishment of my business career? Of my social life? What other business or social accomplishments am I proud of?

What activities have I taken part in, socially or at school, that will help me in business?

What is my aim in life?

Special Preparation

Be ready at your interview for a brief test on skills related to the job, such as typewriting speed and accuracy.

From your personal-data sheet, refresh your memory on names and dates. Pay particular attention to the *Education* and *Experience* sections.

Samples of your work and evidence of your skill are effective arguments. If you have these, prepare a few neatly for presentation.

Some firms ask for a 500-word statement on your experience and abilities. Prepare such a document if you wish. Or prepare an outline, and leave the writing till you know precisely what form the company desires.

Questions to Prepare For. Certain *stock* questions crop up again and again in interviews. Know your answers to the following:

Why are you interested in advertising (selling, teaching)?

Why are you interested in copy (selling tractors, teaching infants, i.e. a sub-division of the larger field)?

When did you first think of —— as a career?

Why do you want to work for us?

What is your strongest qualification for this job?

What are your goals in life?

What accomplishment(s) are your proud(est) of?

Have you ever been dismissed? If so, why?

Are you willing to start at a lower position? At a lower salary? At the bottom?

What is your background? Education?

What were the best courses you ever took?

Were they the courses you did best in?

How long would you plan to stay with us?

What are your hobbies? Amusements? What do you do for recreation?

What have you read recently?

Special Questions. Certain *special* questions or devices may also be used: *The opportunity-to-talk.* The interviewer may turn from questioning you to say 'Just tell me about yourself.' It is a good idea to decide in advance what you will stress if given such an opening.

The problem question. 'You've told us how you would train a school-leaver. Now supposing you had to train a group of middle-aged, casual workers? How would you go about that?'

The judgement question. The interviewer hands you a company product, a business form, or a photograph and asks: 'What do you think of this?' Here, as in the problem question, the interviewer is as much interested in the *way* you answer as in the answer itself. Don't beat about the bush, try not to falter. Quickly make a decision and express it forthrightly, clearly and simply.

The getting-a-slant-on-you question. 'How did you like your previous employers?' 'Which of these two jobs would you prefer?' 'What position would be your first choice? Why? Which would be your second choice? Why? Your third choice? Why? Your fourth? Why?' Obviously such questions are intended to get you to reveal your personality.

The trick question. There is a story that a large American company, interviewing for an important executive position, asked all applicants: 'Supposing there were 100 applicants for this job. What rank would you give yourself among the 100?' Most of the highly competent persons applying, apparently feeling that modesty was a virtue, put themselves in second or third place. But the job, it is said, went to the individual who answered, 'First.' Those who had to stick to their old jobs could comfort themselves with the thought that they really wouldn't want to work for a firm which used such trick questions.

Practice. You will feel more at ease in your interview if you rehearse beforehand. With friends or some member of your family, act out employment interviews. Use several jobs, several situations, as a framework, and play the part of both interviewer and interviewee. Criticize each other. If possible, have an audience of one or two to criticize you both.

As the final item of preparation, decide *exactly* what salary you will *ask* for and the *minimum* amount you will accept.

(2) The Interview Itself

Make an early start for your appointment, planning to arrive at least a quarter of an hour early. Look at the neighbourhood, the building and the office. A walk around the block beforehand taking some deep breaths will be better for your nerves than a last-minute, pell-mell rush.

Leave hat and coat in the reception room, if people are doing this. But if this outer room is too busy and public, carry them in with you. (If there's no rack in the room to which you are sent, beware. The interviewer may be using this as a test. Perhaps you had better then say simply: 'Where would you like me to put my coat?')

As you walk in, try to be confident and relaxed. Say to yourself that your appeal is going to be a positive one: you are there to show the interviewer what you can do for him, not to *plead* for a job.

Your greeting should be friendly and dignified, a simple, 'How do you do?' If the interviewer is a woman, wait to see if she extends her hand for you to shake.

Stand till you are asked to sit; then sit erect and attentive and yet relaxed. Don't slouch. If there are letters on the interviewer's desk, don't let your eyes stray towards them.

Your interviewer may begin with some casual comment, such as one about the weather, to help put you at ease. Respond in kind, keeping the tone casual but polite.

The getting-down-to-business question will come soon thereafter. If it's of the 'tell me about yourself' type, then you know you have the floor for some minutes. Develop the 'selling points' you have planned to stress. Talk freely, but watch your interviewer so that you will know if he wants to interrupt to ask about some detail, or if he is interested in some special aspect of your work.

If the opening is of the 'stock' question type, then you can expect the interviewer to feed you a series of questions. Be specific in your answers, and crisp. Be neither glib nor monosyllabic in your replies.

The interviewer is interested not only in information. He is watching and rating you on your bearing, manners, tact, command of English, responsiveness, alertness, powers of observation, powers of analysis, frankness, initiative, common sense and sense of humour.

Be healthily and objectively confident. Avoid belittling yourself, and avoid cocksureness. Do not brag, 'I can do anything'; do not offer to do 'anything you'd be willing to let me do'. And, of course, be truthful.

Be specific. Don't say: 'I handled a large payroll.' Say: 'I was responsible for preparing and distributing wages and salaries for 1,400 employees.'

Speak up. Use a clear, strong voice, full sentences, good articulation, acceptable pronunciations. Avoid slurring and slang. This is a business conversation, not a domestic chat.

Stay alert and observant. The employer wants people who know what is going on about them.

Show initiative. If the interviewer doesn't mention the possibilities for advancement (and he may refrain deliberately), be sure to ask. But do so in a manner that shows you realize that new employees rarely are promoted to top executive in the first year.

Be responsive. React. But let your reaction also be an adjustment to the interviewer's personality. If he shows you something of the company's of which he is obviously proud, let him know that you understand and appreciate his enthusiasm.

Don't be so awed that you are afraid to smile. On the other hand, don't be facetious and over-familiar.

Be natural. Don't try to be somebody else, to act a part, 'to talk a good line'. A skilled interviewer will quickly spot artificiality.

Some interviewers will do most of the talking. Do not be lulled into inattention by this. You are being tested even though you say very little, for the interviewer will be watching your every reaction. Be an interested, alert listener.

Sales firms, or concerns in other fields where aggressiveness is thought to be an asset, will sometimes keep applicants waiting, or make them appear several times. Show firmness without losing your temper. Show that you can be patient as well as aggressive.

Sometimes you will encounter an inept interviewer, who will conduct other business at the same time or leave you for periods of time. Be patient, meanwhile making up your mind whether you want to work for him, or whether this is merely a minor fault in an otherwise fairly competent employer.

When you sense that the interviewer has asked his last question, rise, thank him, and go. You may ask if he wants any more information, but don't dawdle over your leave-taking. If you catch him eyeing your hat, you will know that you have already stayed too long.

(3) Interviewing the Applicant

In the interview, the employer's task is to find the right person for the job he has to offer. If he has to fill several fairly similar positions, he tries to fit the person into the right job. He must know the facts about the job, learn the relevant facts about the applicant, then match the one set of facts against the other. This tells him whether to appoint, to rule out, or to list the applicant for future consideration.

The employer has a responsibility to the applicant. He must explain the nature of the job carefully, so that the applicant may decide whether the job is the right one for him. The employer who wishes to maintain a low rate of turnover will refrain from overselling the position.

A third function of the interviewer is to 'sell' the company. Even if he must turn the applicant down, he sees to it that the latter leaves with a friendly feeling towards the company and its goods and services.

Preparation for the Interview

Job Analysis. Making a good analysis of the job he is offering helps the employer in choosing between applicants. The analysis should include a description of the general daily duties of the job, its responsibilities and its specific duties. The last include the precise operations the worker performs and the materials, machinery and tools he uses.

From this analysis a list of *specifications* is drawn up: the mental, physical and personality requirements; education, both formal and special; and skill. The last includes type and amount of experience and the degree of precision required, and the amount of time needed for training a beginner to master the skill.

The analysis and list of specifications are based on descriptions by employees and supervisors, time-and-motion studies, and the British Institute of Management Publications (H.M. Stationery Office).

Rating the Applicant. In evaluating applicants, the interviewer will find a *rating sheet* helpful. It focuses attention on the qualities considered necessary for the position, and helps to assure that they will be covered. Items often seen on rating sheets include:

General knowledge, special knowledge, interest in field, skills.
Appearance, bearing, manners.
Delivery, voice, pronunciation, enunciation, choice of words.
Likeableness, sincerity, animation.
Initiative, drive, decisiveness.
Emotional maturity, emotional fitness.
Organizing ability, observation, insight.

Using the above list as a guide, the interviewer should prepare a rating sheet suited to his own needs. He may prepare a *general* sheet, or a series of special sheets, to cover specific positions, containing from ten to fifteen qualities to be rated. Too short a list will prove inadequate; too long a list will prove cumbersome. The interviewer should exclude from the rating sheet qualities such as honesty, loyalty, co-operation, whose rating requires longer and more intimate observation than a single interview allows.

Place for the Interview. The interview is best held in a quiet, private and business-like room, free from telephone interruption. There should be a comfortable waiting-room adjoining.

Planning the Interview. Ample time should be allowed for the interview. If the number of applicants is large, brief preliminary interviews will serve to weed out the unlikeliest candidates. Time should also be allowed for writing up a report on each applicant after his interview.

Arrange the interviews so that they will not be interrupted by other business; and always *keep* the appointment.

The Plan of the Interview. The interviewer will decide for himself, beforehand, which of the three chief types of interview to use:

(*a*) Asking a series of questions (the most usual type)
(*b*) Letting the applicant do most of the talking
(*c*) Doing most of the talking himself.

In the first method, the questions are of two types: simple, 'stock' questions, designed to elicit information and give a broad picture of the applicant's personality; and more difficult 'problem' or 'judgement' questions, designed to probe more deeply.

If the interviewer gives the applicant fairly free rein, he will probably wish to interject questions from time to time. Since these will be unprepared, the interviewer should avoid negative questions ('Didn't you——'); questions which require only *yes* or *no* for answer ('Did you leave of your own accord?'); and questions which imply the answer ('You liked the work, of course?').

If the interviewer does most of the talking, he must be prepared to be a very acute observer of reactions.

In all cases, the interviewer must plan to:

(i) Establish *rapport* with the applicant, i.e. be friendly enough to win his confidence.

(ii) Check orally on at least some of the items covering education and experience in the applicant's letter or application form.

(iii) Test the applicant's skills.

(iv) Arrive at some estimate of the applicant's personality.

(v) Explain to the applicant the duties and responsibilities and possible disadvantages of the job, and supply information about salary, promotion, holiday arrangements, sick leave and company policy.

The employer or interviewer wants to get as true a picture of each applicant as he possibly can. He also wants to treat all the applicants equally fairly and objectively.

The following suggestions will help the interviewer to get closer to the truth about the applicant and to make his judgements as between applicants more reliable.

Use opening remarks to ease tension. Use digressions for the same purposes and also to round out the picture, to help you discover what sort of person the applicant is. But keep your opening remarks brief; don't let the digressions become the substance of the conversation. Keep control of the interview.

Separate facts from inferences. During the interview, concentrate on fact-finding. Build your picture of the applicant slowly, and out of *all* the facts you can obtain by listening and observing. You may miss pertinent facts if you draw inferences too soon; the crucial fact may not appear till late in the interview. Follow leads, of course, and hunches. But don't come to conclusions till the interview is over. Hold up the final decision till all the interviews are completed.

Let your attitudes be in line with your basic functions. You are a judge, a friendly judge—not a critic who tells the applicant what he ought to be; nor a detective looking for incriminating evidence. Nor are you, except when you describe the position, a teacher. Philosophize a bit, if you want, but remember that your homely wisdom is gratuitous and largely for your own enjoyment.

Take the applicant's point of view from time to time. It will help you to judge your own techniques. But don't give him leads that will tell him the sort of response you expect.

Since you must base many of your judgements on the responses you elicit, use questions which will stimulate him to talk, and allow him to qualify and explain his answers. Listen attentively, interjecting an interested 'Yes?' or 'Mmm' when you want him to go on. Maintaining silence after he has made a contribution will practically force him to continue. If you talk a lot yourself, let your monologue be interesting, not soporific.

Don't let your interviews become stereotyped. Vary their form, covering all the points, but covering them in a different order or in different ways. Otherwise, at the end of a half-dozen identical interviews, you will only be going through the motions. You won't get adequate responses from the applicants, and your own perceptions will be blurred.

Watch word-meanings. Make sure you and the applicant are talking about the same thing. The words *engineer* and *mechanic* have many meanings. You will get a true picture of the applicant's experience only if you have him describe his specific skills.

Don't let your general impression of a person bias your ratings on details. Conversely, don't let a single detail, such as a physical characteristic, influence your total judgement. A pleasant smile may betoken a happy disposition; but it may also be a fortunate cast of countenance, an accident of birth. It could just be an irritating fixture.

Try to avoid 'stereotyping' the applicant. Try to see the *individual*. Not all musicians have long hair; not all Welshmen sing; not all Slavs are stolid; not all Janes are plain. Also avoid your pet prejudices. You may believe in long walks, a glass of hot water on rising, and eight hours' sleep. But there may be a place in your organization for someone who is indifferent to walking, can't stand drinking hot water, or who manages very well on six hours' sleep a night.

Finally, be especially alert during the last few moments of the interview. In the easing of tension, in the off-guard comment, in the good-bye and the walk towards the door, there may be significant clues to personality.

(4) The Sales Interview

Salesmanship has been defined as 'the art of providing products that won't come back to customers who will'. It has also been called the act of persuading someone to buy what he would not otherwise have bought.

Both definitions have value. Taken together, they stress that a salesman sells customer satisfaction, that he must always think of future sales as well as the present one, that to be successful he must have know-how.

The good salesman knows the needs of the public, and which of those needs his products will satisfy. He knows how his products satisfy those needs better than the products of his competitors. And he knows how to present his product so that the customer will accept his viewpoint.

Steps in Selling

There are five steps in planned selling: the pre-approach, the approach, the presentation, overcoming objections, and the close.

(*a*) **The Pre-approach.** This is the step in which the salesman goes looking for customers. Its keynote is constant alertness.

The alert retail salesman tries to build a core of steady customers by letting them know, in advance, about the availability of items in which they have a special interest. He displays his stock in an attractive, attention-getting way. He is ever-watchful for the potential customer. As he comes forward to serve a customer, he makes a preliminary analysis of the customer's appearance and actions.

The alert manufacturer's representative keeps in constant contact with dealers and purchasing agents. He aims at complete coverage. He works to please and keep his own customers. He explores to see if he can possibly capture some of his rivals' domains.

The alert salesman or insurance agent keeps building his list of potential customers. For material, he draws on present users, relatives and friends and their friends, acquaintances in clubs and social groups, the businessmen who serve him, and news items and listings. He also tries to attract 'prospects' by demonstrations and exhibitions.

(*b*) **The Approach.** Here, the salesman establishes contact with the 'prospect', obtains further information about his needs, and confirms what leads he already has. He aims to establish a pleasant and positive contact, and to attract attention and interest. He tries to obtain the information efficiently, unobtrusively and accurately, making it clear that his purpose is to serve.

The retail salesman greets his potential customer cordially and promptly. He regards all prospects as customers. If the prospect is looking at the merchandise, the salesman makes some pertinent remark about it: 'This is a special for today.' 'This is a new design by Fowler.' Only to those who look bewildered does he say: 'May I help you?'

Through observation, trial questions and the response to his opening, the retailer tries to discover what types of goods the customer is interested in and at what prices. He notices the appearance of the customer, remembering, however, that the well-to-do may dress plainly, or the poorly-dressed person may be an enthusiast who spends every penny on gramophone records or tropical fish. If a second customer approaches, he greets him promptly with: 'Good morning. I'll be with you shortly.' But he doesn't leave his first customer unless she has great difficulty making a choice, and then only if he secures her permission.

If a representative makes his first contact by phone, he says with a smiling voice: 'This is Arthur Jones, I'd like to speak to Mr. Barton.' (Not, apprehensively, 'Do you think Mr.—er—Barton could possibly speak to me?') His request for an interview is direct, honest and brief.

If this contact is made by letter, the tone is simple and vigorous and stresses the service angle.

When keeping the appointment, do more than announce yourself to the receptionist. Ask her a simple question, such as the correct spelling or pronunciation of your prospect's name. Be very pleasant and courteous here. It will pay to make a favourable impression. Receptionists and secretaries can be important helps or hindrances in your present or future sales efforts.

If you drop in without appointment, try to pick a time when your prospect will not be too busy. But if he is, don't become impatient. Request a definite appointment at some future time.

(c) **The Presentation.** This step, whether short or long, is the one towards which all your preparation has been heading. For here you show how your product or service *satisfies*. You turn your prospect from wanting a product to wanting your brand of that product.

The *major* ingredients of success here are:

(i) *Be confident.* Believe in your product or service. Otherwise how can you expect your prospect to believe in it?

(ii) *Be clear.* Use a vocabulary adapted to the level of your listener: technical, if he is professional; simple, if he is a layman. Use short sentences. Re-state points in several ways. Take up one thing at a time. Demonstrate before you describe. Think of your presentation as akin to the first paragraph of a good newspaper story, covering *who, where when, how* and *why.*

(iii) *Be as complete as is necessary* for the particular prospect. If he can afford only £6,000 for a house, it is foolish to show him £10,000 homes. If he is already half-sold, you may anger him by covering points on which he already agrees with you. Being complete, however, implies anticipating objections he may bring up.

(d) **Overcoming Objections.** Objections may arise at any point during the interview. When they do, meet them in one of the following ways:

If the objection is a serious one, use the 'Yes, but——' technique. Agree with the prospect, and even praise him for his perspicacity: 'That's a very good question,' 'I'm glad you brought that up.' Then show him how the disadvantage he has mentioned is counterbalanced or outweighed. The price is high, but the article has extra sturdiness, and promises fewer repair bills and longer life. Or balance the price against other features—greater safety or ease of operation.

If a strong objection is raised on a minor point, concede the point and do something about it. Offer extra service, replace or change a part, make a special concession or price. The new tyre, costing £5, may sell the second-hand car priced at £995.

If the objection is too formidable, don't argue with the prospect. If the deep-freeze cabinet won't fit in his pantry, it won't fit, no matter how long you talk about it.

If the objection is trivial, ignore it for the time being. The comment may only be a random one, soon forgotten or overcome during the general presentation. Deal with it only if it is repeated.

Deny an objection only when the customer is obviously misinformed. Be cautious and tactful in your denial, and use the objection as an opportunity to educate the customer.

Never try to overcome a legitimate objection by seeming to deny it. If the customer mentions a feature of some other brand, don't tell her that in all your twenty years of selling you've never heard of that brand.

Be brief. Don't magnify the objection by spending much time on it.

Remember, the best way to overcome objections is by anticipating them.

(*e*) **The Close.** The customer has reached his lowest level of resistance and is ready to buy. He needs just a little push to get him to sign on the dotted line. How does the salesman give that last little push?

Be sure to ask the customer to buy. Take the initiative, or the sale may be lost.

Ask him to buy when his interest is strongest. The article he comes back to, the one he looks back at while examining something else, obviously interests him. Judge his interest by the tone of his questions, the look in his eye.

Offer a series of minor choices. Blue or grey, this accessory or that?

Ask questions or make comments which suggest that the article is already sold. 'Would you like delivery next week?' Have the order form on the desk and fill out part of it when you think he is really interested. If he isn't, he'll stop you soon enough; if he is, you'll have closed the sale.

If a sale is impossible, make your close an opening for a next time. 'I'll call again in three months.'

Common Faults in Selling

A variety of faults and what to do about them have been covered throughout this section. But certain faults are altogether *too common*, and deserve renewed attention:

Not emphasizing needs and wants enough. You make the sale only when the potential customer knows his need, feels it strongly, feels that your product satisfies his needs.

Emphasizing price exclusively. Price is important, of course, but sales are not made on the basis of price alone. The person had a reason for buying a car before he started shopping around. Try to find that reason, and address your chief appeal to it.

Failing to show an adequate assortment. You must give the prospect a chance to choose the one thing that is right for him.

Neglecting to explain the use and care of the article you sell. For example, why risk having your customer get angry at your washing-machine because you've neglected to tell him that it has a filter which requires regular cleaning.

Forgetting that suggestion may sell. Not all towns are taken by storm or a frontal attack. But, of course, suggestion selling is more than the stock '*And* something else?'

Overcoming objections in an objectionable way, or not being alert enough to them. Prepare to meet the challenge of the objection whenever it arises.

Not taking the initiative in closing the sale. What is the point of doing everything except sell the item or the service? A salesman's job is to sell, and the last step is as important as the first.

CHAPTER THREE

SPEAKING IN PUBLIC

All too often, a person goes to a meeting, not expecting to do anything more than listen, only to be told on arrival that he is expected to 'say a few words'. Perhaps you are reading this book because you have found yourself in this situation and weren't satisfied with your performance.

This chapter is designed to help you to do better on such occasions. It discusses certain general problems of talking on your feet, such as feeling at ease and using gestures; and certain preliminary matters, such as choosing a subject and analysing the audience. The following chapter takes up the composition of the speech itself—a speech of which you have prior warning. As you gain confidence from your successes in *prepared* public speaking, you will no longer be at a loss when unexpectedly asked to speak.

(1) Feeling at Ease

How to feel at ease before an audience is the chief problem for most people when they take up speaking in public.

'How can I get rid of stage fright?' they ask. And their manner shows that they think of it as some dread disease for which they hopefully seek a wonder-drug.

Actually, the nervousness you feel in making a speech is quite normal. The runner is nervous before his race, the student before his examinations. You would expect to feel nervous when applying for a new job or asking the boss for a rise. Why not then in addressing an audience?

For in speaking in public, as in these other situations, we are going to be tested, criticized, judged.

'But,' you may say, 'the professional speaker doesn't feel stage fright. He's wonderfully at ease.'

To which the reply is, 'Nonsense.' Ask any professional public speaker or actor, and he will tell you that he still feels nervous before a speech or a performance. 'I'm petrified,' some will tell you, 'I can't eat anything for hours beforehand.'

The explanation is that the professional speaker *seems* to be at ease, even though he does feel stage fright. He has had so much experience before audiences that he gets over his fear very quickly, usually at the moment he starts to speak. He has studied this problem and has found ways of reducing excess tension. He has probably even learned how to make use of it.

The problem of feeling at ease, then, is not to cure a disease called stage fright, but to control tension. It has two aspects: to keep tension from mounting into panic; and to put to good use the extra energy which normally accompanies a state of tension.

Always be well prepared. This is probably the most important single rule for feeling at ease.

Being well prepared means thinking, talking, reading about the subject-matter of your talk, organizing and revising what you want to say, and then rehearsing it—several times.

Start your preparation at least a week in advance. Take three or four days for your preliminary work, set aside one day for organizing your ideas, then allow a day or two for ironing out rough spots and trying out your talk on your family or anyone willing to listen.

Don't try to cut down on this preparation. Take more time if you like. Hasty, last-minute planning is bound to be sketchy and may lead to confusion and greater nervousness. Some of Franklin D. Roosevelt's famous speeches took at least three weeks to prepare.

Say to yourself: 'I am not alone.' Comfort yourself with the thought that in feeling nervous about your speech you are like everyone else. Even the greatest of orators, from Demosthenes right up to the present day, were nervous about their speeches—and so is the speaker who sits waiting on the platform beside you.

Say to yourself: 'This is part of the game.' If a public speaker is ever to gain the satisfaction of getting his ideas across to an audience or of moving people to do something, he must be willing to pay the price. Part of the price is this ordeal of feeling nervous. It is rather like having to face an unwelcome visit to the dentist in order to keep one's teeth in good condition.

Think of your audience as friendly individuals. Inexperienced speakers sometimes think of the audience as a ravenous monster, waiting to pick to pieces everything they do or say.

Actually, the audience is composed of human beings. Some will be interested, some apathetic. But unless you are advocating some violent change that means the destruction of the thing they most treasure, the majority of them will feel friendly towards you.

Therefore, talk to individuals in your audience. Pick out the most friendly, most interested face. That's the person you want first to talk to. Then look for another interested person. Talk to him—or her. By the time you've finished talking to half a dozen friendly-looking people scattered throughout the group, you'll feel this is indeed a pleasant audience; and you'll find that you actually enjoy talking to them.

Concentrate on what you have to say. Inexperienced speakers tend to exaggerate the importance of trivialities. A woman fusses over her dress, a man with his tie (the time to think about these is well before the speech). Each imagines that some slip of the tongue has ruined the speech.

If this is your tendency, remember that the audience has come to hear what you have to say. Concentrate on that.

Should a low-flying aircraft pass over while you're in the middle of a sentence, stop and smile and make a remark about the noise if you wish. But the moment quiet returns, get back to your speech.

Relieve your excess tension and use your extra energy. The shaky knees the palpitating heart, the clammy hands you are so conscious of are merely evidence of the changes your body is making to prepare you for your task. Don't fear these changes. Accept them. Try to make good use of them.

Relax while waiting to speak. Sit back comfortably in your chair. Take deep, slow breaths. When you are introduced, walk slowly to the platform or to the speaker's desk. Take your time about beginning. Wait for silence and attention.

Use up some of your extra energy by consciously moving muscles. If you can do so without being observed, clench and unclench your hands several times. Take a drink of water. Make your walk to the platform firm as well as deliberate. Nod to the chairman and the audience. Open your mouth wide and begin talking in a loud, clear, vigorous voice.

If you welcome your nervousness, you will soon find, like the professional, that your extra energy is a source of greater expressiveness and strength.

Put your best self forward. If you are one of those who ask themselves, 'Will I do a good job?' do everything you can to ensure that the answer will be 'yes'.

Look your best (hair tidy, shoes polished). Arrive early, so that you can adjust to your physical surroundings. Then think of past successes you have had involving relations with other people.

Remember that there will always be a next time. Of course, this speech means a lot to you. But its success or failure is not a calamity. The chances are that the sun will rise tomorrow, no matter what mistakes you make.

Do your best, but also keep a proper perspective. If your best is really good, perhaps you will have started yourself on a career of making speeches that will be *really* important—to others as well as yourself.

(2) Basic Concepts

Public speaking is enlarged conversation. There is little difference between talking to one person, to ten people, or to a hundred. You must talk louder; but the talking that goes on around your dinner table does not differ in essence from the talking that goes on at a meeting. The only real difference is that at a meeting the speaker is allowed to talk for a longer time without interruption.

Therefore, think of your speech as a conversation with the audience. Talk *with* the persons you see in front of you. Talk *to* them. But never, never talk *at* them.

It is helpful, too, in preparing and practising your speech, to think of it as a *discussion* with people you know. Imagine that they have asked you an important question and you are doing your best to answer. As you do so, they put other questions to you, and you try to answer these. You explain, tell stories to illustrate what you mean, and cite statistics. Or someone objects, and you offer counter-arguments, and produce facts to back them up. Finally, you sum up everything you've said with a 'There, that's it. That's what I've been saying.'

Thought of and prepared in these ways, your address will be *good talking*.

Public speaking is communication with a purpose. You talk to an audience for a specific reason. You want them to feel, to think, to do something.

Therefore, during your speech, concentrate on this objective. Keep your eye on the ball.

Don't let yourself be distracted by late-comers or noises. Don't let your talking become mechanical. Don't let your attention wander, your manner become absent-minded. If you do, you will not be communicating.

Think about what you are saying while you are saying it. Think about it *hard*.

Then the audience will know that you mean what you say, and will listen.

A good speaker is lively, interested, enthusiastic, vital. He feels alive; he sees his audience as living people. He is interested in his topic and considers it vital to such people.

So he speaks of it with enthusiasm. That's the best way to interest an audience.

A good speaker is earnest. He doesn't talk for talk's sake, to show off his clothes, or his smile, or his diction, or his voice. He doesn't turn on the charm when he stands up only to switch it off as he sits down.

He has something he thinks worth saying and he says it. He is earnest.

A good speaker has a sense of responsibility. He has a sense of responsibility to his *listeners*. He realizes that if he talks for five minutes to 100 listeners he is taking 500 minutes out of people's lives. He tries to say something that will be worth that precious time.

He has a sense of responsibility to *other speakers*. If he has been allotted five minutes, he does not take ten. He takes care not to squeeze others off the programme, or force them to hurry. They, too, may have something worthwhile to say.

He has a sense of responsibility to his *subject*. He doesn't bite off more than he can chew. He doesn't spread it thin.

The good speaker has a sense of leadership. He stands up tall, as a leader should. He talks eye to eye, as a leader should. He speaks responsibly and with authority, as a leader should. He is positive, friendly, straightforward.

The good speaker keeps his head. He doesn't let his enthusiasm carry him too far. He doesn't become a zealot. He doesn't let his confidence become over-confidence. He doesn't let himself get intoxicated with the sense of power that comes with being in the public eye. He tries to be balanced, sane. He keeps his sense of humour.

Be yourself. Say what *you* think, not what some columnist or T.V. personality thinks. Study other speakers, but don't ape them.

Recognize and admire the fine qualities of experienced speakers. But don't feel that these are necessarily the qualities you must have. You must develop your own potentialities, work out your own style, discover what will make *you* an effective speaker.

Know yourself. Do not indulge in wishful thinking about your speaking ability.

Learn to accept criticism and to profit by it.

After each performance, analyse it. Ask trusted friends about it. Try to form some objective estimate of its worth. Discover your weaknesses; don't cover them up. Do something to correct them.

Discover your strengths; then emphasize and develop them.

(3) Beginners' Faults

Inexperienced speakers often show one or more of the faults listed below. It is as well to try and eliminate these right from the start.

The 'er' or 'and-er' habit. All of us are liable to drop an 'er' into whatever we are saying, especially if we are tired, or can't collect our thoughts, or if we've been reading or doing mechanical tasks too long. But 'ers' sprinkled throughout a speech make it tedious.

To correct this fault, take a stop-watch and time yourself while you describe the room you are in as if to a radio audience. Try to talk for 45 seconds without an 'er'. Have somebody with you to check, as it is difficult to hear your own 'ers'. If you make a slip, start again on another 45-second speech.

Describe what you see out of a window, or talk about some news event, in the same way.

The apologetic opening. Only the best speakers can afford to apologize, and they only do it when, for some valid reason, they really have not had time to prepare a speech.

The audience will regard your apologetic opening as a routine; or, if you are too convincing, will start looking for faults.

If you haven't had enough time to prepare, or if you don't know much about the subject, you should not be making a speech. Let someone better equipped do the talking.

Being a copycat. Don't take your speech from, or copy the style of, a newspaper or magazine. Their articles are intended for a reading audience, and their style will sound artificial coming from your lips.

Build your own talks. If a magazine article interests you, read other articles on the same subject, take notes, add your own ideas and observations. Then prepare your speech in your own words.

Fidgeting. Beginners sometimes drain off their extra energy by nervously playing with coins, buttons, keys, pencils, pens or notes. In doing so, they distract the audience's attention.

Don't carry small objects with you to the platform. When you're there, concentrate on your message and use up your extra energy in *vigorous* talking.

Lack of audience contact. Beginners may tend to talk only to themselves or to the front row. Public speaking is *enlarged* conversation, it is communication to *others*. Ideally you should talk to the person in the back row *first*; then talk to the persons closer to you. But if you address the most interested looking faces in turn, as we said earlier, this will help you to make good audience contact.

Jargon. Professional persons tend to use a jargon which is intelligible only to other professionals. This is not a good habit, but what is far worse is that beginners sometimes seem to feel that they will make an impression if they talk over the heads of the audience in such jargon. They will do much better if they use plain, everyday language.

A particularly horrible example, taken from a talk on social work, is: 'Familial societality is already a settled question biologically, structured in our inherited bodies and physiology . . .' This could have been expressed infinitely more clearly, and without any loss of meaning, simply as: 'Family life is born and bred in us.'

Meaningless words and phrases. Avoid *'something or other'*, *'and so forth'*, *'exact same thing'*, *'all that sort of thing'*, *'you know'*.

Be specific. Name names. Say exactly what you mean.

Also avoid *'Before I begin I should like to state . . .'*, *'I could talk on this for hours'*, *'I haven't time to discuss this fully but . . .'*, *'I'll have to leave this for another time'*, *'I hope I'm not boring you with this, but . . .'*

These phrases are useless and irritating. Prepare your talk so well that you won't feel any need to fall back on them.

(4) Visual Factors

An audience sees a speaker before it hears him. It also forms an opinion of him before he says a word. 'Timid', or 'aggressive', it may say to itself, or 'How poised!'

Whether these judgements are valid or not, they are nevertheless made. The speaker must therefore consider how he *looks* to the audience.

Visual factors are important for still another reason: the phenomenon of *empathy*. We tend to 'feel-ourselves-into' what we see. We cheer when a goal is scored; we suffer with the stage heroine. The fidgeting speaker makes his audience nervous. If he is poised, they will relax too. And they will have confidence in the confident speaker.

Posture. A good posture combines both the command 'Attention!' and the command 'At ease!' The speaker will then suggest to the audience that he is both alert and poised.

When addressing an audience you should keep your heels fairly close together, toes turned out somewhat. Heels may be on a line, or one foot may be a bit to one side and in front of the other.

The weight of the body should be on the balls of the feet. If one foot is in front, the rear foot takes the weight, the front foot serving as extra balancing point.

Stand erect. Keep stomach in, chest high, chin in.

Let your arms and hands hang easily at your sides, or put them behind your back. During the course of your speech do not hesitate to slip one hand into a pocket.

The question, 'What shall I do with my hands?' is a psychological rather than a physical one. The answer is: 'Concentrate on what you are saying, and the audience will not notice your hands.'

If there is a speaker's stand, you may grasp it or rest one arm on it. But do not lean over it, or drape yourself on it as though it were a prop to hold you up.

If there is a desk, place your notes on it if you wish. But then stand clear of it. Avoid slumping over stand or desk, or using them as you would a crutch.

In general, avoid stiffness and exaggeration. Strive for naturalness and alertness. Make sure that your basic posture is one from which you may move or gesture with ease.

Exercise No. 4

Try out several of the arm-and-hand positions suggested above, to see which suits you.

Exercise No. 5

Try a heels-on-line stance, a one-foot-in-front stance. Shift your body weight with no foot movement; shift your foot position and your body weight with a minimum of movement.

Movement. Begin your talk standing at, or near, the centre of the platform. Thereafter, move your position only with a purpose. If necessary move forward to emphasize a point, to bring it closer to the audience.

Move to another part of the platform, or turn to face a different part of the hall, when you have finished with one point and are taking up the next.

Avoid the extremes both of standing stockstill and of pacing back and forth.

EXERCISE NO. 6

Practise suitable posture and movement for: 'So much for the political aspects of this question. Now let's take up the economic aspects.' Test the result before a full-length mirror.

Gesture. Gestures, that is, movements of the hands, body or face, should be meaningful.

The good gesture illustrates or emphasizes what is said, strengthening and clarifying it. A speaker may count off points on his fingers; he may point with full arm extended to some object or in some direction. He may outline with his hands and arms contrasting sizes or shapes. He may let his face mimic an emotion, a grimace; or he may use his entire body to simulate some action, such as throwing a ball.

Don't think of a gesture as being just a hand gesture. Get the whole arm, the whole body into it.

Let the gesture precede the word by a fraction of a second.

Don't be half-hearted in your gesturing. Carry the gesture through to the end. But avoid making showy gestures for their own sake. Let the test of the gesture be that it is decisive, significant and unostentatious.

The amount of gesture you use will depend on your personal preference. Today, because of our conversational style of talking, and because of microphones, speakers tend to use fewer gestures than formerly. But do not let this style-preference push you into giving up gestures altogether.

Gestures can be powerful aids to good talking. When you rehearse your speeches, practise appropriate accompanying gestures. After you have tested them, decide whether you will use them or not.

EXERCISE NO. 7

Work out and practise appropriate gestures for:

(a) Contrasting a tiny tot with an all-in wrestler.
(b) 'I demand to be heard!'
(c) 'When I see the Union Jack flying there . . .'
(d) 'Oh! But he was a tight-fisted hand at the grindstone, Scrooge!'
(e) 'You know what a church spire looks like.'

Eye-contact. In conversation, we all tend to look at the person we are talking to. Yet in talking to an audience, many beginners make the mistake of looking at everything *but* the persons they are addressing.

Looking at the eyes of the audience makes people feel that you are interested in them. It also gives you more assurance. Let your eyes sweep around from person to person, section to section, forward and back, side to side.

You need not keep eye-contact constantly; but do not neglect this excellent method of establishing and maintaining *rapport* with your audience.

If you intend to read a quotation during the speech, do not keep your eyes glued to the page. Take in a half-dozen or more words of the text, then look up at the audience as you say them.

Visual Aids. The charts, diagrams or pictures you use should be large enough to be seen and understood from all parts of the auditorium.

If they are hung on the wall, stand to one side as you discuss them. If you yourself hold them, keep them in front of you or to one side. In either case, know the charts so well that you do not have to pore over them to explain them. The charts are for the audience's benefit, not yours.

Elaborate blackboard drawings should be prepared in advance. Simple ones may be sketched quickly during the talk, but practise this so that you can sketch from one side and talk at the same time.

Distribute materials for the audience to look at only if you have enough copies or samples for everybody. To pass around a single copy only causes confusion and distraction.

Notes. There is little use bringing disorganized scribblings to the platform with you.

Your notes should consist of key-words, phrases or brief sentences. These should be written clearly on small, numbered cards, which can be kept in order and held unobtrusively in the hand.

Quotations should be copied out in their entirety, preferably typewritten, and double-spaced. If you plan to read from a book, use a large and obvious marker for your place. Neither you nor your audience will enjoy your search for an elusive page.

Dress. The most important thing about your clothes is that they be appropriate to the occasion. Whether you wear a business suit, sports coat, dinner jacket or mini skirt depends on the time, place and character of the function.

The next most important thing is that your grooming be neat. Untidy or rumpled clothes are as grave a fault as ostentation in dress. And a feathered hat or dangling ear-rings are as distracting as a slip that shows.

(5) Types of Delivery

A speech may be: (*a*) impromptu; (*b*) memorized; (*c*) written and read; or (*d*) prepared in content and structure but not in wording. The last way is called the 'extemporaneous' speech.

(*a*) **The impromptu talk** is the one delivered without preparation.

Beginners sometimes make the mistake of attempting this type of delivery. They feel they will talk better if they leave everything to 'the inspiration of the moment'. The difficulty is that the moment for talking inevitably arrives but the inspiration seldom does.

Only the most accomplished speakers can handle the impromptu talk well. They have made so many prepared speeches that they can readily draw upon this store of experience to make some apt remarks. The story goes that a well-known speaker was asked how he had thought of a particularly magnificent reply to a difficult questioner on the spur of the moment. 'Madam,' he replied, 'I had been preparing for that speech all my life.'

If, through some chance, you are suddenly called on to rise and 'say a few words', choose as quickly as possible some simple message appropriate to the occasion and the audience. This need be merely, 'Occasions like this are always inspiring,' or 'Harry Smith has been one of the best secretaries we've ever had,' or even 'Honesty is the best policy.'

Then, rise and:

   (i) State this message.
   (ii) Say it in another way.
  (iii) Tell a story, or give a few examples, to illustrate your message.
  (iv) Re-state your message in still another way, trying to say it even more strongly than before. Then
   (v) sit down.

You will have said your 'few words' and, having kept them to a few, you will have said them well.

(*b*) **The memorized speech** is also sometimes attempted by beginners. They write out their thoughts and commit them to memory for fear that they will forget what they want to say.

Unfortunately, stage fright affects the memory. Though you may be able to go on for a long time you are apt to break down. You may then be able to continue by going over silently what you have already said, but this makes a sorry spectacle.

Memorizing an entire speech is not recommended for beginners.

(*c*) **The speech which is written out and then read** is encountered fairly frequently today. Statesmen and scientists make use of it because every word may be reported, and even the slightest mistake may call forth severe criticism. Television and radio stations almost always require it.

Yet this type of delivery involves difficulties and dangers which make it unsuitable for beginners. Written style is so much more formal than oral style, that unless great care is taken to avoid it, such a speech will sound more like a schoolboy's essay than a talk. Furthermore, most people today have such little experience in reading aloud that they are likely to do a dull, amateurish job.

Winston Churchill, who was magnificent at this type of delivery, prepared for it very carefully. He dictated his first draft, had his speech typed as sentences rather than as paragraphs, and corrected his type-script. Then he made a recording, and listened to the playback for analysis and self-criticism before delivering the speech.

Though Churchill's speeches are memorable for much more than their delivery, and though they *read* as well as they *sound*, his methods of preparation offer fruitful suggestions for a speech of this sort.

If you *must* write out and read a speech, try for an oral, rather than a written, style. Keep your vocabulary simple; use a conversational, person-to-person approach.

The following is a good example of written style:

'After a regular course of legal education, which lasted five years, the students dispersed themselves through the provinces, in search of fortune and honours; nor could they want an inexhaustible supply of business in a great empire already corrupted by the multiplicity of laws.'

But for speaking purposes, a simpler style is called for:

'Students attended law school for five years. After graduating, the young lawyers scattered through the provinces to seek their fortunes. They did not need to search far for business. There were so many laws that—well, you might even say that the great empire had been corrupted by its laws.' (For help on vocabulary and levels of usage, see the companion volume in this series, *English Made Simple*.)

While writing your speech, test your sentences by saying them out loud. Can you say them easily? If they sound stiff, long or involved, shorten and simplify them, trying for a conversational effect.

When you have finished your writing, practise your speech aloud several times, both alone and in front of family or friends. Keep your tone conversational, and know the speech well enough so that you can look directly at your audience for most of the time.

You can develop your ability to maintain audience contact by looking down at your manuscript for the first half-dozen or so words, but look up at your audience before you actually say those words. Go back to your manuscript only as you are finishing saying what you have previously read.

(*d*) **The 'extemporaneous' speech**—the type prepared in content and structure, but not in wording—is probably the most popular today. One hears it at almost every function where public speaking takes place.

In this type of delivery the main idea of the speech, its structure and materials, and perhaps two or three sentences, are carefully selected and prepared beforehand. But the major portion of what is to be said, the words and sentences that the audience will hear, are left for the speaking situation itself.

This type of delivery is also best for training. It requires talking on your feet, and so is better than the written-and-read speech. It involves memorizing (or jotting down on cards) only a few of the chief ideas, and so incurs less risk of forgetting than the completely memorized talk. It involves careful preparation, and so is more inviting to 'inspiration' than the blank brain of the impromptu speaker.

It provides the opportunity, moreover, for the spontaneity and flexibility which are the essence of speech.

In preparing for an 'extemporaneous' speech, choose the subject and decide on the specific purpose of your talk. Gather your materials by thinking about your subject and reading up on it if necessary.

Organize your materials in a flexible outline. If you prepare notes, use key-words and phrases written in capital letters on small cards.

Practise delivering your speech, trying to change the wording each time. Some key sentences will emerge that you will want to keep. It is a good idea to decide on, write down and memorize, your opening and closing sentences.

Having been through this experience several times, and having criticized your speeches *after* you have made them, you will have gone a long way in developing your speaking ability. (For further details on composing a speech, see Chapter Four.)

(6) Choosing a Subject

In most cases you will know specifically what you must do in your speech: praise an associate who is retiring, nominate someone for office, or describe your firm's stand at a coming exhibition. But if you must choose your subject yourself, the problem need not present difficulties. Once you have mastered a few simple principles, you should be able to decide easily what to talk about even at short notice.

The best choice is a subject which suits (*a*) you, (*b*) your audience, (*c*) the occasion, and (*d*) the length of time you have been allowed.

(*a*) **Choose a subject which suits you.** You will talk best on a subject you know well, or in which you are deeply interested.

Remember, when you are talking you are an *authority*. You ought to know more about your subject than any member of your audience. This should be true if only because you are presenting your personal viewpoint and experience.

Therefore, consider as possible subjects:

    (i) Your job.
    (ii) Your hobby, or your interests.
    (iii) Your past experiences.
    (iv) Your beliefs and convictions.
    (v) Some field of knowledge you've studied.
    (vi) Some idea or process you'd like to explain.
    (vii) Some issue you've discussed with friends.
    (viii) Some project you're interested in.
    (ix) Some desire, or hope, or wish of yours.
    (x) Something you've read that you'd like to give your reactions to.

Such a list might be: accounting; golf; cricket; gardening; trip across France; hitch-hiking; better schools; tax laws; how to pay less income tax; how to buy a used car; safer cars; safer driving; shopping centres; war and peace; the mature mind; better reading habits.

EXERCISE NO. 8

List ten subjects about which you think you have enough information to deliver a talk. List ten propositions which you would enthusiastically defend or attack.

(*b*) **Choose a subject which suits your audience.** Audiences will listen more readily if your subject is one they too are interested in.

They are likely to be most interested in subjects which vitally concern them and are topical.

Certain subjects would appeal to parents but not to youngsters; others to youngsters but not to parents; others to both groups.

Therefore, always think over what you know, or can find out, about your audience. Ask yourself the following questions:

(i) What are they likely to be interested in as *individuals*?

(ii) What are they likely to be interested in as an *organized group*, that is, as teachers, housewives, members of a sports club?

(iii) What are they likely to expect me to talk about?

EXERCISE NO. 9

Jot down subjects you think might interest the groups mentioned above: teachers, housewives, members of a sports club.

EXERCISE NO. 10

Go over the two lists you made in Exercise No. 8 (ten subjects about which you think you have enough information to deliver a talk, ten propositions which you would enthusiastically either defend or attack). From these, select subjects you think would interest: (i) a group of Boy Scouts, (ii) your local Women's Institute, (iii) a group of American visitors to your town.

(*c*) **Choose a subject which suits the occasion.** The demands of the occasion are generally obvious: a Remembrance Day ceremony demands a tribute to the dead and the ideals for which they gave their lives; the annual business meeting calls for reports on the year's activities and perhaps a look at plans for the future

Yet most of us have been bored or annoyed by the speaker who disregarded this principle. He was so wrapped up in his own interests or wanted so badly to get something off his chest that he completely forgot the occasion. At a school speech-day a prominent surgeon got very little applause for his excellent paper on 'Diseases of the Liver'. At the annual general meeting of a suburban photographic society, a defeated candidate for office probably lost all chance of ever being elected by attacking the successful candidates and the election methods.

Keep your subject within the spirit of the occasion.

EXERCISE NO. 11

What subjects would be suitable for: (i) a Christmas party; (ii) the laying of a foundation stone; (iii) the 50th anniversary of a club, a business organization or a college?

(*d*) **Choose a subject which suits your time allowance.** That is to say, be sure your subject is one you can discuss *adequately* in the two, five, ten, 20 or 30 minutes allotted you.

A talk on 'Banking' can hardly be crammed into four minutes. But do not feel that you must give up this subject because you cannot treat it fully.

Narrow a broad subject, or limit yourself to some aspect of it. In this case, 'Origins of the cheque system', 'The Clearing House', or 'Near-cash investments' are certainly relevant subjects which could be treated in a short time.

Conversely, if you merely have to congratulate some volunteers on the success of their fund-raising activities, don't take half an hour at it.

EXERCISE NO. 12

Assume that 'Democracy at the Crossroads' is the theme of an hour-long radio programme. List four subjects which might be discussed by as many speakers under this general heading.

Sometimes all four of the above factors will be of about equal importance in the choice of a subject. Sometimes one, such as the occasion, will be the most important.

Finally, if you are given a specific topic and find, after some thought, that you are not interested in it, suggest another topic that you feel would be more suitable, or refuse the invitation politely. There are times when it is better to remain silent than to speak.

EXERCISE NO. 13

Assume that a Youth Centre has been planned for your town. You have been asked to arrange a short course of three public lectures under the general theme of 'Youth Today'. What would you suggest as three subjects under this heading?

EXERCISE NO. 14

A famous explorer returns from a trip. If he were as good a speaker as he is an explorer, how might he vary the subjects of a series of talks to fit: (i) The Royal Geographical Society; (ii) a horticultural society; (iii) a comprehensive school; (iv) a group of his close friends; (v) a meeting of meteorologists?

EXERCISE NO. 15

Take the lists of subjects you made out for Exercises 8 and 9 and see how you might adapt them to fit the various situations mentioned in this section.

(7) Deciding on the Response You Want

The speaker delivers his speech in order to get a response, a reaction, from his audience.

You will make a better speech and have a better chance of getting the response you want if you define clearly beforehand both (*a*) the general purpose and (*b*) the specific purpose of your talk.

(*a*) **The General Purpose.** On the basis of the general purposes for which they are made, speeches tend to fall into four categories. Keeping your subject in mind, decide into which of the following your speech falls. Do you wish:

(i) **To interest or amuse.** This is the general purpose of many after-dinner speeches, the chairman's or toastmaster's introductions, the preliminary talks before the main speech of the evening, the professional comedian's contribution, the popular travel or 'culture' lecture, and indeed of many so-called 'educational' talks.

In such cases speakers rely mainly on stories, anecdotes and humour. Some introduce touches of wit or excitement.

It is successful when it whiles away the time, when it keeps the audience interested or amused.

(ii) **To inform or teach.** This is the purpose of the classroom lecture, the business report, the training talk given to new or old employees by a manager or supervisor, the paper delivered at a symposium by one specialist to other specialists, the 'popular' lecture given by a scientist or expert to the general public.

This type of speech, besides being interesting or even amusing, conveys information. It discusses, explains or describes events or ideas, or teaches the audience how to do something. It strives for clarity and simplicity. It often uses audio-visual aids—charts, graphs, films or tape-recordings.

It is successful when the members of the audience, besides being interested or even amused, leave the auditorium with more knowledge, understanding or skill than they had upon entering; and when at least some of the listeners remember the content of the speech long enough to put it to use.

(iii) **To stimulate or impress.** This is the purpose of many sermons, of the inspirational talk to salesmen, of the pep talk to athletes, and of speeches made at memorial services, anniversaries, reunions, prize-giving and graduation ceremonies.

This type of speech does not attempt to change people's beliefs, or get them to do something. Rather its general purpose is to strengthen existing beliefs, to get the audience to do more vigorously things which, at the time, they are doing only adequately or even half-heartedly. This is the speech which seeks to substitute earnest effort for lip-service.

As such, it tends more to emotion than to logic, and may contain little or no information. It is frequently accompanied by other stimulants to the emotions: food, flowers, decorations, music, costumes, flags, lighting effects, processions, rituals.

It is successful when the audience leaves feeling exalted, stronger in its faith and eager to fight the good fight.

(iv) **To convince or persuade.** This is the general purpose of the speeches made by the courtroom lawyer, the candidate for office, the salesman, the legislator proposing a bill, the crusader, the reformer, the pleader for a cause, the scientist offering a new theory, the ordinary citizen getting up at a local council meeting or public hearing to argue for something he says will benefit the community.

This type of speech seeks to change an audience's beliefs, to get them to take some specific action. Its appeal may be entirely intellectual and logical, or it may be strongly emotional. It organizes its arguments, backs up these arguments with facts and statistics, and frequently utilizes the methods of the stimulating and impressive speech.

It is successful, of course, when beliefs are changed, when, to some degree, the audience *is* persuaded to do what you ask.

Obviously, a speech whose general purpose is to amuse will differ considerably in content, tone, language and structure from one intended to teach. Both will differ from speeches to stimulate or to convince. Knowing the methods and limitations of each will be a decided help in preparing your talks. (Examples of how narration, exposition and argument are used in various types of speech are given in Chapter Four.)

Exercise No. 16

On the subject of the weather, think of possible speeches you might make whose general purposes would be to interest, teach, impress, persuade.

Exercise No. 17

What were the general purposes of the subjects you listed in Exercises 8 and 9? Could you also deliver other speeches on the same subjects, but with different general purposes?

(b) **The Specific Purpose.** The next step is to phrase as concisely as possible the *specific purpose* of your talk.

Think of the specific purpose variously as the main idea or central thought of your speech; the point you wish to make; what you want your audience to carry away with them; the special angle in your approach.

Boiling down your subject in this way will help you to concentrate your efforts, to eliminate related but distracting details.

Make sure your specific purpose contains one thought and one thought alone, is simple, easily understood, easily remembered, and calculated to arouse interest.

It may be phrased either as a sentence ('High-fidelity equipment will increase your enjoyment of music') or as a question ('How does one clean antique silver?') or the sentence may be implied ('Votes for women!').

Avoid the vague ('Some thoughts on Mexico'), the complex ('How to start a mail-order business') and the lengthy ('Churchill as a young man gave little promise of his later greatness, but when we consider his background we can readily see . . .').

EXERCISE No. 18

What is wrong with the following specific purposes?
(i) The Albert Hall.
(ii) Hints for a long-distance call.
(iii) Savings banks, and investment funds, and stocks and shares, and loans.
(iv) I want you to think about taxation.
Try to improve the statement of these specific purposes.

EXERCISE No. 19

For a general audience, which of the following is the best specific purpose?
(i) Christmas and New Year's Day.
(ii) How to conduct an audit of a commercial bank branch.
(iii) I'd like to help you save a life.

EXERCISE No. 20

Assume you have to speak at: (i) An old folks' home; (ii) The Literary Society of a Public School; (iii) A meeting of members of a theatrical union; (iv) A political rally. Which of the following subjects might be suitable? (*a*) Guidance, (*b*) Children's fears, (*c*) Communism, (*d*) Events in the news, (*e*) Arbitration, (*f*) Television, (*g*) The spoken versus the written word, (*h*) Netball.

Choose good specific-purpose sentences for those subjects you consider suitable. In these situations what subjects would you choose to speak on? What would be your specific-purpose sentences?

(8) Analysing the Audience

Once you have picked a subject which you think will interest a particular audience, analyse your prospective listeners and determine how the speech as a whole can best be *adapted* to them.

A speech in favour of local radio stations might conceivably be made both to a group of sports fans and a group of music lovers. But it could not be the same speech, with the same approach and arguments. What won applause in the one case might call forth hisses in the other.

A speech must be 'pitched' to its particular audience.

Before you give a talk, decide how the answers to the following questions will affect your speech:

(i) **Will the audience be a general or a specialized one?** A specialized audience, such as a group of doctors, requires slanting of the subject to its peculiar interests. The general audience needs a broader appeal.

(ii) **What will be the probable size of the audience?** With a small audience one can be less formal than with a large crowd.

(iii) **What will be the age-range of my listeners?** How far back the experience of your listeners goes will affect your choice of material. With older people, a mere reference to the second World War will elicit an immediate personal response. But for teenagers, those painful years will be known only at second-hand.

(iv) **Will the audience be male, female or mixed?** Material suitable for one sex might not be suitable for the other or for a mixed audience.

(v) **What is the educational and cultural background of the audience?** It is as much a mistake to talk over the heads of the audience as to underestimate their capacities.

(vi) **What social, political and economic prejudices are my listeners likely to have?** Try to find out beforehand the economic level of your audience, the sort of clubs they belong to, their social position. Progressive or conservative, management or workers, homeowners or tenants—each tends to have firmly-held beliefs. The skilful speaker avoids arousing needless hostility. In his arguments, he tries to show that his proposal ties in with principles they cherish.

(vii) **What do they know about my subject?** To cover in detail facts they already know will only bore them. To assume they have knowledge which they do not actually possess will leave them bewildered.

(viii) **What will their attitude be towards my subject?** Some members of your audience will be interested in your subject; others will be indifferent or apathetic; others, if your specific purpose is to persuade, will be hostile. You should try to determine which of these attitudes predominates. Adapt your speech chiefly to this predominant attitude with, of course, appreciation of the other attitudes.

The interested audience needs only to have its interest maintained, so the chief pitfall to avoid here is talking for too long.

The apathetic audience must have its attention caught, its interest aroused and held. A strong opening, the early stressing of what the audience may hope to gain from listening, and the steady, forward movement of your ideas are your best tools.

The hostile audience is, of course, the most difficult to handle. Many skilled speakers follow the practice of delaying, for a considerable time, any direct mention of their specific purpose. They show themselves to be friendly, modest and good-humoured. By their fair-mindedness they let it be known that they expect the audience to be equally fair. They explore all the common ground they have with the audience, they return to points of agreement, before venturing into areas of possible disagreement. In other words, they hope that if the audience gives a series of 'Yes' responses, it will be less disposed to say 'No'.

(ix) **What are they likely to know about me?** If the audience knows little about you, you may tell them some of your past accomplishments.

c

But do so modestly. Whether they know you little or well, avoid the pitfall of boasting. Let the audience learn your worth from the competent way you handle your subject.

Answering the above questions should not be difficult when you are to speak in your local community. The important thing is to adapt your speech to your audience, even though you know its members very well.

When you talk outside your home area, your basic answers will come from the person or committee that invited you, supplemented by such information as you can gather from friends, colleagues and books. Professional lecturers in America often visit a town beforehand, to look it over, talk with townspeople—the butcher, the banker, the farmer, the teacher—to get their views, test their reactions. Borrow this technique if you can, for it helps to show an audience that you know something of them and their special problems.

Keep on the alert, moreover, ready to change your adaptation to the audience up to the last moment. An important event on the afternoon of your talk may change the temper of your audience; the weather may dampen their spirits; or a preceding speaker may say something which you think will influence the audience against the opening you had planned.

Finally, watch the reactions of your audience as you talk, particularly with regard to the special adaptations you have made for them. If you do not get a favourable response, try a different approach.

Exercise No. 21

Select several subjects you might conceivably talk on and determine how you might adapt them to fit the interests and firmly-held beliefs of audiences drawn from the following:

(*a*) A Rotary Club; (*b*) Freemasons; (*c*) A local ratepayers' association; (*d*) A group of company directors; (*e*) A university Socialist Society; (*f*) An anti-apartheid rally; (*g*) A branch of the Communist Party; (*h*) Young Conservatives; (*i*) The National Association of Schoolmasters; (*j*) A Jewish organization; (*k*) A local consumers' association; (*l*) A movement for church unity; (*m*) The Lord's Day Observance Society; (*n*) Young Liberals; (*o*) A motoring organization; (*p*) The British Legion.

(9) Toasts

One of the most likely forms of public speaking you may be asked to perform is that of proposing a toast on some official or private occasion. It is as well to know the correct procedure and apply it as much or as little as the occasion demands.

The Toastmaster

The function of the toastmaster is to establish order and organize the speaking. He checks that the speaker is ready and calls for order; he then announces the name of the speaker. He will use the correct form of address to the audience and the speaker will be correct if he copies this form of address in his introduction.

e.g. *Toastmaster* (banging gavel): 'Your Royal Highness, Your Excellency, my Lords, Ladies and Gentlemen, pray silence for Mr. ——, who will propose the toast of ——.'
(Note: When the toast list is printed in the menu, the toastmaster will not name the toast in his introduction.)
Speaker (rising to his feet after the Toastmaster has finished): 'Your Royal Highness, Your Excellency, my Lords, Ladies and Gentlemen, I have been asked to . . .'

After the toast-speech the toastmaster will repeat the toast and give a definite lead to the company to stand and perform the toast.

The toastmaster usually arrives 30 minutes before the time the function is due to begin and the President or Chairman for the occasion will give him a list of the speakers, toasts and distinguished guests.

Timing

At a formal dinner, the toasts will come when the coffee stage is reached. All service is stopped until after the Loyal Toast has been drunk.

The thing to remember about a toast is to keep it brief and to the point. A toast lasting 2 or 3 minutes is quite acceptable, though a toast-speech (as to a distinguished guest) may last much longer.

When no toastmaster is present

The speaker stands and establishes order by saying 'Ladies and Gentlemen', or otherwise calling for silence. A pause after 'Ladies and Gentlemen' usually has the desired effect. At the end of the speech the speaker gives a definite lead to the company to rise and raise their glasses, repeating the toast itself loudly and clearly.

Form of procedure for a toast

   (i) The speaker stands.
   (ii) He addresses the audience correctly.
   (iii) He states the purpose of the toast; e.g. 'My Lords, Ladies and Gentlemen. It is my pleasure to propose a toast to *the ladies . . .*'
   (iv) He says something complimentary and relevant to the occasion and the person(s) being toasted. (An appropriate story could be included here.)
   (v) He concludes by giving the toast itself; e.g. '. . . and so I ask you to rise and join with me in the toast to *the ladies.*'

Procedure for a longer toast-speech (as to a distinguished guest)

Find out as much as possible about the distinguished guest in advance and make sure that the facts are accurate.

(i) The speaker stands.
(ii) He addresses the audience correctly.
(iii) He refers to the distinguished guest and gives him an assurance of welcome.
(iv) He assures the guest of the honour he does the company by attending.
(v) He gives a brief account of the distinction of the guest.
(vi) He proposes the toast, usually wishing the guest long life and happiness.
(vii) He gives the name of the guest at the end of the toast to give a definite lead to the company.

Replying to a toast

If you are the guest and you are replying you:
(i) Express thanks for the wishes expressed in the toast.
(ii) Express pleasure at being invited (if applicable).
(iii) Wish the organization success (if applicable).

If you are answering on behalf of several guests, again express thanks for the toast and express the pleasure of all the guests at being invited. A short anecdote could be included if applicable. The reply to a toast usually ends with renewed thanks whether one is speaking for oneself or on behalf of others.

It is important when replying to a toast to listen to the words of the speaker who proposed it and use some of his remarks in your reply.

The Loyal Toast

Loyal toasts are usually brief and follow the same form which is subject to the approval of the Queen. Announcements of changing in wording are issued when necessary from Buckingham Palace. The only loyal toasts at present authorized are:

(i) The toast to the Queen.
(ii) The toast to other members of the Royal Family.

Usually only the toast to the Queen is given. No speech is made, and it is only necessary for the speaker to rise and say 'Ladies and Gentlemen— the Queen!'

Even though the toast is brief it is necessary to poise the words carefully, avoiding a sense of rush, to preserve the dignity of the toast.

The second loyal toast can be varied. 'Ladies and Gentlemen, I have the honour to propose the toast of the Duke of Edinburgh, the Prince of Wales and other members of the Royal Family.'

The loyal toast always comes first at all occasions where toasts are to be drunk.

Toasts at a wedding

The usual toasts are as follows:

(i) The toast to the bride and groom, usually proposed by an old family friend who preferably knows both families.

(ii) The groom replies on behalf of his wife and himself and he ends his reply by proposing a toast to the bridesmaids.

(iii) The best man replies to the toast to the bridesmaids and concludes by toasting the health of the parents.

Prepare a toast so that every sentence is clear with carefully-chosen words and balanced phrases. If a story or anecdote is included let it be told in the best language. Know the toast so well that there is confidence and style about the whole presentation.

(10) Using a Microphone

On many occasions, particularly at large banquets, dinners and conferences, a microphone is provided for the speaker. Remember that the microphone is the ear of the listener, so don't shout into it. The amount of volume must be enough to contact the microphone and no more, even though the speaker must *mentally* project to all his audience.

(i) Keep the mouth towards the microphone, and avoid holding papers between the mouth and the microphone as this will distort the sound.

(ii) The microphone will have been placed and adjusted correctly, so there is no need to touch it or move it. Try to disregard the microphone—the speaker must look at the audience and contact them eye to eye.

(iii) When speaking through a microphone to a large crowd, the phrases must be shorter and the pauses longer. Allow time for the listeners to hear and understand.

(iv) If the amplification fails, then project to the back row without raising the pitch level of the voice as this makes the sound strident. Think of 'rolling the voice along the floor'.

(11) Talking on the Radio

Talking on the radio presents special problems. Your audience cannot see you, and yet you want them to think of you as a pleasant, warm and cordial person. You cannot see your audience, can get no immediate response from them. You have in front of you only a mechanical instrument—the microphone.

If you let your gaze and thoughts concentrate on the microphone, you will find it difficult to get the feeling of direct communication with live listeners.

So try to forget the studio equipment and control room. As you talk, think of your listeners. Try to keep up the enthusiasm for your subject, realizing that the microphone will pick up every inflexion and nuance and you can talk as if you were addressing friends in your own living room.

Though you will have many more listeners than could crowd into any hall, they are listening to you *as individuals*. Sit at the table, lean your elbows on it, and talk as if these listeners are sitting at the other end of the table. (Don't rustle your script. Turn the page during a pause which can later be cut by the engineer, if it is being pre-recorded.)

Talk *to*, talk *with* these persons, not at them. Though your script has been well prepared, deliver it in a tone of active, spirited conversation. Let one sentence be a reply to a question. Let the next be an idea that has just popped into your head. Pause as if to find the right word. Think 'because' or 'not at all' or 'in short' before appropriate sentences. Give your audience the illusion that what you are saying is being said for the first time.

Begin with a strong, attention-getting sentence, for your listener can turn you off if you don't interest him. Keep up the attention-getting material. Re-state points at intervals, for some listeners will have tuned in late. Use short sentences, a simple vocabulary, for you are probably talking to the 'average' citizen. But here again you must visualize your audience and make your script appropriate. If you are talking on a scientific subject to a 'highbrow' audience you can use a wide vocabulary and a closely-knit pattern of ideas, though clarity of expression is the main object, whatever the level of the talk.

Let the one or two imaginary persons you are talking to be representatives of the group most likely to be listening at that hour of the day, that day of the week.

Above all co-operate with the producer. He may ask you to make changes in your script, and he may ask you to say things differently. But he is your best guide and is responsible for the programme's success, so try to carry out his wishes.

The Microphone. The studio manager will tell you the best distance to stay from the microphone, whether eight inches or a foot or two. Whatever the distance, keep it. Don't weave from side to side, or back and forth. When you are going to use louder volume at some point, move back a bit. When you are going to talk especially quietly in some section, move slightly closer to the microphone.

Aim your voice towards the centre of the microphone—imagine it to be the ear of the listener. Breathe quietly. Try not to explode b, d, g, p, t, k, too much.

Talk at a rate somewhat faster than you would before an in-the-flesh audience, about 150 words per minute, or between 140 and 180 words per minute. Practise this rate beforehand.

Avoid emphasizing words by saying them more loudly. Instead, emphasize by pitch changes, pauses, and phrasing. Try to achieve flexibility, avoid monotony. Vary pitch, and rate, and quality.

Though you are reading your talk, you should give the illusion that you are talking without a script. Know the material well enough so that you can keep your eyes off the page for at least a third of the time. Unclip your script before you begin. Do not hold it between your mouth and the microphone, and, again, move the pages *quietly* to one side as you finish with them.

Preparation. Double- or triple-space your script. Keep paragraphs small; or better still, separate each sentence.

Underline important words. Indicate pauses by bars (|). Write in directions to yourself in the margin.

Prepare enough material to fill your time allotment, allowing 150 words or from 14 to 16 lines of typescript to the minute. Prepare a little bit extra, for you don't want to run short. Mark off on the script units of three, four or five minutes, whichever is more suitable for the total length of the talk. In the second half, bracket material which can be cut in case you see that you are going to run over time. Be prepared to cut heavily on the next-to-last page, so that you can give full time to the concluding section.

Be prepared for cuts the producer might want. Mark your script as you go through it with him, and don't be surprised if he wants to take out your favourite purple passage, or your carefully worked out ending. The chances are it doesn't *sound* as good as you thought it would. He might even want to cut your beginning which he doesn't think as inspired as you do. You can learn a lot from a good producer.

(12) Talking on Television

On television, talk directly and informally. Face the camera which is being used at the moment (indicated by a light or otherwise). Focus on an imaginary person there and talk to him. As with radio, you will be better received if you think of talking to individuals rather than to a mass audience. Don't let your gaze become unfocused, for then you will seem to be talking *past* or *through* the audience.

Use a lively, conversational style. Do not be too emotional. Try to be sincere and natural. Avoid elaborate gestures, and quick, sudden movements.

Your rate should be the normal speaking one of about 125 words per minute. You need not worry about talking to the microphone for this will be overhead, or hung around your neck, or concealed.

CHAPTER FOUR

COMPOSING A SPEECH

Public speaking, we have already said, is enlarged conversation. By thinking of it that way you will feel more at ease before your audience, and are likely to express yourself more naturally.

But public speaking is a very one-sided sort of conversation. Questions and answers, pauses, examples, transitions, side-remarks—all are yours. So the way it goes is up to you.

You are at the wheel, as it were. Expressions on the faces of your listeners may give you hints of when to slow down and when to increase speed. But the route to follow is for you alone to decide.

Doubtless you have heard the kind of speaker who starts off:

'Well . . . er . . . Let me see now. Before I begin, perhaps I had better explain . . . But it would probably be better if I first tell you what I have in mind. . . . It seems that . . . er . . .'

Such a platform stumbler will wander from one point to another until he finally ends up:

'And so . . . er . . . Oh, yes! There was one point I forgot to mention . . . But perhaps, on second thoughts, we had better skip it now . . . So . . . er . . . Well, that's about all I really have to say. . . .'

A speaker like that may have interesting things to say, but he certainly does not give that impression to his listeners.

As a good speaker, you should know in advance exactly what you are going to talk about. You may leave most of the wording, the pace, and some details of emphasis, to the spirit of the occasion. But you *must* decide well beforehand the main points you will cover and the order in which you will cover them.

The composition of a speech may be divided into three main parts: Introduction, Body, and Conclusion.

A natural thought of most beginners is to start their planning with the first of these. But that is a mistake which can cost you much wasted time.

When the time to face your audience arrives, your first words will be introductory. But preparation is another matter. How you will eventually introduce your speech should largely depend on what its main content is to be. So it is best to work that out first.

(1) The Body of the Speech

If you have followed the advice of the preceding chapter, you will have agreed to speak only about something in which you are really interested and on which you are well informed. The chances then are that you will have more ideas about points to cover than your speaking time will allow.

But do not try to decide what to include and what to leave out until you have jotted down all the likely ideas on cards or separate slips of paper. Postcard-size file cards do very well for this purpose.

Then, spreading these cards or slips of paper out before you on a large desk or table, begin your process of elimination by considering the following:

How does each fit in with the particular approach you wish to make to your general theme? And how is it adapted to the particular audience you are to address?

Let us suppose you are speaking about your favourite sport. Do you wish to talk mainly about its fine points? Or mainly about its great players?

If the former, eliminate notes on the players which do not help to illustrate points of playing technique. If the latter, eliminate notes on technique which do not help to explain the qualities of the players.

Likewise, if the sport is an unusual one and the audience is unfamiliar with it, eliminate anything which assumes an advanced knowledge of its technique. But if the sport is a popular one and the audience consists largely of fans, discard points of elementary explanation.

Or let us suppose you are speaking about job opportunities in your field. Is your main interest in such opportunities in your own locality? Or do you wish to give an overall view of them in the country as a whole?

If the former, eliminate references to situations elsewhere except in so far as they relate to the state of affairs locally. If the latter, do just the reverse.

Likewise, if the processes of your field are little known and your audience is generally unaware of them, there is no point in listing openings for senior technicians. But if its processes are well known to your listeners, you must again be careful to cut out whatever might be too elementary to hold their interest.

Next, sort out those cards which contain the most general points you thought of covering. You may find that you have not jotted down some of your principal headings at all.

Suppose your talk is to be on the fine points of football. You may find that you have a note on the captain always sizing up the weaknesses of each opposition player. You may find that you have another note on how the centre-forward surprises goal-keepers with sudden charges. But you may have no note covering the general strategy of the game.

Adding such notes as needed, you will find yourself with a number of cards with entries like:

> *Fine points of defence*
> *Fine points of passing*
> *Fine points of goal-keeping*

In what order should you organize these?

Generally, several possibilities will present themselves. There is no more reason why an explanation of the fine points of football should start with defence than with passing or any other aspect. The choice may be a toss-up; or it may depend on your own feelings on the game.

Yet, once you have made your choice of a starting point, you cannot go on from it in just any order whatsoever. To proceed from goal-keeper to centre-forward, to full-back, to winger is literally 'jumping all over the field'.

If your listeners follow you on such meanderings, it will be in spite of your organization rather than because of it. So keep arranging and re-arranging your separate notes until they bring out your ideas in an order which makes good sense.

As you do so, you may change your mind altogether about what main headings to use. Or, you may combine some and sub-divide others. For example, those mentioned above may eventually end up something like this:

> (a) *Goal-keeping*
> (b) *Defending the wings*
> (c) *Covering the mid-field*
> (d) *Passing and attacking*

On another plan:

> (a) *Attacking and scoring*
> (b) *Passing the ball*
> (c) *Running and covering the opposite player*

On a still different plan:

> (a) *Individual positions*
> (b) *Teamwork*

In any event, these are only the *main* headings. You will next need to sort out the rest of your notes to group the more general remaining ones in the same way. Under the third heading in the first preceding arrangement, for example, you may have:

> (c) *Covering the mid-field*
>   (i) *Playing centre-forward*
>   (ii) *Playing inside-forward*

    (iii) *Playing left-winger*
    (iv) *Playing right-winger*
    (v) *Playing full-back*

Another plan might be:

    (*c*) *Covering the mid-field*
      (i) *Tackling centre-forward*
      (ii) *Covering main wingers*

But all this relates only to the larger framework of the body of your talk. You will finally need to group all your usable remaining notes on specific points, according to how they fit into such a general scheme.

You might, for example, end up with an arrangement which starts something like this:

BODY OF TALK

(*a*) *Goal-keeping*

    (i) *Basic techniques*

      A. *Dealing with the ground shot*
        1: *Importance of keeping legs together*
        1.1: *Example from* 1966 *World Cup Final*
        2: *Importance of seizing ball firmly in both hands*
      B. *The chest-high shot*
        1: *Body square-on to ball*
        2: *The sideways dive*
        2.1: *Example from* 1969 *Cup Final*
      C. *The high shot*
        1: *Catching the ball*
        2: *Bringing ball down to chest height*

    (ii) *Reducing danger area in front of goal*

      A. *Anticipating movement of opposing forward*
        etc., etc.

With your ideas thus jotted down as separate notes and spread out before you, you can rearrange them at will. You can see at a glance how all that you mean to say fits together in each possible presentation. And it is a simple matter to add points, take them out, or shuffle their order.

The platform stumbler who omits such written preparation tries to do this very same thing, as he says, 'in his head'. But he usually does it inadequately and too late—with his audience watching his embarrassment while he fumbles with 'mental notes'.

After you have become a seasoned speaker, you may well be able to cut some corners on this routine. If you are to speak on a familiar theme, you may be able to jot down your notes directly. But then you will be drawing upon past experience.

Meanwhile do not be deceived into thinking that outlines are unnecessary. Any good artistic job appears to flow so smoothly and effortlessly that it *seems* to have been produced spontaneously. But that is only because the trials and errors of many false starts do not show in the finished product. The many discarded plaster models for a marble statue, the many discarded pencil sketches for a mural painting, the many tentative drafts of a poem, play or novel—these are never seen in the seemingly inspired result. They have been washed away with that 90 per cent of genius which is perspiration.

And the same is true of the art of speaking. Eloquence is rarely spontaneous. But you are much more likely to sound *as though* your speaking was the inspiration of the moment if you sweat out your problems of composition over your notes well before you get to the platform.

Exercise No. 22

With the above suggestions on outlining in mind, analyse the texts of speeches you read in the newspaper. In the case of the body of each:

What are the main points?

What general plan of organization appears to have decided the speaker to present these points in the order he does? Is it a good order? What other arrangements would be as good, or possibly better?

How is each main point explained, illustrated, or developed by minor points, anecdotes and other such material? Could different materials have been better used?

Try drafting the complete body outline of the most worthwhile of these speeches as it may well have been prepared by the speaker himself. Experiment with different rearrangements of the same material and note how different the effect of the speech would have been on each plan.

As far as possible, try to do the same for speeches to which you actually listen.

In the preceding chapter you listed ten subjects for possible talks. Using the suggestions of this chapter, now prepare an outline for the main body of several of these talks. Save your work for additions to be made later.

(2) The Introduction

After working out the main body of your speech, the next step is to plan its introduction, or beginning.

Your first need in this phase of the speech is to arouse your listeners' interest. Fascinating or important as your subject may seem to you, the audience may not at first take the same view. Until they start paying close attention to what you have to say, you will be up there talking to yourself. And there are few sounds more disturbing than the louder and louder shuffling of feet, the growing buzz of conversation, while you are trying to get your point across from the platform.

Interest will of course remain a problem throughout the entire course of your speech. But the moment when you first address your audience is your best single chance to do something about it. Even those members of the audience whose minds have already wandered to other matters are likely to take notice when a different speaker is about to begin. That is the time, therefore, to make your most carefully considered attempt to get their attention.

One standard device is to choose an opening which points a human interest angle in vivid or dramatic form. John Betjeman often uses this type of beginning. Here is one for a speech on church architecture.

'There's something much kinder about a house which has been lived in for generations than a brand-new one. Apart from the fact that an old house is better built than a new one, it's part of England, not a bright red pimple freshly arisen on its surface. An old house reflects the generations that have lived in it. Your mother's tastes for frills and silk lamp-shades, your grandmother's passion for framed watercolours, your great-grandmother's needlework and heavy well-made furniture. It may be a bit inconvenient and muddled, but it is human.

But of all the old houses in England, the oldest and most interesting are . . .'

This example illustrates the device of starting from the known and understood and then progressing to the unknown. The speaker has captured and stimulated the attention and imagination of the listeners by talking about something which most listeners will know from experience and from this opening he begins to develop his theme.

Another device is to connect what you have to say with some current event which has already caught public attention. Thus, a speech on football might start off with comment on a coming or recent World Cup Series. Or a speech on job opportunities might open with some recent statistics on employment trends, especially if the trend is down.

Humour is another standard device of introduction. A good joke or an amusing story has almost universal appeal. A weary audience appreciates the brief break of a good laugh even more than an attentive one.

Lady Megan Lloyd George, speaking about her father, started in this way.

'When my father first became Chancellor of the Exchequer he said to my mother: "It will be a very peaceful job. There is only the Budget." My mother smiled and shook her head and said: "Well, I will wait until I see you at the Treasury." How right she was. There was only the Budget but it took from April to December to get through the House of Commons, and was the cause of two General Elections.'

Adlai Stevenson established quite a reputation in America for his witty introductions when he was campaigning for the presidency. Speaking on foreign policy, he began:

'I want to share with you, if I may, a letter from a California lady who knew my parents when they lived here fifty years ago. She writes that after Grover Cleveland was nominated for the Presidency in 1892 and my own grandfather was nominated for Vice President, she named her two kittens Grover Cleveland and Adlai Stevenson. Grover, she writes, couldn't stand the excitement of the campaign and died before the election. But Adlai lived to be a very old cat.

'And this, my friends, is obviously for me the most comforting incident of the campaign so far. . . .'

Note how the anecdote used here ties in with the theme of political candidacy. A joke which is just another funny story and relates to nothing else that is said, may actually distract your audience's attention from your main subject.

Another thing to be careful about is the question of propriety. On a truly solemn occasion humour can strike a discordant note. Moreover, different people draw the line on humour at different places. For such witticisms as Adlai Stevenson's above, some people questioned whether he was serious enough to be a good presidential candidate. So even a joke must be carefully considered beforehand by the speaker who plans to use it on a public platform.

Certain formalities of the speaking occasion should also be attended to in your opening. It is rude not to reply to a polite introduction. It is courteous somehow to acknowledge that it is to your immediate listeners that you are speaking rather than to the world in general.

Yet, a routine handling of these formalities may get a speaker off to a weak start:

'My good friends, I am most unworthy of the too flattering introduction which your distinguished chairman has just given me. Nevertheless, I regard it as an honour and privilege indeed to address this splendid gathering on this great occasion . . .'

Such stale platitudes make us shudder. Especially when uttered mechanically, they lead us to expect the worst.

Experienced speakers, on the other hand, may use effective references to the speaking occasion as their means of first establishing contact with the audience.

When the late American President Eisenhower spoke at his home-coming celebration at Abilene, Kansas, he started off with these words:

'Governor Arn, Ladies and Gentlemen: we are of course experiencing today a Kansas shower, but I assure you there's not half as much water here today as there was in the English Channel eight years ago today. Moreover, in Kansas we can use this rain—it's okay by me.

'Today I return to the home of my boyhood to join with friends and family in reunion, to see again familiar faces, to receive an inspiring welcome.

'No man can experience these things without deep gratitude and humble thanksgiving for the benefits and kindness he has enjoyed. He realizes anew what he owes to those who guided him in his youth—who taught him—who gave him a share of their own spirit and heart and soul. For such things he strives through the years to repay dear ones and friends—yet he can never entirely erase the debt. He can only testify what he owes.

'Here and now I have the opportunity to speak out . . .'

This speech went on to review the major phases of American national policy. Yet it was effectively begun with these warm personal remarks intimately associating the speaker with his listeners. Some observers had thought the bad weather was going to 'spoil the whole affair'. But the speaker made it an opportunity to show his good humour, to reveal that he remembered what rain meant to the Kansas farmer, and incidentally to remind his audience of his part in the great events through which he first became well known to them.

There are times, of course, when a well-meaning chairman gives you such an excessively flattering introduction that you are actually put at a disadvantage. In such a case, it is just as well to put your relations with your audience back on a more reasonable person-to-person basis by your own opening remarks. Note how the Reverend Harry Emerson Fosdick does it in the following extract:

'I warmly appreciate that far too generous introduction. I do not deserve it. But I am comforted by the remark of a friend of mine: "Flattery never hurts anybody unless he inhales." You see, the Chairman and I have been friends for a long time, and I am affectionately devoted to him and to his wife—I married them—so that he is not prepared to speak objectively about me. He is an honest man, but I don't believe half of what he has just been saying; nevertheless, I warmly appreciate it.

'Frankly, I have been apprehensive about speaking here today. I know nothing about running a business, and for me to talk about economics or politics or business administration would be nonsense. My only hope is that you have been talked to so much about your specialized problems that it may not be altogether unwelcome to have someone speak here about something else altogether. And there is something else which concerns us: the moral situation in our country . . .'

This introduction is warmly, even intimately personal. At the same time it reveals maturity of mind which can raise serious questions without being self-consciously solemn.

Such a beginning invites our attention no matter what the subject, because it commands respect for the speaker himself. A man like that we instinctively feel, must have something worthwhile to say.

The final need of your introduction is to direct attention to the main body of your speech. Otherwise the interest it arouses in other matters may actually serve to defeat your real speaking purpose.

Reviewing each of the above examples of effective introduction, you will see how each also has a good transition, or carry-over, to the main theme.

The very word 'introduction' comes from two Latin words: *intro* meaning 'into', and *ducere* meaning 'to lead'. It is literally a 'leading into'. What it should lead is the audience's interest. But it should lead this interest into the main body of the speech which is to follow.

Exercise No. 23

With the above explanations in mind, analyse the introductions of each of the speeches you have considered in the preceding exercise. In each case:

How do they arouse, or fail to arouse, interest? Is a single device used? Or a combination of devices? And how effectively?

Do they attend to formalities of the speaking occasion? How? Is the effect a loss or an increase in possible audience interest?

Do they tend to distract attention from the main theme? Or do they have effective transitions? And by what means do these transitions carry interest over to the main body of the speech?

Analyse in the same way speeches to which you actually listen.

For each speech for which you have already prepared a Body outline in Exercise No. 22, now prepare an Introduction outline.

(3) The Conclusion

If first impressions are the most striking, last impressions are often the most lasting.

Your very first words may determine what kind of a hearing your speech will get. But your very last words may decide how it will be remembered or acted upon by your listeners.

The experienced speaker is careful, therefore, to save some appropriate material from the body of his speech in order to clinch it effectively at the end. He would no more think of beginning a speech without knowing how he was going to finish it off than of building a house from incomplete plans.

The easiest type of conclusion is a summary of what has been said. A certain old rustic, with very little formal education, when asked the secret of his success as a story-teller, replied:

'Well, I'll tell you. First I always tells 'em what I'm goin' to tell 'em. Then I tells it to 'em. Then I tells 'em what I've just told 'em.'

'Tellin' 'em what you've just told 'em' gives your listeners a chance to reflect back and realize how all you have been saying finally ties-in or comes together. This is most obviously necessary when your talk centres on detailed technical information.

If the purpose of your speech is inspirational, however, a mere recapitulation may weaken its final effect. In that case you will find it more effective to end with a general re-statement of your theme in strongly inspirational terms.

Here, for example, is the conclusion of Adlai Stevenson's speech from which the introduction was quoted above:

'Some may say to you that this is visionary stuff. To this I reply that history has shown again and again that the self-styled realists are the real visionaries—for their eyes are fixed on a past that cannot be recaptured. It was Woodrow Wilson, with his dream of the League of Nations, who was the truly practical man—not the Old Guard who fought him to the death. And in the fateful summer of 1940 it was the vision of a Churchill that saw beyond Dunkirk to victory.

'I say that America has been called to greatness. The summons of the twentieth century is a summons to our vision, to our humanity, to our practicality. If these provide the common purpose of America and Asia, of our joint enterprise, of our progress together, we need have no fear for the future. Because it will belong to free men.'

EXERCISE No. 24

With the above explanations in mind, analyse the conclusions of each of the speeches considered in the two preceding exercises.

So far as possible, do the same for speeches to which you actually listen.

For the speeches for which you have already prepared Body and Introduction outlines in the two preceding exercises, now prepare conclusion outlines.

So far we have taken up only the elements of speech composition. Introduction, Body, and Conclusion have each been discussed separately in general terms.

Now we shall illustrate in more detail, how all these elements need to be combined in types of speeches you may have occasion to make.

(4) Narration

Everybody loves a good story. Almost any kind of a point can be made in story form. That is perhaps why narration—story telling—is one of the oldest and most popular forms of public address.

It also happens to be the easiest kind of speech to organize, and therefore the best to start practising on.

But you might not think so to hear the way some people handle it:

'A friend of mine told me the funniest story when he heard I was going to speak here tonight.

'It seems that these two men (Which "two men"?) were coming into a building at the same time . . .

'Now wait a minute! I should have said in the first place (Why didn't he, then?) that the man who was going to the basement had just got out of a taxi. And the man who was going upstairs—he was the one who really found the briefcase—had just got off a bus . . . Or maybe it was the other way around . . . Oh, well, it really doesn't make any difference . . .

'Anyway, as I said before (Did he?), they were both late and . . .' etc., etc.

There is really no excuse for 'scrambling' a narrative like this.

In other kinds of speeches, the problem of what order to follow is more difficult. To tell about the game of football in *general* you can start with its origins, rules, personalities, or a dozen other possible points of departure. And each such starting point limits you in different ways as to how you can go on from there.

But events—real or imaginary—take place in time. They occur in succession. Clock and calendar can settle the elementary problems of order for you.

To tell the story of a *particular* football game should be a simple matter. From the kick-off to the final whistle, each highlight follows the one before and precedes the one after. All you need do is follow the sequence of events.

Why, then, the difficulty which some people have with narration?

Perhaps the most common fault lies in how the *introduction* is handled.

The beginning of a narrative must, of course, serve the usual purpose of arousing interest. But like the first act of a play (which is just a story acted out) it must also identify the characters and set the scene for what is to follow.

Narrators who start off with unclear references to 'these men' or 'this girl' would do well to recall the technique of the first stories they probably ever heard:

'Once upon a time there was a boy named Jack who lived with his mother in a little cottage. His father was dead, and they were very poor . . .'

The subject-matter of such old fairy tales may seem childish. But not the technique of their telling.

Their narrative beginnings give you at once a clear picture of recognizable individuals. There is never any danger thereafter that you will mistake Jack for the Giant, Mother Bear for Goldilocks, or Aladdin for the Genie.

Most of these characters are pictured, moreover, against a *background* which is equally clear. Each indicates a certain atmosphere—simple poverty, forest wildness, oriental splendour—which gives added poignancy to what is to happen.

The intended effect of a *mood* story—horror, mystery, adventure or the comic—may depend almost entirely on striking the right note at the outset. But even the most straightforward narrative usually needs some kind of preliminary explanation of circumstances before your listeners can fully appreciate the point of whatever else you are relating.

If you are telling about a football game, for example, you need to mention, as soon as possible, the names of the teams, the occasion, and perhaps some of the players in the line-up. Mention of the gate receipts and a spot description of the fans' excitement in the stands might also help to sound the intended keynote.

Then you will be free to go ahead with the play of the game in any needed detail. You will not have to backtrack for explanations, and you can be reasonably confident that your listeners are able to stay with you.

There is, of course, an artful way of beginning in the middle of a tale and then filling in the background later. Known as the *flash-back technique*, it is sometimes used by experienced story tellers to grip their audience's attention at once with a tantalizing foretaste of the later action.

On such a pattern, your account of a football match could start with the last five minutes of the second half. Interrupting at a crucial point, you could then review the first half, the previous games of the season or of other seasons, even the parallel schoolboy games of the same players, before returning to the situation with which you had started.

But that is, essentially, a dramatic method. You can have lots of fun experimenting with it *after* you have had some experience with direct narration.

Perhaps the most common error in handling the body of a narrative is failure to focus attention on what is really significant.

The problem of *focus* in narrative arises from the fact that, to be truly tellable, a tale must first be disentangled from a thousand and one trivial incidents which have no real bearing on its point.

Even the most exciting football match you ever saw must have had its comparatively dull stretches. In order to highlight main events, therefore, you need to give relatively brief treatment to relatively long periods of intervening time:

The first half of the game was quite uneventful. The few attempts at goal-scoring were accidental and not planned by any deliberate strategy— and the home side's defence was sent into disarray by these accidental attacks. Then, just before the first-half whistle, Bobby Charlton went through the visiting team's defence without any opposition whatsoever and scored with a fantastic left-foot drive which sent the fans wild with enthusiasm . . .

Or:

The first few days we spent fishing those waters were as dull as any I have ever spent. No matter what kind of bait we tried, we caught nothing. There just didn't seem to be any more fish left in the sea. But we had no sooner let out our lines on the fourth day when Bob got a bite which nearly pulled the rod right out of his hands . . .

Note in each of these examples how much irrelevant routine is telescoped into a few terse sentences. Unsuccessful attempts to get near the goal, days of fishing and changing bait to no avail—it is pointless to go into detail on matters like these.

If you do so you only draw on your audience's reserve of interest. So never try to give a full, ball-by-ball or blow-by-blow account in any ordinary narrative. Always plan your material so that the time you give each part is in proportion to its importance.

Another helpful device is to organize the events you are narrating into several related groups or phases.

A familiar pattern in fiction runs somewhat as follows: (i) An opening phase in which things are running smoothly. (ii) A phase of foreboding in which signs of trouble appear. (iii) A phase of complication in which things become worse and worse. (iv) A phase of climax in which matters come to a head. Then (v) a final phase in which the problem is resolved.

There may, of course, be double climaxes, pessimistic tales which are grim from the very beginning, or other variations of pattern.

The important point is that by organizing the events of your narrative into some such groupings, you will not only keep them more clearly in mind without looking at written notes, but you will also make it easier for your listeners to follow the thread of your story.

Psychologists have recently 'discovered' that we grasp things better when we can perceive them in recognizable patterns. A number like 9481 is harder to keep in mind than the number 2468 which sticks in our memory because we see in it the familiar pattern of the table of two's.

But ever since ancient times, good story tellers have understood this principle well. Although they may not have written books about it as a technique, they have applied it in the plots of their tales.

Your touring holiday may not have been high drama. But if you are to give a talk about it, you might well group its several phases on a comparable plan or plot. For example:

(*a*) *Getting ready*
(*b*) *The route out*
(*c*) *Crossing the Channel*
(*d*) *Sightseeing in Paris*
(*e*) *The route back*
(*f*) *Homecoming*

As for the conclusion of your narrative, the main thing is to make it short and simple.

The Greek slave, Æsop, always appended a moral to his fables. But there is reason to suspect that he did it as a deliberate dig at the intelligence of the Roman masters for whom he wrote. 'All's well that ends well' may make a good title. But it makes a lame ending.

If you have really told your story effectively, it will point to its own conclusion. What you add may only detract from the final effect. So, unless there are the most urgent reasons to do otherwise, break it off sharply at the end.

EXERCISE NO. 25

If any of the speeches you analysed for the three preceding exercises included narratives, review them now in the light of what has been discussed here. In each case:

Does the introduction serve to identify the characters and set the scene, as well as arouse interest?

Are the events organized in their proper time sequence? Are they grouped in appropriate phases?

Are flash-back methods used? If so, to what effect?

Does the conclusion allow the story to speak for itself?

As far as possible, analyse in the same way, narratives to which you actually listen.

Review in the same way any narratives you may have outlined for the three preceding exercises. If necessary, add new ones now which are narrative in form.

If you have young brothers or sisters, or if other children are available to you as an audience, arrange to 'tell them stories'. It will be entertaining for them, and excellent practice for you. If you can draw on your own experience or imagination for such tales, so much the better. If you have to get them from books, do not try to follow the published stories exactly as they are written. The illustrated page may use quite different techniques than the speaker. So re-work the outline, as suggested above, to adapt them to your purpose.

In such a venture you will find audience analysis more important than you may at first suspect. If your stories are the least bit 'too old' for the group, they will promptly let you know they are bored and restive. If your stories are the least bit 'too young' for them they will be positively indignant. In particular they will not stand for anything they believe to be 'sissified'.

But if you can strike just the right level, you will have a rewarding experience.

Children are also more responsive than adults to the manner in which stories are told. If you are getting across to them, they will sit with mouth and eyes wide open. If not, they will act out their boredom. At

every change of tone, pace, expression, wording, material, you will see
the results at once.

Thus you will get valuable experience in the feel of the live speaking-
situation. Especially if you lack practice in speaking to adult groups,
you will find yourself a lot more at ease before youngsters. And you
may well be able to carry that feeling of confidence over to adult
occasions.

(5) Exposition

Exposition is explaining—telling about, telling why, telling how.

It is what you seek when you consult your lawyer or stockbroker or
any other expert, when you want a better understanding of child psy-
chology, business cycles or atomic energy.

It is what you are asked for when new employees need to be 'shown
the ropes' at your shop or office, when your next-door neighbour seeks
pointers on growing chrysanthemums, when your children ask why the
moon shines only at night or where babies come from.

It is 99 per cent of the work of our schools, 90 per cent of the work of
our armed forces in peacetime, and a much greater percentage of the
work of all industry than is commonly realized.

Few speaking assignments can be easier under one set of circumstances.
Few can be harder under another.

It may take a qualified building contractor only two minutes to tell a
team of experienced carpenters how to carry out repairs to a building.
But he may never be able to explain to the satisfaction of a white-collar
client why it took them so long or cost so much.

The important difference again is your relation as a speaker to your
audience. Take the following passage as an example:

*The ratio of the coupling impedance to the geometric mean of the im-
pedance of corresponding elements in the two meshes is called the
coupling coefficient.*

To an audience of electrical engineers, this is perfectly clear. To any
other, it is mumbo-jumbo.

If you are a surgeon explaining a new surgical technique to other
surgeons, you will doubtless start with the physiological conditions to
which that technique has been applied, the special instruments needed,
and the types of anaesthesia recommended. Then you will describe the
steps to follow, merely mentioning the more common ones, and elabor-
ating upon the more unusual ones. Your conclusion may cover post-
operative care of the patient, statistics of recovery and mortality, and a
final summary of the special precautions to be taken.

Perhaps, in such a case, you can make what you say more clear with
good diagrams and fuller explanations of details. But your main prob-

lems of organizing what you have to say are taken care of by the lecturing routine of your field.

When you try to tell a group of laymen about surgery, however, you face an entirely different problem. You can no longer take knowledge of technical terms, familiarity with routines, or even interest, for granted.

The more enthusiastic you are about your subject, the harder it will be for you to realize that your listeners may find it dull. The better you yourself understand what you are talking about, the harder it is for you to grasp what your listeners may not understand about it.

The first question to ask yourself is: why should the audience consider this matter at all? Yes, it means a lot to me. But what can it mean to them?

If you are a surgeon, you must talk of hospitals not as places where you operate, but as places where most people go only when they are seriously ill.

If you are a builder, you must talk of houses, not as job sites for your workmen, but as homes in which people dwell.

If you are a professional footballer, you must talk of the game not as a means of earning a living, but as a sport which most people enjoy as amateurs, spectators or fans.

You must set aside, temporarily, your insider's point of view. You must make every possible effort to see your subject from your audience's outside point of view.

This applies not only to the preliminary question of arousing interest, but to the very heart of the explanation itself.

Perhaps the greatest single mistake of speakers on technical subjects is to use *technical jargon* without explaining it.

We have all had experience of fakes and show-offs who do this deliberately to 'impress' their listeners. Whenever such quackery does not just confuse or annoy an audience, it leaves them suspicious that the speaker is really trying to camouflage his ignorance. The general public is less easily taken in than it used to be by learned double-talk with nothing behind it.

But it is easy for you to commit a similar error quite innocently. In so unpretentious a matter as explaining how to bake a particular kind of cake, you may unthinkingly say: 'Then fold in the whites of two eggs.' Neither you nor any other experienced cook may be aware that any technical term has been used. But the listener who 'folds' only letters and newspapers may have a very grotesque picture in his mind of what you mean by 'folding in egg-whites'.

This is not to say that you must *never* use any such expressions. That would be unnecessarily awkward, if not impossible. But do try to use technical terms sparingly.

Unless there is some real point in doing otherwise, call a common cold a 'cold' rather than an 'acute upper respiratory infection'. Or call common table salt just that, not 'sodium chloride'.

If technical terms are unavoidable or serve a real purpose, explain them simply as you go along. Preferably, describe the action or object *before* you use the term itself.

If you are telling your audience how weather is predicted, you may conveniently speak of 'precipitation' once you have mentioned that it means 'either rain, sleet, hail or snow'. But then remember that your listeners do not have before them a written copy of what you are saying. They cannot check back if something has slipped their minds, as they could if they were reading your speech. So remind them of technical definitions whenever they are likely to need such help.

It is also a good idea to anticipate in your introduction *common mistaken attitudes* towards your subject. Are you talking about 'wonder drugs'? Some people have been so over-impressed by them as to think ordinary health precautions are no longer necessary.

Is your subject golf? Many think of it as 'an old man's game' in which 'you just keep chopping at a ball until you hit it, and then spend the rest of the day walking around looking for it'.

Have you been asked for a popular explanation of psychiatry? Some still regard it as treatment only for raving lunatics.

You will do well, therefore, to clear away such popular misconceptions as soon as possible.

A more basic need is somehow to connect matter unfamiliar to your listeners with something familiar to them. A common example is the kind of explanation the astronomer gives of astronomical sizes and distances in a popular lecture. He may compare the sun to a golf ball, and then say that, on the same scale, the Earth would be no larger than a grain of sand, 19 inches away, while the star, Alpha Centauri, would be a similar ball 1,000 miles away.

When Albert Einstein gave a *popular* explanation of relativity theory, he did not use differential equations, as when addressing other scientists. He referred instead to what we experience when riding in lifts or trains; and he went on from there by other simple analogies.

Pumpkins, peas, miles, lifts going up and down, trains passing each other on parallel tracks, these are things our minds can grasp more easily than 'light-years' or 'relatively accelerated co-ordinate systems'.

Even commonplace facts and figures need special treatment when the listener does not have them spread out before him as when reading a book. Charts and diagrams are helpful if they are large enough for the audience to see.

But there are times when you cannot have such visual aids on hand for the audience to look at while you are speaking. Then you must make up for the lack of them by the way you present your figures.

The simplest device is to *round off* numbers of many digits. Do not say:

'Three million, one hundred and twenty-eight thousand, four hundred and thirty seven; or seventy-nine, point six one eight per cent.'

Say, rather:

'Well over three million, or very nearly eighty per cent.'

Better still, express your statistics in a form which strikes the imagination of the listener and drives home to him what they mean *in concrete terms.*

For example, you might have occasion to point out that your morning newspaper contained 122,000 words of editorial matter. Unless your audience is made up of journalists, such a figure would have little effect. But if you point out that your morning paper contained as many words as a *long novel,* all your listeners can appreciate what a significant achievement this is.

Figures expressed in such a manner do not put an audience to sleep; seven-digit columns often do. Make your statistics meaningful.

You can do much the same sort of thing with other kinds of ideas. Even when they are not obscure to begin with, you will make the points you wish to emphasize more vivid to your listeners, and easier to remember, if you illustrate them with some striking *example, analogy* or *anecdote.*

Charles E. Wilson, president of General Motors, began an address to an audience of management consultants as follows:

'The title I have chosen for my talk, as most of you know, is "The Camel's Nose is Under the Tent". The expression comes from an old Arabian fable, and to an Arab it spells trouble and disaster. The fable of The Arab and His Camel goes something like this:

'One cold night, as an Arab sat in his tent, a camel gently thrust his nose under the flap and looked in.

' "Master," he said, "let me put my nose in your tent, for it is cold and stormy out here."

' "By all means, and welcome," said the Arab, and turned over and went to sleep. A little later he awoke and found that the camel had not only put his nose in the tent but his head and neck, as well.

'The camel, who had been turning his head from side to side, said, "I will take but little more room if I place my forelegs within the tent. It is difficult standing without."

' "You may also plant your forelegs within," said the Arab, moving a little to make room, for the tent was small.

'Finally the camel said: "May I not stand wholly within? I keep the tent open by standing as I do."

' "Yes, yes," said the Arab. "Come wholly inside. Perhaps it will be better for both of us." So the camel crowded in.

'The Arab with difficulty in the crowded quarters again went to sleep. The next time he woke up he was outside in the cold and the camel had the tent to himself.

'Independent of how he got there, the important point is that the camel of government control now has his nose under the tent of free competitive industry and is crowding in. We will all have to watch him or he will take over the tent . . .'

The comic picture of a clumsy quadruped nosing his drowsy master out of his own quarters is, of course, only a starting point. It does not 'prove' anything. It remains to be justified in terms of something which is not a fable. But it does inject new life into the statement of a point of view to which many listeners had long since stopped paying much attention.

Note that this last example of expository technique is also a narrative. We may distinguish different types of speech in terms of the speaker's main intent. But there is no hard and fast difference between the several kinds of speech composition themselves.

Just as narration may serve the purposes of exposition, therefore, both may also serve the purposes of argument.

(6) Argument

Argument is speaking to persuade. Its practical purpose is to win support for points of view or proposals for action.

For the salesman the outcome may mean the booking of a big order. For a club member, it may mean the soundness of his organization's policy. For a political party it may mean the winning of an election. At the level of international statesmanship even the grim issue of war or peace may be at stake.

In such cases 'the chips are down'. Our convictions, our very hopes and fears are often involved. What then makes argument so important also makes it difficult.

To begin with, there are certain basic ethical questions as to means and ends.

It would be pointless to ignore the fact that there *are* well-established ways of 'pulling the wool over people's eyes'. The very word *sophistry*—which means deliberately deceptive argument—goes back to certain rhetoricians of ancient Greece who, over 2,000 years ago, professed to teach how to speak so as 'to make black appear white, or the worse the better cause'.

Admittedly, the sophists and their followers have been doing a brisk trade ever since. Deliberate quacks, frauds and demagogues do sometimes have their day.

On the professed theory that 'there's a new sucker born every minute', Barnum amassed a fortune. After Adolf Hitler published his belief that the speaker should tell such colossal lies that the simple-minded public is overwhelmed by them (*Mein Kampf*), he gained enough popular support to be able, in a moment of manufactured crisis, to seize control of the German government. Such examples can be multiplied many times over.

Now what about such methods of persuasion?

In one set of circumstances, the answer is obvious. A speaker who is peddling Hokum's snake-bite remedy will have to talk fast or the yokels will have a chance to think. One who seeks to gain notoriety by stealing the limelight does not let common decency stand in his way. One who is inciting a mob to riot against the processes of justice will have to work on his listeners' most vicious prejudices and depraved passions.

But how about the speaker who sincerely believes that he is defending all that is sound and good against the attacks of folly and evil?

It is an elementary social fact that many shades of different opinion are sincerely held by different people. Even when standing side by side, looking at the same things, we may see them with different eyes. Depending on our different past experiences or constitutional make-ups, we view the same scene with different sensitivities, different habits of perception.

'This is a wonderfully large doughnut!' says the optimist.

'It has such a terribly big hole in the centre!' objects the pessimist.

'We have achieved one of the highest standards of living in the world!' the Government boasts.

'It is not half of what it could, or should be!' the Opposition complains.

There is such a thing as genuine disagreement in the face of identical evidence. In view of the importance of the ends for which we argue, then, are not all devices of persuasion equally legitimate? So long as we really believe in what we are speaking for, are we not within our rights to use cajolery or trickery to win others over to our side?

One attitude is to regard all arguments as ammunition in a war of ideas. The front-line soldier has no choice. He must use his rifle and bayonet as best he can. Otherwise, he will end up as a casualty himself.

According to this view, the world of opinion and policy-making is a jungle. You fight with words and ideas as does a beast with tooth and claw. Otherwise your beliefs will become extinct. And then what good is it to have been fair and reasonable?

A book on the art of speaking is, of course, not a place to preach virtue. Yet, the techniques which a speaker uses in argument so obviously depend on his ethical principles that they cannot be discussed realistically as though they existed in a moral vacuum.

If yours is the jungle view of human nature, you will study how best to exploit the ignorance, stupidity and emotional immaturity of your listeners. You will devise 'trick cases' and 'loaded definitions'. You will distort evidence or fabricate your own from rumour and gossip. You will practise the theory of 'the big lie repeated loudly enough and often enough until people lose their power to doubt it'.

Whenever possible, you will confuse the attempts of others to think critically by intimidation and emotional appeals to prejudice. And to do all this more easily, you will shift the ground of consideration from real problems to false 'isues' of your own making.

However, even if this is your view of human nature, you cannot afford to forget Abraham Lincoln's famous maxim:

'You may fool all the people some of the time; you can even fool some of the people all the time; but you can't fool all of the people all the time.'

Although this statement has often been made fun of, the more you think about it, the more good sense you are likely to find in it. Yes, sophistry does work, perhaps more than many of us would like to admit, but most people 'catch on' sooner than the cynics realize. There is, as the Americans say, little repeat business in the wooden-nutmeg trade.

An on-the-level salesman may lose a big order to a tricky competitor. But if he has a good product and has represented it honestly, who is more likely to get the repeat business over the years?

Hitler may have had a meteoric rise. But the truth eventually over-threw his big lies, and his name lives only in infamy.

You may lose many of your arguments when you feel you should have won them. But if you have kept your listeners' respect, your credit will still be good with them for the future.

This does not mean, however, that you can ignore the *legitimate* biases and special interests of your listeners. On the contrary, careful audience analysis is particularly important to this kind of speaking.

In trying to put your case on a sound logical basis you should not forget that logic itself is, in a sense, relative. It is mainly a way of being consistent with yourself. If you start from different *premises*—basic assumptions—you will arrive at different conclusions by the very same logical steps.

A well-known professor used to tell his students the story of a mental patient who was quite rational except for one thing: he was convinced that he was dead.

On one occasion a number of psychiatrists were experimenting with this patient to see if there was any way of reasoning him out of his absurd notion.

One of the doctors finally took the patient's hand, pricked the skin on the back of it with a surgical instrument, wiped off the blood with a piece of cotton, and showing him the bright, red-stained swab, demanded: 'Can you look at that and still insist that you believe you are dead?'

With the evidence literally thrust under his nose, the patient was deeply disturbed. His brows knitted in a frown, he bit his lips, and there was obviously a struggle going on in his mind. It looked for a moment as though he had been reasoned out of his delusion. But suddenly his face cleared and he answered: 'Why, that only proves dead men bleed!'

Granted his assumption, of course, the patient was perfectly logical. His reasoning went like this: 'I am dead. I am bleeding. Therefore a dead man is bleeding.'

When we are too naïve about reasoning, our evidence often has the effect of helping others to such unintended conclusions.

The structure of your argument should, indeed, be a logical one. That is the basis on which you should try to arrange your notes as recommended at the beginning of this chapter. But you cannot expect to work solely from your own personal premises.

The chances are that you will never, in a lifetime, persuade a real opponent that his premises are wrong. *Conversion* is a remarkable thing —because it so rarely happens.

The most you can realistically attempt in any one speech is to gain the support of those listeners whose minds are not yet fully made up. If you are both effective and fortunate, you may then also persuade some other listeners that your conclusion is more acceptable to them than they had realized. But you are not likely to achieve either of these results unless you start from those aspects of your audience's genuine interest and conviction which are most closely related to yours.

Suppose, as a parent living in a district where there are no playgrounds you feel that something should be done to provide recreational facilities for children. Your original concern in the matter may be simply that of a parent for the well-being of his own children.

But let us suppose further that, by means discussed in the next two chapters, you have an opportunity to present a case for such a playground before the following audiences:

(i) A group of your neighbours who are also parents.
(ii) A meeting of a local ratepayers' association.
(iii) A meeting of a local businessmen's association.
(iv) An open meeting of your town council.

In each of these groups there may be several individuals who will sympathize with your desire as a good parent to see your youngsters have as happy a childhood as possible. But that will not be their main concern. And that will not be what they are there for.

To build a playground takes time, trouble and money. It will mean work and expense for many people as long as it operates. You need more than a few nods of sympathy.

Your problem in each case is to show how what you happen to be urging is in the interests of your audience.

The first group will doubtless be easiest to persuade. As parents themselves, some may already feel as strongly as you do the need for such a project. They may merely be waiting for someone like you to take the initiative in speaking up for it.

Still others in the same group may have given their children's welfare less thought. They need to have their attention called to the dangers of children playing in the street, how many have been injured in this way, and how well other communities have been provided with safe playgrounds.

Here your main obstacle is mere inertia. As a speaker you need only to awaken dormant interests.

The composition of the second audience may overlap the first. But the ratepayers will also include people who have no children, or whose children are grown up. Why should they bother about playgrounds? Would they get anything out of it for their money besides the satisfaction of doing good deeds?

The modern ratepayers' association is an alert civic group which seeks mainly to ensure that money collected as rates is used to the best possible advantage. If you can appeal to them on that basis, you may well find them with you as a matter of enlightened self-interest.

How about your playground as a community asset? Can you show that areas without such facilities tend to run down? Can you show that property values tend to go up in neighbourhoods with such facilities?

Next comes the businessmen's association. Some of its members are parents and some are ratepayers, but is there anything in this project to appeal to the group specifically as businessmen?

When a community runs down due to inadequate facilities, is that not as bad for local business as it is for property owners? When the community level improves, is that not as good for local business interests as for any other?

Is there not, moreover, an established relationship between lack of playgrounds and juvenile delinquency? When children have nowhere to work off their energy, are they not more likely to go in for vandalism and shop-lifting?

If you can show that support of such a project as yours is also a good business investment, you will have more than a personal appeal to offer. You will be putting your proposition on a sound commercial basis.

Before the local council, finally, you may offer all these arguments. But then you should also emphasize whatever moral support you have been able to get from the other groups.

Summarizing, then, your overall case may look something like this:

(a) *Existing playgrounds are inadequate.*
(b) *The proposed new one would be good for the community's children.*
(c) *It would be good for local ratepayers.*

(*d*) *It would be good for local businessmen.*
(*e*) *It has responsible popular support.*

This is the kind of arrangement of main points which might well come from an early organization of your notes as suggested at the beginning of this chapter.

The first contention would probably be a necessary part of any talk you might give. The others might also at least be mentioned on most speaking occasions. But the amount of time you would spend on each of the last four would most certainly depend on your analysis of your listeners' main concern in each case.

How, next, will you back up these contentions?

Argument (*a*) may be common knowledge, or it may not. Can you get or make a survey of how many children of different ages there actually are in your area? Can you get comparative figures for other areas? Can you also get the figures on the number of acres of playground, swings, tennis courts, etc., in the other areas.

The more exactly you prepare such data, the less likely is your proposition to be confused with the vague proposals of fuzzy minded 'crackpots'.

Argument (*b*) is not wholly a factual matter in the same sense. It involves some less tangible considerations which you will have to present in more personal terms:

'After all, one is only young once. We do not want our children to look back over the years on bleak memories of street corners and back alleys. . . .'

But perhaps you can also get statistics of accidents to children playing in the streets, or of cases of juvenile delinquency traced to unsuitable gathering places. These will help to make it clear that you are talking sense and not sentimental rubbish.

For arguments (*c*) and (*d*), you may well have to look into the estimated costs of acquiring, equipping and maintaining a playground. No sound business group is likely to sign a blank cheque even for the worthiest cause. So you will need to calculate the total cost of the project and the estimated increase in property values which should result. If the resulting figure is higher than you had realized, you may then have to compare it with estimated costs of vandalism, of other delinquency, of injury due to accidents, etc.

For contention (*e*) finally, the best evidence is signed petitions or officially prepared copies of resolutions passed at the ratepayers' and businessmen's meetings. If you can get them, newspaper editorials supporting your cause are first-rate ammunition.

Wherever possible, give your evidence in specific numerical form. Reliable statistics on a wide range of questions like those of populations, national income, employment, exports, imports, economic productivity, etc., can be looked up in such convenient sources as *Whitaker's Almanack.*

Other issues, of course, do not admit of such treatment. Is euthanasia (mercy killing) in accord with our major moral and religious traditions? This is the sort of question on which we are much more likely to be guided by authoritative opinion. Looking up such topics in sources like *The Times Index* or *British Humanities Index*, you can find articles by people whose specialized study or official connexion gives their judgement more weight with an audience than your own personal assertion.

Be careful, though, not to cite 'authorities' outside the field of their real competence. Prominent people voice views on all sorts of questions. But it is no more appropriate to quote a general on the merits of modern art than it is to quote a glamorous film-star on the strategic value of atomic weapons.

It is one thing to think out a case in plausible general terms. But it is quite another to back it up with *evidence*. Without good organization on your part, your listeners may not even get the point of the data you present to them. But without concrete indications of the grounds on which you maintain your position, they may fail to see any reasons for it. Your preparation should anticipate both of these needs.

(7) Composition as Feeling for Form

We have so far considered speech composition only in connexion with the organization of specific parts, or specific kinds, of speeches.

But the question of how to organize a speech is merely a special case of the more general problem: how to put first things first, last things last, and everything in between in its proper place. The more we have cultivated our sense of form, direction, structure or purpose, in other areas, the more easily can we apply it in what we say.

Avoid the idea that speaking is something apart from whatever else you do. Try to carry over to your speaking any skill or insight you have already gained in other activities. For example, when you look at a painting or photograph you particularly like, ask yourself the following questions:

Does it catch the eye at once?

After the first general glance, is your eye drawn by the composition to some sharper focus of attention?

Are there elements in the picture which keep distracting your attention from the central point of interest? Or do all secondary objects lead back to the main focus?

Does any part of it seem to have no connexion with the rest of the picture? Or does all of it obviously belong within the same frame?

If you prefer music, consider some of your favourite pieces. Listen to them again, asking yourself:

Does it take some time to arouse your interest? Or does it catch your ear with the very first notes?

Do the first bars so arrest your attention that you tend to hum them over rather than listen to the rest of the composition? Or do they rather lead your attention to what follows?

Is the same melodic theme repeated monotonously. Or is it given interesting new variations as the composition progresses?

If there are several melodic themes, do they tend to clash with each other? Or are they so inter-related as to contribute to a common, musically interesting effect?

Is the composition padded out? Or does it conclude gracefully before your attention is fatigued?

At the finale are you at all uncertain whether it has actually reached its end? Or does it finish off with an unmistakable final cadence?

You can ask similar questions for sculpture, poetry, novels, short stories, films, plays, radio or television programmes—anything that requires design or any kind of artistic contrivance.

Note particularly that most of the questions asked above are in pairs. If your answer is 'yes' to the first in each pair, the work you are considering does not have *good structure* for you. For you it is in some respect awkward, confused, jumbled, incoherent, ill-organized, or otherwise badly composed.

If your answer is 'yes' to the second question in each pair, the work you are considering is *well composed* so far as you are concerned. You find it clear, consistent, unified, focused, harmonious, well-organized.

Each of the art forms considered above has certain elements in common with the art of speaking. All the above questions could be re-phrased to apply to public address.

The first eye-catching quality of a painting or the first ear-catching quality of a musical composition corresponds to the interest-arousing phase of the introduction to a speech.

Elements in each which distract attention correspond to a speaker's rambling off on matters which have no bearing on his main theme though they may be interesting in themselves. And so on down the line. Go back to the above questions and note the parallels for yourself.

Finally, you should ask yourself questions like those above whenever you are considering any performance which is planned, designed, or in any other way artistic. The more you cultivate your sense of form and order in all matters of art, the more readily will you be able to distinguish between good and bad structure in speech.

D

CHAPTER FIVE

FORMAL SPEAKING PROCEDURE

In most civilized countries there are thousands of organizations—social, political, religious, welfare, business, trade-union, and civic—which hold business meetings regularly. And when attending their meetings we need to be able to stand up and say what we think about what goes on.

When matters which concern *you* are being discussed, do you sometimes hesitate to speak until it is too late? When you rise to the occasion, are you sometimes cut short with the ruling that you are out of order? When you have your say without interruption, do you sometimes find that the discussion goes on as though you had not spoken at all?

If any of these things happen, what do you do about it?

All too often, many of us grumble that the organization is being 'run by a clique'. In protest, we attend meetings less regularly. In the end we may drift away altogether from affairs in which we would like to play an active role.

But the so-called *clique* often consists of overburdened members carrying on to the best of their ability. They may want to consider the views of those who drop out. But they have no direct way of knowing what these views are. They may even wish to be relieved of some of the responsibilities of office and committee membership. But they get re-elected and reappointed because no one else seems to show ability for such jobs.

So the grumbling makes them feel misunderstood. 'Why don't the grumblers speak up at the right time and in the right place?' they ask.

Some meeting groups, it is true, are run in such a way as to discourage participation by the full membership. They *have* been 'taken over' by a minority. But again it is our fault that we let this happen. When the general membership knows its rights and speaks up for them, no such thing can occur.

Are you seriously concerned with the aims of the organizations to which you belong? Then doing your bit includes having your say and speaking your mind.

What does that require?

Careful organization of ideas, clear use of language, effective devices of explanation, good vocal resonance, distinct articulation—all of these help. All are taken up elsewhere in this book.

But you also need to know some basic things about the special speech situation at a business meeting. You need an understanding of the rules of procedure, according to which business meetings are conducted.

(1) Rules of Order

Rules of order are those laws of procedure by which discussion at meetings is regulated. Collectively they are called *parliamentary law* because of their origin in rules worked out over the centuries in the English Parliament.

Many handbooks have been written to adapt the rules of governmental legislative bodies to the needs of ordinary business meetings. One of the best known is *The Chairman's Handbook*, by Sir Reginald Palgrave, first published in 1877, but still valid as an excellent guide.

The simplified account of parliamentary procedure in this chapter concentrates attention on the more basic principles which you will have occasion to apply as a member of a democratic organization.

(2) The Chair

The Chair is the office of the Chairman who presides over a meeting. The term is used to distinguish the office from the personality of the individual who occupies that office.

Special Rules

(*a*) The Chair should preserve order in the meeting and regulate its procedure by applying the rules of order impartially to all members.

(*b*) While occupying the Chair, the Chairman should refrain from speaking for or against controversial motions. If he feels an urgent need to speak on a controversial question, he should vacate the Chair and speak on the same basis as any other member.

(*c*) The Chairman should not vote unless a secret ballot is being conducted, or unless a tie has resulted by other means of voting.

(*d*) Under *formal procedure* (see Chapter Six), the Chairman should avoid use of the pronouns, 'I' and 'me', but should use such expressions as 'The speakers will please refrain from cross-conversation and address all questions to the Chair.'

(*e*) Under formal procedure, members should address the presiding officer as 'Mr. Chairman', or 'The Chair'.

Not: 'Arthur, I think your decision is all wrong.'

but rather: 'Mr. Chairman, I move to appeal from the decision of the Chair.'

More is involved here than a mere fussiness over words. The distinction between the office of the Chair and the personality of the Chairman is based on the fact, expressed in rule (*a*), that the Chairman is expected to apply procedural law impartially at a meeting.

Like everyone else, the Chairman has his own personal views, interests, friendships and possibly antagonisms. But he is not supposed to allow these to influence his official actions.

Like everyone else, the Chairman also has his own individuality of character. A warm, friendly disposition is of course an asset; and patience is almost an essential. But he is supposed to apply these desirable personal traits to all members alike.

Rule (b), which prohibits him from joining in debate, is to help protect an erring Chairman from himself. The remaining rules are to help protect a good Chairman from others.

When you are Chairman, it may seem artificial to say to your best friend: 'The Chair calls the speaker to order.' But the formula also says in effect: 'It isn't really me who is calling you down like this, Jim old chap, but just the responsibility of the Chair which you yourself helped vote me into.'

When the same formula likewise requires an angry member to address you as 'Mr. Chairman', it again avoids needless personal unpleasantness.

Notwithstanding such practices, many a Chairman of a mixed meeting has gone home to face the anger of a wife or husband for having ruled against spouse in favour of 'that busybody who lives down the street'. It is just such hazards of the office which the rules attempt to keep to a minimum.

Moreover, an impersonal attitude towards the Chair helps keep a proper tone in discussion at times when it might otherwise be difficult to do so. A good Chairman is a blessing at any meeting. He keeps things moving by his energy and obvious fairness. But sometimes a weak personality gets elected to preside over the best of organizations. Then the established tradition of respect for the Chair can give it needed authority which the Chairman cannot command for himself.

These explanations illustrate the important general point that no matter how artificial certain rules of order may appear, they are never mere formalities. They usually embody the practical wisdom of generations of deliberators who have tried to give sense and system to their ways of talking things over.

EXERCISE NO. 26

A session of a Court is a special form of meeting in which the presiding officer is the Judge. In view of what has been said above, consider the following:

What 'rules' is the Judge required to apply equally to all parties to a trial?

Is the Judge supposed to prejudice the outcome of a trial in any way?

Why does the Judge customarily say: 'The Court rules . . .' rather than 'I rule . . .'?

Why does the Judge customarily refer to those in Court as 'The Witness', 'Counsel for the Defence', etc., rather than by their names?

Why do others customarily address the Judge as 'Your Honour' rather than by his name?

If you do not think highly of the personal ability or character of the Judge, may you speak to him disrespectfully in his official capacity in Court?

Does the personal ability or character of the Judge have anything to do with a citation for Contempt of Court?

In answering the above questions you will find parallels between the Court and other meeting situations. Because the Judge is expected to be impartial, all parties must respect his official role as the presiding officer. Contempt of Court has nothing to do with any individual's personal qualities. It is an act of disrespect for the Court as an institution of justice.

The same considerations apply to respect for the chairmanship of a meeting. It is, in effect, respect for the worth and dignity of the meeting organization itself.

(3) Rising to be Recognized

No one other than the Chairman may normally address the meeting unless called upon or 'recognized' by the Chair.

If you wish to speak, therefore, you must first rise to be recognized. Formally, this means standing. In small, informal meetings it is usually enough to raise your hand.

Ordinarily you may not interrupt a speaker to do this. The most basic principle of accepted procedure is that *only one speaker can be properly heard at a time.* (Certain privileged or emergency exceptions to this rule will be explained later.)

Other things being equal, the Chairman will generally recognize that member who rises first.

EXERCISE No. 27

If you were the Chairman, whom would you recognize in each of the following cases:

(i) A member who has already spoken twice on the same question. A member who has not yet spoken on the question.

(ii) A member known to agree with the views just expressed by the preceding speaker. A member known to disagree with those views.

(iii) A young member who is often quick to his feet. A senior member who rises seldom and with physical difficulty.

In each of these cases you would do best to recognize the second choice because:

(i) Whenever possible, members who have not yet had a chance to speak should be recognized in preference to those who have.

(ii) Fair practice requires each side to be heard in turn.

(iii) Considerations of common courtesy apply. Getting recognition should never become an athletic contest with the reward to the nimblest.

(4) Having the Floor

Once you have been recognized by the Chair you are said to 'have the floor'. This means that no other member may interrupt you except for certain privileged or emergency purposes.

Subject to any standing time-limits which your organization may have set on individual speeches, you may then continue speaking so long as you remain 'in order'. This means that what you say must be *proper* and *relevant*.

The question of the propriety of your speech is no different at a meeting than in any other social situation. The general rule is that you may not use language offensive to your listeners. This obviously implies a flexible standard. Words which would outrage a meeting of Sunday School teachers may sound tame at a gathering of trawlermen.

The thing to remember is that the most sensitive member of any audience is entitled to have his reasonable sensibilities respected. So let your policy be: 'in case of doubt, cut it out'.

Beyond that, make sure not to impugn the character, motives or personal affiliations of a fellow-member. The only exception to this is discussion on an actual impeachment or censure measure, when character judgement becomes relevant. Even then you should have such proof of your statements as would stand up in Court.

The relevance of whatever else you say depends upon a number of things such as the *Order of Business* and *Precedence of Motions* discussed later in this chapter.

The general principle is: one question at a time, and each in its proper turn.

If the Chairman has asked for additions or corrections to the minutes, don't bring up a committee report unless it is in connexion with the way the minutes have been written (see *Reading and Approval of the Minutes*, below). If the building of a new clubhouse is being discussed, you will be out of order in speaking of a membership drive, unless you do so in connexion with the building project. And no matter what is going on, you may not tell about your fishing trip except on the unlikely chance that it has a reasonable bearing on the business at hand.

But if *the floor is clear* of other business, and if the agenda otherwise permits (see *The Order of Business*, below), you may introduce a new item of business. You do so in the form of a **motion.**

(5) Making and Seconding Motions

This is the general procedure for making and seconding motions:

Member A (rising to be recognized): 'Mr. Chairman.'

Chairman: 'The Chair recognizes Mr. A.'

Member A (after brief explanation of his purpose): 'I move that such and such be done.'

Chairman (if it is in order): 'It has been moved that such and such be done. Is there a seconder?'

Member B: 'I second the motion.'

Chairman: 'It has been moved and seconded that such and such be done. Is there any discussion?'

Special Rules

(*a*) When a motion has been *properly* made and seconded, the Chairman must refer it to the assembly for discussion.

(*b*) No other discussion is then in order except in connexion with motions which properly precede the one thus introduced (see *The Precedence of Motions*, below).

Explanation

The formality of requiring a specific motion is for the purpose of focusing discussion. It serves to establish what is being talked about.

Even with this requirement in force, and even in the best-regulated meetings, discussion may wander far afield. Some speakers manage to twist almost any topic to their own pet themes. Others get so concerned with side issues as to forget the main point.

When this happens, an alert Chairman will remind the assembly what the question before them is. If the Chairman fails to do so, any member may ask him to.

Sometimes an embarrassed assembly has to wait while the Secretary searches his transcript to find out what the motion before them really is. The practical need for the above formalities then becomes strikingly clear.

'Seconding' is simply co-sponsoring a motion. It assures that at least one other person is interested in a question before it is considered. But it is not always required.

(6) The Order of Business

The question of whether what you say is in order (see *Having the Floor*, above) is partly determined by the order of business of the meeting.

An organization's order of business is the basic plan which its constitution (see *Constitutions*, in Chapter Six) requires its meetings to follow. This plan or scheme consists of a number of consecutive *items* covering routine business.

An **agenda** is the order of business with specific *sub-items* entered under the main headings.

The general rule is that you may not speak on any item at a time when a different item is being considered. To do so is literally *out of order*.

The main items on a typical order of business are set out below, with **examples of** how they are introduced and of what discussion they allow.

(a) The Call to Order

Chairman (rapping with gavel): 'The meeting will please come to order.'

Explanation

Until the meeting is thus officially *called to order*, nothing that is said, even though it may be addressed to everyone in the room, has official status for consideration. The records of the meeting begin with this call.

(b) The Minutes

The Secretary of an organization has the duty of noting all important transactions which take place at a meeting, and writing them down in an official permanent record called the *Minutes*. His reading of the minutes of the previous meeting is usually the first business of a meeting after it is called to order. For example:

Chairman: 'Will the Secretary please read the minutes of the last meeting.'

Secretary: 'The regular monthly meeting of the Oxbridge Traction Engine Club was called to order by the President, Mr. John Jones, on Wednesday, August 8th, at 8.15 p.m. in the King's Head Hotel . . . etc.'

After the reading of the minutes, they must be *approved by the membership*. For example:

Chairman: 'Are there any additions or corrections to the minutes?'

Member A: 'Mr. Chairman (pause for recognition), I wish to say that I think this group made a very bad mistake when it passed the second motion the Secretary just read . . .'

Chairman: 'Mr. A., you are out of order. This is not the time to debate that again. Unless you have some question as to how the minutes have been recorded, the Chair must ask you to be seated.'

Member B: 'Mr. Chairman (pause), didn't you include Mrs. D. in your appointments to the Ladies' Committee at the last meeting? I don't believe I heard her name mentioned on the list as it was read to us in the minutes.'

Secretary: 'No, Mr. Chairman, I don't have Mrs. D.'s name down.'

Chairman: 'Mrs. D. was included in the appointments, Mr. Secretary. Will you please add her name to the list. Are there any other additions or corrections? (pause for reply) If not, the minutes will stand as read.'

Explanation

Only questions of the completeness or correctness of the record may be raised when the minutes are to be approved.

If there is any serious debate about the correctness of the minutes, they cannot be approved so informally. The procedure then is:

Chairman: 'If there is no further discussion concerning the minutes, the Chair will now entertain a motion that they be approved as corrected.'

Member E: 'I so move, Mr. Chairman.'

Member F: 'I second the motion.'

Chairman: 'It has been moved and seconded that the minutes be approved as corrected. All in favour . . .'

In small informal meetings it is usual for the Chairman to use a modified form of procedure.

Chairman: 'If there is no further discussion concerning the minutes, may I sign them as being approved? All those in favour?'

(c) Reports

Reports by officers and committees are usually heard in the following order.

Officers: President, Vice-President, Secretary, Treasurer.

Committees: Standing Committees, Special Committees.

As an example of this procedure, let us consider the following:

Chairman: 'Would the Treasurer please make his report?'

Treasurer: 'As of the last report of the Treasurer, our cash balance was . . . Receipts since then were as follows . . . Payments since then were as follows . . . The cash balance is now . . .'

Chairman: 'Are there any questions concerning the Treasurer's report?'

Member A: 'Mr. Chairman (pause for recognition), now that the question has come up again, I'd like to ask why the Society has appropriated so much money for so-called welfare purposes. We need our funds for . . .'

Chairman: 'Sorry, Mr. A., but the Chair must rule you out of order. That question does *not* come up at this time. We are not now reconsidering our past appropriations. We are merely hearing the Treasurer's report of his custody of our funds. Are there any other questions?'

Member B: 'Mr. Chairman (pause), I should like to ask if the balance given by the Treasurer includes an estimate of membership subscriptions due but not collected.'

Chairman: 'Will the Treasurer please answer that question?'

Treasurer: 'In accordance with the By-laws, Mr. Chairman, our accounts are kept on a cash basis. No subscriptions are recorded until actually collected.'

Chairman: 'Thank you, Mr. Treasurer. Are there any other questions? (pause) If not, the Treasurer's report will be referred to the Finance Committee as usual.'

Committee reports sometimes include recommendations for action. A common error of some chairmen in these circumstances is to ask for a

vote to *accept the report*, without meaning to have these recommendations thereby put into effect. This practice is subject to misinterpretation.

A report is *accepted* merely by being heard. Any vote taken should
be on the question of whether to put its recommendations into effect.
The only exception to this is a vote on a motion to thank the committee
members for their work.

Chairman: 'You have just heard the report of the Finance Committee
recommending that membership subscriptions be increased by one
guinea per member per year. Since this would involve a change in the
By-laws (see *Constitutions, etc.*, in Chapter Six), it may not be considered until after it has been announced as a question at a previous
meeting. Do you now wish to move that it be so announced as the first
general order of business (see below) for the next regular meeting?'

Member A: 'I so move, Mr. Chairman.'

Member B: 'I second the motion, Mr. Chairman.'

Chairman: 'It has been moved and seconded . . . etc.'

(*d*) General Orders

A general order of business is any motion proposed for consideration
at the first opportunity in a given meeting. This means immediately
after all reports have been heard. For example:

Chairman: 'As the first general order of business tonight we have to
consider the recommendation of the Finance Committee at the last
meeting that the membership subscriptions of this Society be increased
by one guinea per person per year. Is there any discussion?'

Explanation

Passage of the motion to consider this question at the previous meeting, makes it unnecessary to go through the routine of moving and
seconding it at the present meeting.

Legislative bodies and some large organizations also include *special
orders of business* in their agenda. These differ from general orders only
in that they set a definite time for the consideration of the question.
This would interrupt any other business, except another special order,
which the meeting happened to be considering at that time.

Most organizations obviously do not have to commit themselves to
so inflexible an arrangement. Unless there are exceptional reasons, do
not try to fix your order of business by the hands of the clock.

(*e*) Unfinished Business

Sometimes a meeting ends without disposing of a motion before it.
This motion then becomes *unfinished business* which the next meeting
must take up immediately after general orders. For example:

Chairman: 'When we adjourned last week we were considering the motion to discontinue regular business meetings from June 30th to September 1st. Is there any further discussion of that motion now?'

Explanation

At any given meeting, unfinished business comes up in the same automatic manner as general orders. For that reason, the two items are sometimes combined in a single order of business under either heading, or under the joint heading: 'General Orders *and* Unfinished Business'.

(f) New Business

If you have a proposal to bring up for consideration for the first time, wait until 'New Business' is called for, before rising to be recognized.

It is a good idea to have the exact wording of what you propose written out in the form of a motion. No matter how well you may be prepared to back up your proposal, stumbling over its wording gives the impression that you do not know what you are talking about.

Moreover, phrasing a motion unclearly because you are doing it on the spur of the moment, gives it a bad start. The discussion that follows often then turns on the question of what you really mean and how better to state your meaning, rather than on the merits of your proposal.

For ordinary purposes, keep the wording of your motions as short and simple as possible. For example:

'Mr. Chairman, I move this Sports Club appropriate ten guineas to provide a trophy as first prize in its annual fly-fishing tournament.'

But, if what you propose is unavoidably complicated, or is intended to come to some kind of official attention, you may need to word it more formally. For example:

'Mr. Chairman, I move the following resolution:

"Whereas, Loamshire County Council has constructed no public playgrounds in this parish; and

Whereas, Loamshire County Council has constructed adequate public playgrounds in neighbouring parishes; and

Whereas, public playgrounds are an essential public facility for the general welfare of the community; therefore be it resolved:

that this Residents' Association petition the County Council to take all necessary measures promptly to provide this parish with adequate public playgrounds; and be it further resolved:

that the Executive Committee of this Residents' Association be authorized and instructed to call upon all candidates for office in the forthcoming County Council elections to determine and report to this assembly their policy with regard to action upon this petition." '

Discuss your motion informally beforehand with some other member who is likely to be willing to second it. An embarrassing pause in the proceedings of the meeting while waiting for the motion to be seconded can thus be avoided.

If possible let the Chairman know in advance—before the call to order—that you intend to ask for the floor for that purpose.

Some organizations require that members desiring to make motions under New Business, hand them in writing to the Secretary beforehand. In such cases they may be included in the agenda accompanying reminder-notices of the meeting.

For further details concerning this item of business, see *Main Motions* (below).

(g) Adjournment

Once a meeting has been called to order, it remains in session, except for *recess*, until it is *adjourned*.

A recess is a temporary interruption of a meeting. This may be for such purposes as refreshment or conference among groups of members. At a set time, the *same meeting* reconvenes.

Adjournment is the formal end of a meeting. On the basis of motions explained later in this chapter, it is formally announced by the Chair: 'The meeting is now adjourned.'

Nothing said after adjournment can become part of the official proceedings of a meeting, even though addressed to everyone in the room. Should a group be called back to order after being adjourned, what then takes place is, strictly speaking, a new meeting and it should be so recorded in the minutes.

EXERCISE NO. 28

Under which item of the order of business would it be appropriate to consider each of the following:

(i) A question as to how many members are in arrears with subscriptions.

(ii) A motion to hold a special social function.

(iii) A question as to what events the Programme Committee has so far arranged for the coming season.

(iv) Further discussion of a question under consideration when the previous meeting adjourned.

(v) The President's account of his visit to the organization's national headquarters.

(vi) A correction to the official title recorded for the guest speaker at the previous meeting.

(vii) A proposal to launch a membership recruiting campaign.

(viii) Current recommendations by the Ways and Means Committee.

(ix) Support of a motion specifically assigned for consideration at the present meeting.

(7) Explanation of the Table of Motions

Most of the remaining technicalities of parliamentary procedure are summarized in the accompanying *Table of Motions* (page 100). Glance at the Table briefly for a general impression of its format and contents, then proceed to the following explanations of the entries in its nine columns.

Column 1—Precedence

The precedence of motions is a set of rules of order whereby discussion of certain motions may claim priority over discussion of certain other motions. Thus, precedence is another aspect of parliamentary procedure which determines what speaking is *in order* at any given time.

In general, any motion is said to *precede,* or *have higher precedence* over another, if the rules permit it to be introduced at a time when the other motion is already being discussed.

Conversely, any motion is said to *be preceded* by, or *have lower precedence* than another, if the rules do not permit it to be introduced when the other motion is under consideration.

The 24 most important types of motions—those likely to come up in the meetings of most organizations—are tabulated in column 1 of the accompanying Table of Motions (page 100).

Of these, the first 21 are listed in the order of their *relative precedence.* Speaking on any of these motions is *in order* when any motion *below* it is being discussed. Speaking on any of these motions is *out of order* when any motion *above* it is under consideration.

The three motions in the last group at the bottom of column 1 have special orders of precedence (explained in the notes of column 8, and also in the separate explanations of each of these motions given on the pages referred to in column 9).

Column 2—Authority to Interrupt

Nothing is more basic in parliamentary procedure than the practice of allowing only one member to speak at a time. Hence the requirement that you rise and be recognized by the Chair before you may have the floor.

Sometimes, however, you may have legitimate reason to interrupt a speaker. You may have an urgent *Point of Personal Privilege* to raise (see explanation of Motion P4); or a serious objection to make to the way the meeting is being run (see explanation of Motion I1).

In such emergency cases you have a right to speak up without waiting for another speaker to finish. Where such interruptions are allowed is indicated in column 2 by the entry, *Int.* (May Interrupt).

For all other motions, of course, you must wait your turn.

Column 3—Need for a Seconder

Although it is general practice to have a motion seconded before it is further considered (see *Making and Seconding Motions*, above), there are also cases where such a requirement would not be sensible.

For example, you may question the Chair's decision as to a voice vote and may want to have a more accurate count (see explanation of Motion I4). Or you may wish to ask for pertinent information in order to follow what is being said on the floor (see explanation of Motion I5).

In such cases parliamentary procedure does not require that you be seconded. This is indicated by the omission of the entry, *Sec.* (Seconder required) in column 3.

Column 4— Debatability

Most parliamentary procedure is concerned with ensuring that debate can go on in an orderly manner. But there are times when it can, or must, operate so as to terminate debate.

There are cases where you may reasonably object to the consideration of motions made and seconded (see explanation of Motion I7); or, when it is reasonable for you to move that debate on a question be closed (see explanation of Motion S2).

If either of these motions of yours were to be themselves debatable, their purpose would automatically be defeated. The question to whose consideration or continued discussion you objected would, in effect, continue to be considered or discussed in the debate over your motion.

Parliamentary rules therefore provide that only those motions may be debated for which debate is appropriate, as indicated in column 4 by the entry, *Deb.* (Debatable).

Column 5—Amendability

Likewise, some motions may properly be amended, whereas others may not. Those motions which may be amended are indicated in column 5 by the entry, *Amd.* (Amendable).

For a general discussion of amendments, see the explanation of Motion S5.

Column 6—Required Votes

Since usual democratic practice is majority rule, the usual requirement for the passage of a motion is a simple majority vote. This is indicated in column 6 by the entry, *Maj.* (Majority) for motions which require no more than a majority vote to be carried.

But suppose a simple majority vote could prevent consideration of any motion you made (see explanation of Motion I7), or could stop debate on any motion in which you were interested (see explanation of Motion S2). It would then be possible for a bare majority-of-one, in your organization, to prevent your ever getting a chance to speak on the floor for your proposals.

To avoid situations like that, certain motions must have a two-thirds vote to pass. They are indicated in column 6 by the entry, *2/3*, after them.

Column 7—Renewability

Suppose there were no parliamentary restriction against moving and seconding a motion again after it had been defeated. A single pair of persistent members could then obstruct the entire procedure of a meeting by repeatedly proposing the same unpopular measure each time it was voted down. To avoid such an obstacle, there is a general rule that no motion may be renewed immediately after it has been disposed of.

It is reasonable, however, to allow many kinds of motions to be made again after conditions have changed.

For example, a group which at 10 p.m. votes down a motion to limit debate or to adjourn, may want to reconsider such motions at 11 p.m.

This possibility is recognized by a provision for renewability in certain cases. All such motions are indicated in column 7 by the entry, *Ren.* (Renewable).

Column 8—Special Notes

Certain motions in all the columns from 1 to 7 may carry the entry, *(8)*. This refers you to column 8 where special explanations are given.

Column 9—Page References

The last column (9) of the Table refers to the pages where additional explanations of items may be found.

Use of the Table of Motions

If you have some previous acquaintance with the rules of public meetings, you can use the Table of Motions in this book as a convenient quick reference to decide questions of procedure. Take the book with you to meetings for that purpose.

All you need to remember are these few simple abbreviations:

Int. for 'May interrupt'
Sec. for 'Needing a seconder'
Deb. for 'Debatable'
Amd. for 'Amendable'
Maj. for 'Majority'
Ren. for 'Renewable'

As you read the explanations of the various kinds of motions in the rest of this chapter, keep turning back to the Table to revise the

	1	2	3	4	5	6	
	Motions in Order of Precedence (Groups P, I, S, and M only)	Authority to Interrupt	Need for a Second	Debatability	Amendability	Required Votes	Re ab
PRIVILEGED MOTIONS							
	P1 To Fix Time and/or Place of Next Meeting (8)	—	Sec.	(8)	Amd.	Maj.	●
	P2 To Adjourn (8)	—	Sec.	(8)	—	Maj.	R
	P3 To Recess (8)	—	Sec.	(8)	(8)	Maj.	R
	P4 Questions of Privilege	Int.	—	(8)	(8)	(8)	R
	P5 To Call for the Orders of the Day	Int.	—	—	—	(8)	R
INCIDENTAL MOTIONS							
	I1 Points of Order	Int.	—	(8)	—	(8)	
	I2 Points of Inquiry	Int.	—	—	—	(8)	
	I3 To Appeal from the Decision of the Chair	Int.	Sec.	(8)	—	Maj.	
	I4 To Call for a Count of the Vote (8)	Int.	—	—	—	(8)	
	I5 Points of Information (8)	Int.	—	—	—	(8)	
	I6 To Suspend the Rules (8)	—	Sec.	—	—	2/3	●
	I7 To Object to Consideration (8)	Int.	—	—	—	2/3	●
	I8 To Consider as a Whole or by Parts (8)	Int.	Sec.	—	Amd.	Maj.	
	I9 Request for Leave to Withdraw a Motion	—	(8)	—	—	(8)	R
SUBSIDIARY MOTIONS							
	S1 To Close Debate (8)	—	Sec.	—	—	2/3	R
	S2 To Limit (or Extend) Debate	—	Sec.	—	(8)	2/3	R
	S3 To Postpone for a Definite Time (8)	—	Sec.	Deb.	Amd.	Maj.	R
	S4 To Refer (8)	—	Sec.	Deb.	Amd.	Maj.	R
	S5 To Amend (8)	—	Sec.	Deb.	(8)	Maj.	▶
	S6 To Postpone Indefinitely (8)	—	Sec.	Deb.	—	Maj.	
MAIN MOTIONS							
	M All Main Motions	—	Sec.	Deb.	Amd.	Maj.	
REVIEW MOTIONS							
	R1 To Reconsider (8)	(8)	Sec.	(8)	—	Maj.	
	R2 To Repeal (8)	—	Sec.	Deb.	Amd.	(8)	
	R3 To Renew (8)	(8)	(8)	(8)	(8)	(8)	

HIGHEST PRECEDENCE · LOWEST PRECEDENCE · SPECIAL PRECEDENCE

Int. = 'May interrupt'   Sec. = 'Needing a seconder'   Deb. = 'Debatable'
Amd. = 'Amendable'   Maj. = 'Majority'   Ren. = 'Renewable'

8	9
Special Notes: *Explanations of entry* (8) *in other columns*	*Page* *References*

(1) Privileged only when no time and/or place have yet been set. (4) Debatable only if no other question is pending. (7) Renewable only to change time and/or place.

107

(1, 4) Privileged and undebatable only when made for immediate adjournment.

(1) Privileged only when made for immediate recess. (4) Debatable only when floor is clear. (5) Amendable only as to length of recess.

108

(4, 5, 6) Usually decided by Chair. Only a resulting motion is debatable, amendable, or needs majority vote.

108

(6) The Chair normally complies, but a 2/3 majority is needed to postpone a special order.

109

(4, 6) Debatable and in need of majority vote only if appealed from the decision of the Chair by I4.

110

(6) Answered by Chair with help of others if needed.

111

(4) Debatable only when point is not one of decorum or order of business, or when pending question is debatable.

111

(1) Also known as: 'Call for a Division of the Assembly'. (6) No vote is needed since Chair must comply.

112

(1) Must be addressed to the Chair and must be a genuine request for information.

113

(1) Applies only to certain rules (see page 115). (7) May be renewed only by unanimous consent.

114

(1) Should be limited to grounds of relevance or propriety. (7) Renewable only by opposition to consider.

115

(1) Also known as: 'To Consider *in Toto* or *Seriatim*'.

115

(3, 6) Granted by Chair if there is no objection. Otherwise needs a seconder and requires a majority vote.

116

(1) Also known as: 'That the Question be now put'.

105

(5) Amendable only as to time-limit proposed. Otherwise identical with S2.

104

(1) The preferred motion for postponing consideration without ulterior strategic purposes.

105

(1) Wording should fully specify to whom referred, which committee, how appointed, etc.

104

(1) See column 5 for which motions this one is applicable to. (5) Amendments may themselves be only once amended.

102

(1) Applies only to Motions M and P4. See page 106 for strategic implications of this motion.

105

(7) Once defeated, may not be renewed until second session following.

117

(1) An emergency motion to be made only at same meeting or at meeting following one at which original motion passed. (2) May interrupt only for entry, not for consideration. Hence dual precedence. (4) Is debatable only if original motion was.

118

(1) Also known as: 'To Rescind'. Not in order when R1 is. (6) Needs 2/3 majority unless notice is given at previous meeting. (7) May not be renewed until next meeting.

119

(1) Applicability shown in column 7. (2, 3, 4, 5, 6, 7) Has same status in all columns as original motion.

120

important points. This will help fix in your mind the relation of each type of motion to the others.

The Classes of Motions

Motions are usually divided, as in the Table, into five general classes: *Privileged, Incidental, Subsidiary, Main* and *Review* (see general explanation under *Incidental Motions,* below).

Of these, Main Motions are the most basic, and Privileged Motions have the highest precedence. But since the practical applications of Subsidiary Motions require the least prior understanding of the others, we shall begin our more detailed study with them.

(9) Subsidiary Motions

Subsidiary Motions are those which apply to other motions. Having no independent purpose of their own, they serve to help dispose of other motions. We shall consider them here in groups according to the several ways in which they do this.

Motion to Amend

A motion *To Amend* (S5 in the Table of Motions) is subsidiary in that it proposes changes in other motions. It may do this for the words, sentences, or paragraphs of an original motion by:

(*a*) Striking out,
(*b*) Inserting, or
(*c*) Striking out and substituting.

For example:

(*a*) 'Mr. Chairman (pause for recognition), I move to amend the motion "that we be willing to meet earlier hereafter" by striking out the words "be willing to".'

This improves the sense of the motion. The words, 'be willing to' are unnecessary and can be misconstrued.

(*b*) 'Mr. Chairman (pause), I move to amend the motion "that we meet earlier hereafter" by inserting the words "one half hour" between the words "meet" and "earlier".'

This makes the motion more specific.

(*c*) 'Mr. Chairman (pause), I move to amend the motion "that we meet one half hour earlier hereafter" by striking out the word "hereafter" and substituting for it the words "during the months of February and March".'

This changes a detail of the motion, but in the spirit of the orginal intent and in a manner more likely to get approval.

The following special rules apply to the motion To Amend:

(*a*) It may be applied only to those other motions indicated in column 5 of the Table of Motions.

(*b*) It takes its relative precedence from the motion to which it is applied.

(*c*) If may itself be amended only once.

(*d*) It should relate to the motion amended and not have the effect of making a different motion.

Sometimes you may be in favour of most of the provisions of a motion, but object to certain details. Or, you may favour the general intent of a motion, but question whether that intent is correctly expressed by its wording.

If there were nothing you could do about this you might find yourself obliged to vote against motions with whose purpose, or with most of whose provisions, you agreed.

The motion To Amend is a means of finding out whether the original proposal can be brought more into line with your way of thinking. So do not hesitate to use the device of amendment whenever you believe it will serve to clarify debate.

Members supporting the original motion may appreciate your help because they find your amendment better expresses what they had in mind. Or, even if they do not wholly agree with it, they may be willing to accept it to gain the additional backing of members who think as you do.

The motion To Amend is sometimes called an *Appendage Motion.* This means that it takes its relative precedence from the original motion to which it applies.

The precedence order shown for it in the Table of Motions holds when it is applied to a *Main Motion* (see below). But the motion at the very top of the precedence list is also one which can be amended. A motion to amend motion P1, with regard to the proposed time or place of next meeting (see below), will therefore precede any other motion which can be made.

Special rule (*c*), limiting amendments to one further amendment, is to avoid excessive complication. When you get to the stage of putting patches on patches, it is a good idea to start over with a fresh article.

The purpose of requiring an amendment to relate solely to the original motion is to prevent it being used to change the original subject of discussion. For example:

Member A: 'Mr. Chairman (pause for recognition), I move to amend the motion "that we meet one half hour earlier" so as to read "that we place a time-limit on long speeches in order not to have to get here so early".'

Chairman (laughing): 'We all understand how you feel about that, Mr. A. But your motion is not a proper amendment and the Chair cannot accept it for consideration.'

Member A is, of course, only joking. But what he says is technically out of order because, in the form of a motion to amend, he is making a different proposal. In effect it is an argument against the original one. But the same thing is often attempted seriously.

Motion to Refer

A motion *To Refer* (S4 in the Table) is subsidiary in that it proposes to turn consideration of another motion over to a committee for study and recommendation. For example:

'Mr. Chairman (pause for recognition), we have been debating for the last half hour whether this organization should sponsor these social events. But no one present can now give us enough facts about costs, available halls, and questions like that. I therefore move that we refer the question to our Programme Committee for study, and ask that it report its findings and recommendations at our next meeting.'

When you sense a situation such as the one described above, do not hesitate to use this motion. It may save much time and pointless discussion.

The motion To Refer should specify the committee to which the original motion is to be referred, and what that committee is to be instructed to do with it.

This motion is sometimes used *strategically* (see Chapter Six) with the purpose of removing an original motion from discussion never to be taken up again. This is known as 'burying it in committee'.

You can avoid such 'burial' of a motion in which you are interested if you insist that any motion To Refer state *when* the committee is to report back.

Lastly, bear in mind that no motion can ever be referred to any sub-group for *decision*.

A motion can be passed only by the regular procedure of voting at a meeting. A committee can serve only to help the membership do this by reporting its *factual findings* and *recommendations*.

(9a) Motions Regulating Debate

The two motions below (S2 and S1 in the Table of Motions) are subsidiary in that they relate to the debating of other motions.

Motion to Limit (or Extend) Debate
For example:

'Mr. Chairman (pause for recognition), I move that we limit debate on the question before us to one more speech of at most five minutes for each side.'

Or:

'Mr. Chairman (pause), I move that we extend debate on the present question one half hour.'

Motion to Close Debate

For example:

'Mr. Chairman (pause for recognition), I move to close debate.'

Or:

'Mr. Chairman (pause), I move that the question now be put.'

Both the above motions require a two-thirds majority vote.

Both the above motions also have the same status in all other columns of the Table of Motions, except that the first may be amended as to the proposed time to which debate is to be limited or extended.

If it were not possible to limit or close debate, a minority could prevent any motion from being passed by talking on and on to prevent a vote from being taken.

On the other hand, if it were too easy to limit or close debate, a small majority could always shut off opposition to their motions by moving to close debate on them at once. Hence the requirement of a two-thirds vote. This makes it impossible for a majority of less than two-thirds to silence the minority, or for a minority of less than one-third to prolong discussion.

Most often however, these motions serve a more simple routine purpose. When both sides to a debate begin to repeat themselves, or when the whole discussion begins to go round in circles, you can use them to get on to other business.

(9b) Motions Postponing Consideration

The remaining two motions of this general class are subsidiary in that they relate to ways of postponing consideration of other motions.

Motion to Postpone for a Definite Time

'Mr. Chairman (pause for recognition), the hour is getting late and there is an urgent matter of new business which I should like to bring before this meeting. I therefore move that consideration of the motion now before us be postponed to the next meeting.'

This motion (S3 in the Table of Motions) may be debated or amended. It creates a *general order* (see *Order of Business*, above) if in the form of the above example. It creates a *special order* if a definite hour is specified, in which case a two-thirds majority vote is needed to carry it.

Motion to Postpone Consideration Indefinitely

'Mr. Chairman (pause for recognition), I move to postpone consideration of this question indefinitely.'

This motion (S6 in the Table) applies only to *Main Motions* and to *Questions of Privilege* (see below). It may be debated.

Since both of these motions have the effect of postponing consideration of an original motion, there is a question of which one you should attempt to use in any given case where you would like to put off debate on a question.

For an answer, consider first the main facts about each of these motions with regard to their status in columns 1, 4 and 5 of the Table of Motions.

S3 *To Postpone for a Definite Time*	S6 *To Postpone Indefinitely*
Medium Precedence	Low Precedence
Debatable	Debatable
Amendable	Unamendable

Which of these subsidiary motions can most readily be used in an emergency to clear the floor for other business?

Which of the above motions would be fairest to use under normal circumstances?

Obviously the first, To Postpone for a Definite Time. It provides for a specific time to reconsider the original motion. And it admits of both debate and amendment, thus assuring that a generally acceptable time for reconsideration may be set.

The normal purposes of any member who wants to have an original motion considered at a later time, are therefore well enough served by the first two motions above.

Why, then, the other motion, To Postpone Indefinitely?

This is a *strategic motion* (see Chapter Six) in that it is never used for what it seems to be for, but always for an ulterior end. The key fact is that it is debatable just as the original motion is. By moving it, therefore, the opposition to the original motion has something to gain and nothing to lose.

If the motion To Postpone Consideration Indefinitely is passed, the opposition has achieved its purpose of preventing the original motion from passing. Moreover, it does this without a commitment for reconsideration, as would be implied in a motion To Postpone Consideration for a Definite Time.

Even if this strategic motion is not passed, however, the opposition is still no worse off than it was before. Indeed, as the motion is debatable, it may even have gained some advantage.

First, the opposition will have gained debating time to speak against the original motion without being subject to time-limits to which discussion on that original motion may later be subject.

Secondly, the opposition will have had an opportunity to learn its strength and weakness by the positions which other members take, and by the count of the vote on the subsidiary question of postponement.

Thirdly, the opposition will have delayed final action on the original question for a period of time which may be long enough to enable them to gather more strength.

Lastly, the opposition will have been able to do all this without the risk of a vote on the original motion—for this remains to be debated and voted on after the subsidiary motion is disposed of.

Never be fooled by the motion To Postpone Consideration Indefinitely. It is simply a *delaying tactic*.

This does not mean, however, that it is always obstructive. It can also serve to further good democratic procedure.

It has found a place in parliamentary procedure because well-organized minorities sometimes try to rush unpopular measures through at meetings where they happen to have a temporary majority. In such cases, the delaying feature of this motion may be used to postpone action until the normal balance of the voting membership is restored.

To summarize:

You will find the motion To Postpone for a Definite Time, the fairest way of putting off debate under normal circumstances, and the least subject to abuse for strategic purposes.

You should be on your guard against the motion To Postpone Consideration Indefinitely being used as a delaying tactic. But do not hesitate to use it yourself if you find a temporary majority trying to take advantage of the absence of members whose views you share.

(10) Privileged Motions

Privileged motions are those which deal with the basic arrangements for a meeting and with comfort and personal rights of the members attending.

The fact that privileged motions have the *highest precedence* (see page 100) does not necessarily mean that they concern the most important items of business. On the contrary, they may relate to minor matters such as the opening of a window for ventilation, or mere details of routine such as the formal ending of a meeting when its real business is finished.

Yet, the reason they are given right of way over more important questions will be clearly seen in each of the following cases.

Motion to Fix the Time and/or Place of Next Meeting

'Mr. Chairman (pause for recognition), I move that when we adjourn we do so to meet next at this same place at 8.30 p.m. tomorrow evening.'

This motion (P1 in the Table) is privileged only when no time and/or place have yet been set for the next meeting. It is debatable only if no other question is pending. It is renewable only to change the time and/or place.

This motion has the highest precedence because it is a necessary preliminary to the motion to adjourn. Since no official action may be taken after adjournment, an organization could theoretically abolish itself by adjourning without a set time and place to meet again.

Most organizations, of course, have regular meeting times and places, so they do not normally need this motion at all.

Motion to Adjourn and Motion to Recess

Explanations of these terms, and an example of the motion *To Adjourn*, have been given under *The Order of Business* (see page 91).

The two motions (P2 and P3 in the Table) have privileged status only when they provide for *immediate* adjournment or recess. When privileged, they may not be debated. They may not interrupt a speaker or a vote.

The high precedence of these motions is based on the common-sense idea that members cannot usefully be kept at a meeting when they feel that they must, or would rather, go elsewhere.

The rule against interruption keeps the motions from being used to deprive a speaker of the floor, or to avoid the tally of a vote.

Questions of Privilege

An *Ordinary* Question of Privilege (P4 in the Table) is one which relates to the comfort or convenience of the members at a meeting. It requires a formal motion only when challenged. For example:

Member A: 'Mr. Chairman (interrupting if necessary, and not waiting to be recognized), I rise to a question of privilege.'

Chairman: 'What is your question?'

Member A: 'Will the Chair please ask the speakers in the front of the room to speak up more clearly so that we can hear them in the back of the room?'

Chairman: 'By all means. The Chair asks all speakers to comply with the member's request. And will the last speaker please repeat what he just said for the benefit of those in the back of the room.'

Second example:

Member B: 'Mr. Chairman (interrupting if necessary), I rise to a question of privilege.'

Chairman: 'State your question.'

Member B: 'Will the Chair please ask all candidates for election to leave the room while we discuss their qualifications?'

Member C: 'Mr. Chairman (also interrupting), as a point of privilege,

I object to our being asked to leave the room while our candidacies are being discussed.'

Member B: 'In that case, Mr. Chairman, I should like to make my original question of privilege a formal motion.'

Chairman: 'It has been moved as a point of privilege that all candidates for election be asked to leave the room while their qualifications are being discussed. Is there any discussion on the privileged question?'

A question becomes one of *Personal Privilege* (also P4 in the Table) when it involves the reputation or standing of a member. For example:

'Mr. Chairman (interrupting if necessary), I rise to a point of personal privilege. . . . The speaker has just misquoted me in a way that reflects upon my personal reputation as a loyal member of this organization. I ask that he correct that impression immediately, or else that I be given the privilege of taking the floor at once to make clear the facts of the matter in so far as my personal reputation is concerned.'

Note that anyone raising a Question of Privilege may interrupt a speaker if necessary. Note also that no vote is required unless a motion is involved.

The high precedence given to Questions of Privilege is a matter of common sense in all routine applications. Members should not hesitate to raise them for reasons of their comfort and convenience in following the course of business.

The high precedence given to Questions of *Personal* Privilege reflects the importance properly attached in democratic procedure to an individual's personal dignity and security from slander. It is best for any organization, however, to try to avoid the need of raising these questions.

Call for the Orders of the Day

The general plan of a meeting's *Order of Business* has been discussed in detail on page 91. But sometimes a Chairman does not follow this order or he allows others to depart from it on the floor. A member may then Call for the Orders of the Day (P5 in the Table). For example:

Member A: 'Mr. Chairman (interrupting if necessary, and not waiting to be recognized), I call for the orders of the day.'

Chairman: 'In what particular, Mr. A?'

Member A: 'The Chair has just asked for reports from committees. But we have not yet heard the Treasurer's Report.'

Chairman: 'Thank you Mr. A. That was an oversight. The Treasurer will please make his report.'

Second example:

Member B: 'Mr. Chairman (interrupting, etc.), I call for the orders of the day.'

Chairman: 'In what way, Mr. B?'

Member B: 'The speaker is introducing new business. But at our last meeting there was a general order of business voted for consideration today.'

Chairman: 'Is that the case, Mr. Secretary?'

Secretary: 'Yes, Mr. Chairman, it is.'

Chairman: 'The Chair will then have to ask the speaker to yield the floor. Will the Secretary please read the general order of business'. . . etc.

Any member calling for the Orders of the Day needs no recognition or seconder. Moreover, he may interrupt a speaker, if necessary.

If the Chairman does not use his authority to keep discussion to the proper order of business, this motion is your means of getting him to do so.

(11) Incidental Motions

The traditional distinction between *Privileged, Incidental* and *Subsidiary* motions may be summarized as follows:

Privileged Motions are a special group of motions concerning matters of such urgency at the moment that they require a special priority for consideration.

Subsidiary Motions are those which are applied to other motions for the purpose of disposing of them.

Incidental Motions are those relating to questions which arise out of the consideration of other motions.

This division is clear enough as far as Privileged and Subsidiary motions are concerned.

But the so-called 'Incidental' motions are much more similar to those in the other two groups than their formal definition would suggest.

For example, *Leave to Withdraw a Motion* is practically a *Question of Privilege*. Yet, *Leave to Withdraw a Motion* is also just as much a way of disposing of another motion as any motion usually classed as *Subsidiary*. And in many similar instances there are really no hard and fast lines of division between these so-called classes of motions.

You will therefore find it simpler to think of 'Incidental' motions either as more privileged subsidiary motions or as more subsidiary privileged motions.

Points of Order

Sometimes the question of correctness of procedure depends, not on the *Order of Business* (see page 91), but on some other parliamentary rule. For example:

Member: 'Mr. Chairman (interrupting if necessary, and not waiting to be recognized), I rise to a point of order.'

Chairman: 'Please state your point of order.'

Member: 'The alleged amendment which the speaker has just offered is not a true amendment to the main question. In effect, it is a proposal of an entirely different measure instead of the one we are now considering.'

Chairman: 'Quite so, Mr. A. The Chair must ask the speaker to reword his motion in the form of a proper amendment or else yield the floor.'

Note that anyone raising a Point of Order (I1 in the Table) may interrupt a speaker and needs no recognition or seconder. Note also that the Point of Order is decided by the Chair and is not debated unless the Chair's decision is asked for.

Like a *Call for the Orders of the Day*, this motion makes it possible for you to help keep the Chair alert to correct parliamentary procedure.

You should be careful, though, not to abuse it. Unless the point is of practical consequence, you will only antagonize others by calling constant attention to minor technical slips.

Points of Inquiry

A point of correctness of parliamentary procedure may be put in question form. For example:

Member: 'Mr. Chairman (interrupting if necessary, and not waiting to be recognized), I rise to a point of inquiry.'

Chairman: 'Please state your question.'

Member: 'Is the present speaker in order in offering an amendment to my motion at this time?'

Chairman: 'Yes he is. A motion to amend takes precedence over the main motion. The speaker is therefore quite in order and may continue.'

Note that anyone raising a Point of Inquiry (I2 in the Table) may interrupt a speaker, but should not do so for trivial reasons.

If the Chairman cannot answer the question he may refer it to the assembly, but a debate is not in order.

You should know enough about the rules of debate not to have to raise frequent questions of procedure. You are entitled, however, to have your reasonable questions answered officially by the Chair.

You may also use the form of a parliamentary question even when you know the answer. It is a tactful way of calling for the Orders of the Day or of raising Points of Order without embarrassing the Chairman.

To Appeal from the Decision of the Chair

Appeals from decisions of the Chair (I3 in the Table) must be made promptly after the decision has been made, and may interrupt a speaker if necessary.

They require a seconder and are debatable unless the question is one of decorum or order of business, or unless the pending question is undebatable.

The question is always put to vote as one of sustaining the decision of the Chair, as in the following examples:

Member A: 'Mr. Chairman (interrupting if necessary, and not waiting to be recognized), I appeal from the decision of the Chair.'

Member B: 'I second the motion.'

Chairman: 'The decision of the Chair has been appealed. Is there any discussion?'

(Discussion)

Chairman: 'If there is no more discussion, the question is: "Shall the decision of the Chair be sustained?" All in favour . . .' etc.

Or, if the question is not debatable:

Member C: 'Mr. Chairman (interrupting if necessary, etc.), I appeal from the decision of the Chair.'

Member D: 'I second the motion.'

Chairman: 'The decision of the Chair has been appealed. The question is: "Shall the decision of the Chair be sustained?" All in favour . . .' etc.

The ruling of the Chair on points of order is normally accepted. But it does not have to be.

If you believe the Chair to be in error on an *important* point, you may appeal against the decision by means of this motion. Here again, you should not do so for trivial or merely technical reasons. Keep your parliamentary powder dry, for the time when it is really needed.

To Call for a Count of the Vote

The motion for a count of the vote is also termed a *Call for a Division of the Assembly*. (I4 in the Table.)

The usual practice is for a voice vote as illustrated below. Because some people answer louder than others, however, it is often hard for you to tell which side has carried by a voice vote, especially when the vote is close.

Chairman: 'All those in favour of the motion will please say "Aye".'

Response: Chorus of 'Ayes'.

Chairman: 'All those opposed to the motion will please say "No".'

Response: Chorus of 'Noes'.

Chairman: 'The "Ayes" have it. The motion is carried.'

Member A: 'Mr. Chairman (interrupting if necessary, and not waiting to be recognized), I call for a count of the vote.'

Chairman: 'The member calls for a count of the vote. All those in favour of the motion will please hold up a hand.'

(The Chairman appoints a teller for the 'Ayes' and a teller for the 'Noes'. The tellers count the number of hands held up and write the number down. The same procedure then takes place for those who voted against the motion. The Chairman, with the written number of votes for and against the motion, then rises and announces the number of votes and the decision of the meeting.)

Note that anyone calling for a Count of the Vote may interrupt a speaker if necessary; he needs no recognition or seconder.

If he is in doubt, the Chairman himself may ask for a show of hands, or a standing vote. But you are also entitled to a careful count if you question the Chairman's decision, and you can ask for it by means of this motion.

Points of Information

In the following example, Member *A* is speaking:

Member B: 'Mr. Chairman (interrupting if necessary, and without waiting to be recognized), I rise to a point of information.'

Chairman: 'Does the speaker mind?'

Member A: 'Not at all, Mr. Chairman.'

Chairman: 'You may state your question, Mr. B.'

Member B: 'Is the speaker taking the figures he has been quoting from our last year's Balance Sheet?'

Member A: 'No, Mr. Chairman, I am sorry if I failed to mention that these figures are from the Treasurer's current records.'

Member B: 'Thank you, Mr. Chairman. That was what some of us were wondering since we could not find them on the last Balance Sheet.'

Member C: 'While such questions are in order, Mr. Chairman, I'd like to ask one. Do you realize, Mr. A., that those figures you have been quoting are misleading because of the unusual expenses we have had this year?'

Chairman: 'Sorry, Mr. C. That is not a proper point of information. The Chair will be pleased to recognize you next if you wish to raise such an issue. But Mr. A. has the floor now and may proceed.'

Points of Information (I5 in the Table) should be limited to genuine inquiries.

You need not first be recognized to rise on a point of information, but the speaker may decide whether he will yield the floor to hear your question.

Both questions and answers must be addressed to the Chair. In the above example, Member *C* was out of order also in addressing his question directly to Member *A*. Cross-conversation is not allowed in formal discussion.

The high precedence given to a request for information is to help you follow what the speaker is saying. Member *B* is *in order* in the above example because he is making a genuine inquiry.

Member *C* is *out of order* because he is obviously trying to use this high-precedence motion to get speaking time for which he should properly wait his turn.

If someone rises on a point of information while you have the floor, you must decide whether you will agree to hear his question. When your time is limited and you have important points still to make, you may be reluctant to do so, since both question and answer will be clocked against you in limited debate.

The question to be asked, however, may be troubling other members as well. Answering it may help your case more than saying what you had planned to say. You will do well, therefore, to yield to members from whom you can expect intelligent questions.

To Suspend the Rules

Many of the preceding motions provide means of keeping the procedure of a meeting regular. This motion and the following one, however, provide emergency means of avoiding usual procedure.

The fact that there is a general class of motions, *To Suspend the Rules* (16 in the Table), does not mean that all rules can be suspended by any organization. Each society's constitution or by-laws (see Chapter Six) specifies which rules, if any, can be suspended at its meetings.

It is commonly possible to suspend rules which relate to:

(*a*) The order of business.

(*b*) Limitations on debate.

(*c*) Exclusions of non-members from attendance of discussion.

It is generally *not* possible to suspend more basic rules which relate to:

(*d*) The rights of members.

(*e*) Voting requirements.

(*f*) Rules of parliamentary procedure not specifically excepted.

As an example of a permissible move to suspend:

Member A: 'Mr. Chairman (pause for recognition), in view of the importance and complexity of the motion on the floor, I move to suspend the rules in order to extend debate on it beyond the limits imposed by our By-laws.'

Member B: 'I second the motion.'

Chairman: 'It has been moved and seconded . . .' etc.

As an example of a motion to suspend which is not permissible:

Member C: 'Mr. Chairman (pause for recognition), the motion which was just barely defeated required a two-thirds majority. In view of the importance of the action, I move to suspend the rules in order to make a simple majority vote enough to pass it.'

Chairman: 'Sorry, Mr. C., but the Chair cannot entertain such a motion. A rule of voting is not one which can be suspended.'

Note that a motion to Suspend the Rules is limited to specified rules. It may not be debated or amended, and it requires a two-thirds majority vote.

This motion is more limited than is generally realized. It is strictly a special-purpose measure for setting aside minor regulations when there are good grounds for doing so. It is *not* a way of getting around really basic parliamentary principles.

The rules governing it assure that no time will be lost on it, and that it will not pass without substantial majority support.

To Object to Consideration

Member: 'Mr. Chairman (interrupting if necessary, and not pausing for recognition), I object to consideration of this motion.'

Chairman: 'Objection has been made to consideration. Do you wish to consider the original motion to which objection has been made? All those in favour of considering the original motion please say "Aye" . . .' etc.

Note that this motion (I7 in the Table) should be made when the original motion is first presented.

It should be based upon a presumption of bad taste or irrelevance in the original motion.

It requires no seconder and cannot be debated or amended.

It is put to vote by the Chair in the form illustrated above, and a two-thirds vote in the negative excludes the challenged motion from further consideration.

Most rules of debate are designed to give all members and all points of view a fair chance to be heard. Sometimes, however, a minority may take advantage of this fact to impose upon a meeting motions out-of-line with its purpose.

For example, a pair of members of a social or business club may repeatedly introduce resolutions for 'world peace' or 'clean living'. You may have no objection to these in themselves, but may well feel that they are out of place at that meeting.

To Consider as a Whole or by Parts

In the older manuals of parliamentary procedure this motion is usually given the Latin phrasing: Consideration *in toto* (as a whole) or *seriatim* (in a series, and so part by part). (I8 in the Table.)

It is customary to consider any motion as a whole unless a motion is passed to consider it by parts. For example:

'Mr. Chairman (pause for recognition), discussion of the motion before us is becoming so complicated, I move to consider it paragraph by paragraph.'

If this motion is passed, separate votes are taken on the separate parts into which the original motion is then divided.

By moving to consider a complicated motion by parts, you may obtain *two advantages*: (i) you can speak for or against each part separately in debate; (ii) you can register your support or opposition on each part separately when the vote is taken.

Thus you can help to keep separate issues from being confused, and can better express just where you stand on each part of the original question. Give its possible use careful thought whenever debate becomes too involved.

Where necessary this motion may be applied to break down an original motion, sentence by sentence or phrase by phrase.

Request for Leave to Withdraw a Motion

If there are no objections, the situation is simple:

Member A (Original Mover): 'Mr. Chairman (pause for recognition), in view of what has just been said by the last speaker, I should like to withdraw my motion.'

Chairman: 'The member requests leave to withdraw his motion which we are now considering. Are there any objections? (Pause for response) If not, that leave is granted and the floor is now open for other business.'

But there may well be objections, as in the following example:

Chairman: 'The member requests leave to withdraw his motion. Are there any objections?'

Member B: 'I object, Mr. Chairman.'

Chairman: 'In that case the Chair will have to ask if anyone is willing to move that Mr. A. be granted permission to withdraw his motion.'

Member C: 'I so move, Mr. Chairman.'

Member D: 'I second the motion.'

Chairman: 'It has been moved and seconded that the member be granted leave to withdraw his motion. All in favour . . .' etc.

In this motion (I9 in the Table) note that only the mover may request leave to withdraw a motion.

The Chair can grant the request only if there are no objections: when there are objections, a formal motion to grant it must be made, seconded, and voted on without debate.

No one but you can reasonably be allowed to withdraw a motion which you have made. In the absence of objection, it can be regarded as your personal right to do so.

Since other members have accepted consideration of your motion, however, the rules give them the right to object to your trying to take it back from them.

(12) Main Motions

Original Main Motions supply the grist for the parliamentary mill because they introduce those basic proposals of action for which the organization exists.

The other classes of motions considered above—Privileged, Incidental and Subsidiary—serve merely to help an organization to function so that it can deal with these basic motions more efficiently.

Typically, an Original Main Motion is the kind you may most properly make as a point of *New Business*. In that connexion (see page 95), we have already given as examples: the proposal at a meeting of a Sports Club to purchase a contest trophy; and a proposal at a meeting of a Residents' Association to petition council officials for the construction of a playground.

Look back at these examples for formal wording and for recommendations as to what preparations you should make before trying to introduce such motions.

Motions to introduce main points of new business, however, are not the only ones included in this general class. There are also *Incidental Main Motions*.

Consider, for example, the question of when and where the next meeting of an organization will be held. We have already seen (page 108) that, if this question has not been decided, a motion concerning it is classified as 'Privileged' and has the highest precedence.

Yet, if a time and place have already been set for the next meeting, a motion to propose a different time or place is not so privileged. It then has no more priority for consideration than an ordinary Original Main Motion.

Moreover, even when such a motion is privileged, once it has been introduced it becomes a main motion in the sense that subsidiary and incidental motions may be applied to its discussion. If the floor had been clear at the time when it was introduced, it would be treated like any Original Main Motion so far as parliamentary routine is concerned.

The same is true of a motion *To Adjourn* if it is not for *immediate* adjournment; or of a *Question of Privilege* once it has been put as a motion before the meeting.

All such motions are therefore classed as *Incidental Main Motions*— 'Incidental', to distinguish them from 'Original' main motions introducing essentially new business; and 'Main' because incidental and subsidiary motions may be applied to them.

Main motions are last in order of precedence. The low precedence means that none can be made while any other motion including another main motion, is being discussed.

E

This may at first seem unsound, since the most important business considered at a meeting must be introduced by means of main motions. Why put first things last in order of priority?

Subsidiary, incidental and privileged motions take precedence over a main motion, however, only because they enable a meeting better to consider the more basic proposals which are contained in a main motion.

Beyond that, the purpose of the rule of precedence is simply to assure that no more than one main motion be discussed at a time.

(13) Review Motions

Review Motions are those which direct attention back to a motion previously considered. You may therefore quite correctly think of them as a special class of Incidental Main Motions.

The form which they take, and their precedence order, depends on the manner in which previous discussion of the original motion was ended.

Motion To Reconsider

If previous discussion ended in the *passing* of the original motion, that motion may be reviewed, under certain conditions, by means of the motion *To Reconsider* (R1 in the Table). For example:

'Mr. Chairman (interrupting a speaker, if necessary), having just learned from a late arrival that the Borough Surveyor has declared Oxbridge Assembly Rooms unsafe for large gatherings, I move to reconsider our vote earlier this evening to hold our next meeting there.'

A motion To Reconsider may be moved only by a member who voted for passage of the original motion, and only during the same meeting, or the meeting immediately following the one at which the original motion was passed.

The proposer may interrupt a speaker on any other motion.

Once seconded, the motion To Reconsider automatically stops all action carrying out the motion to be reconsidered.

Discussion must await clearance of the floor, but precedes any other main motion not actually under discussion.

The motion To Reconsider may not be renewed.

The reasons for the above rules are that the motion To Reconsider, is primarily an emergency measure. Its main purpose is to stop action on a previous motion when new information puts that action in a different light.

Like other devices for quick action, however, this motion can be abused. The rules which limit its use to supporters of the original motion and forbid its renewal if defeated, are intended to prevent a defeated side from using it to block action on a motion.

But sometimes a scheming minority will have some of its members vote along with the majority just in order to make them eligible, later, to delay action by moving To Reconsider.

Likewise, a scheming majority will sometimes automatically move To Reconsider a motion which they have just passed themselves. Their purpose in doing this is to make it impossible for *real* opposition to the original motion to stop action on it later.

For comment on all such parliamentary manœuvres see the section on *Strategy* in Chapter Six.

Motion To Repeal

After the meeting following the one at which it is passed, an original motion can no longer be reached by the motion To Reconsider. If you then wish to discuss the action approved by a previous vote, you must do so through the motion *To Repeal*, sometimes called *To Rescind*. (R2 in the Table.)

Under either name, this is a motion to undo whatever was done by the original motion, and so it is reasonable only when the previous action is one which *can* be undone. For example:

Member A: 'Mr. Chairman (pause for recognition), I move to repeal the motion we passed two years ago increasing membership fees by 10s. 6d. per year.'
Member B: 'I second the motion.'
Chairman: 'It has been moved and seconded . . .' etc.

Second example:

Member C: 'Mr. Chairman (pause for recognition), in view of the recent conviction of the Trustees of the Z Foundation for misuse of funds, I move to repeal the motion we passed last year making a donation to the Foundation.'
Chairman: 'Many of us regret that action as much as you do, Mr. C. But in accordance with our instructions, the Treasurer forwarded a cheque to the Foundation the next day and it has long since been cleared through the bank. So I do not see how the Chair can entertain a motion such as you offer now.'

Note that a motion To Repeal has the same precedence status for entry as any other main motion. Note also that it requires a two-thirds majority, unless notice of consideration has been given at the previous meeting, in which case only a simple majority vote is required.

Any action is subject to quick review within a reasonable period of time by means of a motion To *Reconsider* (see above). But if past actions could always be so easily revived, it would be theoretically possible for a conspiring minority to reverse an organization's entire past policy at a single meeting in which they chanced to have a temporary majority.

Once the period of the motion To Reconsider has expired, therefore, the revision of past actions is made more difficult. The rules governing *Repeal* motions give them the lowest possible precedence rank to ensure that an organization's considered policy shall not be too easily reversed.

Motion To Renew

Strictly speaking, there is no such thing as a separate motion 'to renew consideration'. But when a motion is made again, after having been previously moved and defeated, the new motion is said *To Renew* the original one. (R3 in the Table.)

The conditions under which each type of motion may or may not be renewed are indicated in the *Table of Motions* and discussed in the explanation of *Renewability* (see page 99).

First example:

Member A: 'Mr. Chairman (pause for recognition), I should like to move once more as I did earlier this evening, that . . .'

Chairman: 'Sorry, Mr. A., but that motion was defeated when you first introduced it. We may therefore not take it up again until the meeting after next when the Chair will be glad to have you reintroduce it if you then wish to.'

Second example:

Member B: 'Mr. Chairman (pause for recognition), I again move to reconsider the motion we have passed to appropriate . . .'

Chairman: 'Sorry, Mr. B., but you are out of order. Since a motion to reconsider cannot be made a second time after it is once defeated, the Chair can entertain no such motion.'

Third example:

Member C: 'Mr. Chairman (pause for recognition), a full hour has gone by since my motion to close debate on this question was defeated. I therefore again move to close debate.'

Member D: 'I second the motion.'

Chairman: 'It has been moved and seconded to close debate. All in favour . . .' etc.

CHAPTER SIX

DISCUSSION TECHNIQUES

(1) Formal and Informal Procedure

Perhaps the most commonly misunderstood aspect of speaking in public is the difference between formal and informal procedure.

When strictly following the formalities described in the preceding chapter, you may at times have felt stiff and unnatural. Taking your cue from such experiences, you may have departed from such formality at other times only to find yourself called to order.

What, then, is the best policy to follow in this matter?

As a general rule, you should keep to formal procedure when the meetings you attend are (i) large, or (ii) concerned with major issues; and when the members of the audience are (iii) not well acquainted with each other, or (iv) sharply divided in opinion.

Any one of these factors alone may decide the question. There is a limit to how casual a large assembly can be without becoming too disorganized to accomplish anything. And even two people tend to be more formal in their attitude when they are comparative strangers, when they are engaged in serious dealings, or when they are not seeing eye-to-eye.

Conversely, the procedure may become more informal when the members at your meeting are (i) few in number, (ii) well acquainted, (iii) dealing with routine matters, or (iv) in agreement as to views.

Most of these factors are of course relative. We could say that a meeting has few participants when less than some arbitrary number like 15 are present. But the questions of how well acquainted or in agreement with each other people really are, is a matter of nice judgement.

In doubtful cases it is always best to err, if you must, on the side of formality. You can soften the strictly correct formulas of speech with a smile and a casual tone of voice. The ludicrous effect of over-formality, after all, is as much a matter of how you speak as of what you say.

Then, if the general tone of response seems to justify it, you can shift to less formal wording later.

As a Chairman you should be particularly sensitive to this problem and give the speakers some indication of how to proceed.

Whenever informality seems possible, you can use it to speed matters up by cutting corners. But when objections arise you must be prompt in returning to strict procedure. For example:

Member A: 'Mr. Chairman (pause for recognition), in view of the information that has been brought out in the discussion, I move to amend the main motion by striking out the word "Wednesday" and substituting for it the word "Thursday".'

Chairman: 'Perhaps that change will be acceptable to Mr. B, who made the motion. If so, we won't need to take time for discussion and vote on the motion to amend.'

Member B: 'Yes, Mr. Chairman, that would be perfectly all right with me.'

Member C: 'Mr. Chairman (pause, etc.), I wonder if Mr. B would also be willing to have his motion read "next September" instead of "next August".'

Member B: 'No, Mr. Chairman, I most definitely would not agree to any such change!'

Chairman: 'In that case, Mr. C, the Chair must ask if you want to put what you have in mind in the form of an amendment to the motion.'

In this example the Chairman was able to save time by treating A's formal action informally. But on seeing that C's informal suggestion could not be handled in the same way, he correctly put the discussion back on a formal footing.

The main error to avoid is that of confusing informality with *irregularity.* When your meeting is conducted informally, you should do substantially the same things as under formal procedure, only in a more relaxed and streamlined manner. Never use informality as an excuse for avoiding the substance of the rules of parliamentary procedure.

For example, at a regular business meeting:

Chairman: 'Support for this appropriation measure seems to be so strong that I don't believe we need bother taking a vote on it. The Secretary can record it as passed.'

The Chairman in the above example is not just being informal. He is being highly irregular. Unless there has been a proper majority vote, any dissenting member has the right to charge that there has been a misappropriation of funds.

The second example is taken from the quarterly meeting of the 450 members of the Suburban Tenants' Association:

Chairman: 'Will the Secretary please read the minutes of the last meeting.'

Secretary: 'Nothing much happened at the last meeting. I don't think we need take the time to read the minutes. I have a copy of them here on my desk if anybody wants to look at them on the way out.'

Here the Secretary is being much too informal for the occasion. He cannot reasonably expect that many people to read a document of any length while walking past it on their way home at a late hour. Moreover, it is a long time between quarterly meetings, and those who attend them may need reminders of what took place at the last one.

The third example is taken from a luncheon meeting of the four like-minded members of the Competitions Committee of a Fishing Club:

Committee member A: 'Mr. Chairman, I rise to a point of inquiry.'

This is, of course, absurdly over-formal. The member was, we may hope, joking over the cocktails.

(2) Parliamentary Strategy

In the explanation of different kinds of motions in the preceding chapter, attention was called to the *strategic* possibilities of several.

In certain cases such tactics are strictly irregular. For example: attempts to change the intent or substance of a motion by *Amendment* (see page 102), or attempts to interrupt a speaker and gain debating time by improper *Points of Information* (see page 113).

An alert Chairman should prevent such abuses. Or you can influence him to do so by the use of *Points of Order* and *Appeals from the Decision of the Chair* (see pages 110 and 111).

But other strategic moves are perfectly regular. Perhaps the most unblushing example of this is use of the motion *To Reconsider*, so as actually to prevent the possibility of reconsideration (see page 118). Its purpose, as we have seen, is to enable action to be stopped, for emergency reasons, on a motion previously passed. However, a majority may take advantage of the fact that this motion is un-renewable: they may themselves immediately move and vote down the motion *To Reconsider*, thus making it technically impossible for others to reconsider the same action later.

Moreover, by the motion *To Refer*, a bare majority can side-step consideration of a proposal at will (see page 104).

By the motions *To Limit Debate*, *To Close Debate*, or *To Object to Consideration*, a two-thirds majority can confine discussion of any question as they wish, even to the extent of preventing it altogether.

The motion *To Postpone Consideration Indefinitely*, we have also seen, is always a tactical move to delay action on a main proposal (see page 106).

Each of these motions, including the last, has a perfectly legitimate purpose. Yet, the very effectiveness of such motions for their intended use makes them subject to misuse. And there is no formal parliamentary means of distinguishing between their intended and unintended application. So the question is: what should be *your* policy regarding them?

One thing should be perfectly clear in any case. You should fully understand the possibilities of such tactics if only to be prepared to *counter* them when used against you in formal discussion.

Do not hesitate to challenge *Amendments* which tend to change the substance of motions in which you are interested.

Do not allow improper *Points of Information* to interrupt your speaking or be clocked against your allotted debating time.

When a motion is made *To Refer* a proposal in which you are interested, see to it that, through discussion and amendment, it is referred to a committee which will really work on it and report back its recommendations in due time.

Do not hesitate, moreover, to use any of these motions yourself for their legitimate purposes. As we have seen, there are often reasonable grounds for moving *To Close Debate*, *To Object to Consideration*, or *To Postpone Indefinitely*.

But what about the purely obstructive use of such motions?

A book of this sort is not the place for exhortations to virtue. Still, it can be reported as a fairly clear lesson of practical experience that parliamentary skulduggery tends to defeat itself in the end. In our imperfect world, tactics of this kind sometimes enjoy a limited success. But in the long run, they satisfy those whom they serve no more than those whom they frustrate.

When you are working with a comfortable majority, it may seem an easy matter to force a measure through by arbitrarily closing off debate. But there are several questions which you should ask yourself.

What happens to your respect for those who join you in such an action? How, then, must it affect their respect for you? And what kind of a basis is that for working together in the future?

What kind of precedent does it set for your organization as a way of handling its business? This time it may have worked out to your advantage. But how about the next time? And the next, and the next?

What is the effect of such an action on the minority of the moment who are over-ridden? Do you want them as loyal, interested members of your group for other projects? Is this kind of treatment calculated to make them such?

Reasonable consideration of the points listed above leads to the conclusion that a measure must be very, very important indeed to be worth winning by questionable means.

You are advised to study tactical devices with great care. But you will do so most profitably if you go at it in the spirit of the law-abiding citizen who takes up judo 'just in case'.

It is worth mastering the technicalities of the rules of order explained in the preceding chapter. Then you will know how to speak up at the right time and in the right way, You will have the assurance that goes with knowledge. You will be spared the embarrassment of being found out of order. And you will be able to block irregularities of others, disadvantageous to the motions you are interested in.

Do not, however, make the opposite mistake of becoming a 'stickler' for technical trifle—sa parliamentary show-off who parades his knowledge of the rule book.

Many so-called 'irregularities' are as harmless as they are innocent. They are the fumblings of people who have not yet learned the correct procedures. If you are Chairman when such individuals blunder on the floor, you will accomplish little by lecturing them. Often all that is needed is a tactful suggestion:

'Perhaps, Mrs. Smith, you would like to put what you are saying in the form of a motion to . . .'

Or:

'I wonder, Mr. Jones, if you would explain the point you are making later on, when we come to the question you have in mind under Unfinished Business.'

Thoughtfulness like this may be appreciated even though it *is* educational.

Or, if you are not the Chairman, consider the possibilities of a *Point of Inquiry* before you raise a *Point of Order*. Better still, do not raise either, unless the irregularity is really serious or appears to be made with malicious intent.

Even the best speakers make occasional slips, and you may have more than one occasion to be grateful for similar thoughtfulness on the part of others.

(3) Organizing an Action Group

Much of the instruction given to the speaker advises him how to find the right things to say to a given audience. But in certain practical situations your problem may be the very different one of finding the right audience for a given speaking purpose.

Here are three typical examples of speakers whose difficulty is getting the kind of hearing which will make their speaking effective.

(i) *Mr. K.* and *Mr. L.* are neighbours on a new housing estate. Over the back fence they complain to each other about the Council's delay in putting lights in the streets, extending the school-bus service to the new community, and other such matters. Mr. K.'s letter to the Council has gone unanswered; Mr. L.'s visit to the Town Hall got him nowhere.

(ii) *Mrs. M.* and *Mrs. N.* often meet at the day-nursery which looks after their children while they are at work. They agree that the equipment in the nursery is inadequate and that supervision of the children leaves much to be desired. They have told the matron of the nursery that they would be glad to share the costs of more equipment and more supervisors. But the matron's abrupt answer was that she did not want to 'get into anything like that'.

(iii) *Mr. P.* and *Mr. Q.* run small shops in a London suburb. At lunch, in a local restaurant, they compare notes and find that an increasing number of their old customers are doing their shopping at the big supermarkets. Neither has been able to do much by himself to recover the lost trade.

The chances are that none of these people will get very far merely by organizing their ideas better and expressing them more forcefully. So long as their audience is confined to individuals they can buttonhole, their words will be without effect.

What they all need is the kind of audience to whom they can bring their facts and figures with some hope of getting action. Their first job is to call a public meeting of people willing and able to back them up.

If you find yourself in such a situation, this is the way to go about it.

First sound out others who face the same problems, with a view to forming an Organizing Committee with a temporary Chairman.

Mr. K. and *Mr. L.*, for example, might spend a few evenings calling on their immediate neighbours. *Mrs. M.* and *Mrs. N.* might begin with the other mothers who use the day-nursery. *Mr. P.* and *Mr. Q.* can call on other local tradesmen at lunch time or during the slack hours of the day.

Be ready, if you can, to make a fairly specific suggestion—the formation of a Residents' Association, a Nursery Project Group, a local Better Business Bureau. But avoid giving the impression that you have everything worked out and just want the other fellow's backing.

The other fellow may have better ideas than yours, or he may not. In either event, he is more likely to respond if you give him reason to believe that he has a part to play.

Do not make the mistake of 'pressurizing' obviously reluctant individuals. If you keep their goodwill they may tag along later. But if you are too insistent at the outset, you may antagonize them permanently. The popularity ratings of the 'know-all' and the busy-body are low. So be careful not to be officious or pushing.

The best technique is to ask the right questions. 'Do you feel that the Council has been giving us a fair deal? Have you ever had any experience with a Residents' Association? How do you suppose one would work out for us here?'

In the answers to such questions you may find broader experience than your own with such matters, and better ideas as to how to deal with them.

Remember, also, that an Organizing Committee has work to do. Never load it up with indifferent, half-hearted or obviously incompetent people. Invite into it only the best talent you can get.

This is especially important in the case of the Chairmanship. You may be of the stuff of which leaders are made. So do not hesitate to accept the responsibility if you are willing to carry the ball, and if the others obviously show that they expect you to.

On the other hand, if it is results you want rather than doubtful glory, be ready to support for the post of Chairman the man who seems most to command the confidence of the others. He may not be the one you know best. He may not even be one of the founding members. But if he has what it takes to put the plan over, you will serve your cause best by supporting him.

Once an Organizing Committee is thus formed, it should plan an *Organizing Meeting*.

This means, first of all, arranging an appropriate time and place—details, which are not as simple as they may seem.

No time is ever really convenient for everyone. The chief mistakes to avoid are conflicts with people's working hours, periods of religious observance, or previously arranged events likely to interest the same potential audience.

Beginning too early discourages those who arrive home late. Beginning too late discourages others addicted to the maxim of 'early to bed . . .'

Try to canvass a typical sample of the people you would like to reach. Find out their commitments and preferences. Then settle on the least inconvenient time for the greatest number.

The possibilities of a place to meet may be even more limited.

If there is no alternative to the local school hall, the matter is settled. If you are fortunate enough to have a choice, pick a hall which will be large enough to seat all comfortably, but not so large that a good turn-out will look like poor attendance.

For non-partisan and non-sectarian groups, you should avoid meeting places with a partisan or sectarian atmosphere. And do not choose a room in a public house if you hope to recruit people who are diffident about such surroundings.

These arrangements are only the beginning of your job. The Committee should also prepare a brief, pointed *announcement* of the Organizing Meeting.

This should cover not only such details as the time and place, but the purpose of your Committee in calling the meeting, and what you hope to accomplish by it.

The announcement should also be an invitation not merely to come and listen, but to present ideas as well. 'We want to hear from YOU!' is a good approach whether the individual wishes to speak or not. Just as long as he feels welcome to put forward his own point of view, he is more willing to hear what others have to say.

The Committee's preparations should, of course, include careful planning of the Organizing Meeting itself.

Your purpose will be little served by a big attendance if you have failed to organize the programme. Each member of the Committee should know exactly what he has to do, and when, without any need for last-minute consultations.

Start promptly. A wait of more than five or ten minutes before starting a meeting makes an audience restless. 'If these people can't even start on time,' they begin to think, 'what good can come of the whole thing?'

Bear in mind also that a meeting such as this has no regular authority as yet. The Committee members extended the invitation, but they have no more to say about its outcome than those who appear by invitation.

The proper thing is for an agreed-upon member of the Organizing Committee to stand up before the audience, call the meeting to order, and nominate an agreed-upon person to serve as temporary Chairman. This motion should be seconded promptly by another agreed-upon Committee member, then the first one can put the question to a vote.

Normally, the election of a temporary Chairman for a not-yet organized group will go through automatically. The temporary Chairman can then proceed to the election of a temporary Secretary to record the minutes.

Next, the temporary Chairman should explain the general purpose of the meeting and sum up the thinking of the Organizing Committee as to what it might accomplish. Or, he can call on some other agreed-upon member of the Committee to do this.

If the responsibility falls to you, be careful to take account of the possible interests and apprehensions of your listeners. What most of them want to know is why they should take part in this sort of affair at all. Address yourself to that question first.

Anything vague like: 'Some of us thought it might be a nice idea if we were to get some kind of group organized around here . . .' will very likely draw the reaction: 'Why bother?'

On the other hand, do not try to deliver a complete 'pre-packaged' programme. Avoid the attitude that all the others need to do is to have the good sense to come along and back it up. Most people like to be addressed as adults who might have a few good ideas of their own, and the chances are that many of them do.

The test of your meeting will be the reaction you get *from* the audience. Let them understand that you honestly want to find out what they know and think about the situation. Keep your own speaking brief enough to leave them time to have their say.

Once the discussion is started, the Chairman will do well to recognize as many different speakers as will volunteer from the audience. He can remind the long-talkers and the repeaters, in a friendly way, of the number of others who have not yet been heard from.

Members of the Committee should stand by, ready to speak up in case of a lull. But as far as possible they should let others make the points.

Finally, be careful that the discussion does not deteriorate into a general airing of grievances. You are there for a more important purpose than just blowing off steam.

As soon as it is clear that a need for organization is widely felt, and as soon as all present have had a reasonable chance to have their say, an agreed-upon member of the Committee should introduce a motion that a permanent organization be formed. For example:

'Mr. Chairman (pause for recognition), in view of what has been said here tonight, I wish to propose the following motion:

' "Whereas we residents of Airy Acres believe that our community interests would be better served by a permanent civic association; therefore, be it resolved, that the Chair appoint a committee of five to draw up a proposed constitution for such an association; and be it further resolved that we meet again at the same hour four weeks from today to consider the recommendations of that committee for such a constitution." '

The original Organizing Committee should, of course, be prepared promptly to second this motion and speak in explanation and support of its previously agreed-upon text. But they should be careful not to give the impression of trying to force something through by pre-arranged plan.

The purpose of the advance preparation of the motion is to make sure that discussion will not dissipate into mere talk. If you depend on inspiration, you may lose your chance to get action started at the opportune moment. But that does not mean you are committed to a conspiracy.

The audience may want to load the 'Whereas' clause with a list of grievances, make the committee larger or smaller, and meet again sooner or later. This may, or may not, be wise. But it can be done by amendment and consideration by parts (see Motions S5 and I8 of the Table of Motions on page 100), and it is the right of the assembly to do so if they think best.

Do not make the mistake of being obstinate about mere details of your plan. That would risk arousing distrust for the entire project. If this organization is to accomplish anything, its members will have to compromise their differences in a spirit of give-and-take.

For a committee such as is proposed by the above motion, a gathering will normally draw on the experience and interest already shown by the

Organizing Committee. But the members of this initial group will also do well to try to bring others into responsible jobs as soon as possible. Once you give the impression of trying to hold on to the ball, others may decide to let you run with it—all by yourself.

The temporary Chairman should therefore call for volunteers and try to appoint members of the audience who have shown intelligent interest in their contributions to the discussion. But he should also know, by previous agreement, in what order to call upon the members of the Organizing Committee as they are needed.

Use the interval between the first and second organizing meetings for further promotion and canvassing.

If all goes well, the *Second Organizing Meeting* will end the work of the Organizing Committee.

The temporary Chairman should preside over the opening of this meeting, calling first for the *minutes* from the Secretary, and next for the proposed *constitution* from the Constitutional Committee.

Procedure may be as at any meeting of an established organization. The main motion before the assembly is the proposal to approve the constitution. It may be amended, considered by parts, and otherwise treated as described in Chapter Five.

If the constitution is referred back to the Constitutional Committee, a third organizing meeting will be necessary to continue discussion in the same way.

Once a motion to adopt the constitution is passed by a majority vote, however, qualifications for membership will have been determined.

All those eligible and willing to join should then do so by signing the approved draft of the constitution and paying whatever subscriptions are required by it.

This may be done during an interval when the meeting is in recess. When the meeting is called back to order, the temporary Chairman should call on the Secretary to read the list of members. These are the people now eligible to vote for the permanent officers provided for by the constitution.

The temporary Chairman's last responsibility is to conduct the election of the President, as provided for in the constitution. Once elected, the President takes over as chairman, conducts the election of the other officers, and a new organization is on its way to do its part of the world's work.

Exercise No. 29

In the preceding text, three examples are given of pairs of individuals who face the need of forming an appropriate action group. Consider in detail how you would apply each step of the recommended procedure to their organization problems.

(i) Whom should they sound out to form an organizing committee? And how should they go about contacting these people?

(ii) What would be a good text for their announcement of an organizing meeting? What likely time and place should it propose? How should they follow it up by personal interviews?

(iii) What would be the text of a good resolution to introduce at each organizing meeting?

(iv) With what arguments would you support such a text?

(v) What details of such a text should you stand ready to have modified by amendment?

(4) Constitutions, By-laws and Rules

The basic regulations which govern the procedure of any meeting are those contained in the organization's constitution, by-laws, charter, or standing rules. If you are to take an active part in the formation of any democratic group, you will need to know what they should contain.

Even if all the organizations to which you belong are well established, you still need to get to know their basic rules. Officers or older members may refer to their provisions as reasons why you can or cannot make particular proposals. So you should have more than a general awareness of what they are about.

The *Constitution* of any organization is a document containing the basic laws or rules by which that organization is governed.

Some older societies with a complicated structure have only a few articles in their Constitutions, with such headings as

- Name of the organization
- Purposes of the organization
- Requirements for membership
- Officers and their election
- Provisions for meetings
- Method of amending the constitution.

In such cases, other basic regulations are contained in a separate document and are known as By-laws. For example:

- Duties of officers
- Standing Committees and their duties
- Methods of admitting members
- Custody of funds
- Definition of a Quorum (The number of members who must be present to hold a meeting and cast valid votes.)
- Parliamentary authority (The standard work on parliamentary law to be followed at meetings.)
- Method of amending the by-laws.

More commonly, however, all the provisions belonging to either of these are now combined in one known as *either* the Constitution *or* the By-laws. The first name is of Latin origin; the second of Anglo-Saxon origin. There is just about the same difference between the two words as between 'residence' and 'home'. Although they mean the same thing, however, you should, in each case, use whichever term appears in the document itself.

Standing Rules usually cover such additional matters as:

- Set hours and places of meeting
- The order of business
- Limitations on debate
- Limitations on attendance or speaking by non-members.

These are usually the only 'rules' which may be suspended by the motion *To Suspend the Rules* (see page 114).

If your organization is a local branch of a larger body, it may have a *Charter* instead of either a Constitution or By-laws.

This is a similar document, issued by the parent organization, and authorizing your group to operate locally under the name and Constitution of the parent organization. Its provisions will therefore be much the same, except that they will also state in what ways the local group is responsible to the larger one.

Whatever the basic documents which govern your organization, they should state in black and white just what your rights and responsibilities are as a member, and they should do the same for all the officers and major committees.

Study them carefully. You may well be able to quote them to good effect later.

Exercise No. 30

If you do not have copies of the Constitution, By-laws, Charter, or Standing Rules of any organization to which you belong, get a copy from the Secretary. Then check the text carefully with such questions as these in mind:

(i) What is the stated 'purpose' of the organization? Is that the purpose for which you joined it? Are most of its meetings conducted in the spirit of such a purpose? Have most of the motions it has recently passed tended to carry out that purpose? Do some recent actions of the organization have a contrary effect? Can you think of any proposals that would better carry out the stated purpose?

(ii) What are the stated 'duties' of the officers? Are your officers, in fact, fulfilling those duties? Are they in some cases, perhaps, overstepping their authority? How about yourself, if you are an officer?

(iii) What *standing committees* are provided for, and what are their duties? Are they functioning as they should? Or have some tended to become 'paper committees' while others took over? Is this a better arrangement? If not, what might you say at meetings to correct the situation? Or, what amendment might you propose to clarify it?

(iv) What is defined as a *Quorum* to conduct business at your meetings? Are that many members always actually present? If not, what should be done about it? Should you support a drive for better attendance? Should those who do not attend be removed from the membership roll? Or should the quorum requirement be cut by amendment?

(v) What handbook is used as *parliamentary authority*? Is it being followed? Does your Chairman need to be reminded of its provisions?

(vi) Are there any stipulated *limits on debate*? Are these observed by you and your fellow-members at meetings? If not, would it be better to do so, or to amend the limitations?

(vii) Which rules, if any, may be *suspended* by a motion to do so? Are any others ever side-stepped at your meetings? Have you always realized and made use of allowed suspensions yourself?

On the model of the texts examined above, try drafting proposed constitutions or by-laws for one of the proposed new organizations in the preceding part of this chapter.

(5) Platform Debates

As a matter of general interest to the membership, your Programme Committee might arrange a *platform debate* on a current topic.

In that case the question is called a **proposition,** and you should word it in a way that admits of a simple *yes* or *no* answer.

A mere topic, such as 'Local Radio' or 'A local radio station for Oxbridge' would not do because it invites explanation rather than argument.

'Resolved, that the City of Oxbridge accede to the popular demand for a local radio station' is an improvement. Yet this wording illustrates the different error of *loading* the question. Whether there is *in fact* a popular demand is what the debate should be about. So never put any such prejudicial terms in the proposition itself. In this example the proposition should be 'That the City of Oxbridge set up a local radio station'.

Speakers who support the proposition are called the **Affirmative.** Those who oppose it are called the **Negative.**

There may be no more than one speaker on each side. Two is usually the best number for general interest value. You are quite sure to have planned badly if you want more than three. And of course there should always be the same number on both sides.

The customary form of debate is divided into two general parts—presentation and refutation.

In the *presentation* phase each speaker for and against the proposition is given an equal amount of time to present his constructive case.

The Chairman for the occasion introduces the debaters to the audience in the order: speaker for the motion, speaker against the motion, seconder for the motion, and so on. The idea is that the speaker for the motion begins and that the sides alternate thereafter throughout the presentation.

You should, of course, relate what you say in such a speech to what the other speakers are saying. But you are supposed to concentrate on the more positive aspects of your own case.

As a speaker for the motion, you should emphasize your positive reasons for supporting the proposition. As a negative speaker you should emphasize equally positive reasons for opposing it.

A much-repeated saying which you may have heard is that 'the burden of proof is always on the affirmative'. On this theory, a smug negative will sometimes assume that it has nothing to do but wait for the affirmative to put up an argument, and then criticize it.

This makes some sense in a court of law where our legal tradition presumes a man to be innocent until proved otherwise. The proposition before the court is that the accused is guilty. The defence (speaker against the motion) technically has no obligation except to show how the prosecution (for the motion) is in error.

But elsewhere the circumstances can be quite different. A popular proposal may easily be carried, unless an aggressive opposition builds up a very strong case against it. That could be the situation, for instance, with regard to the above proposition to set up a local radio station.

Thus, in practical situations, the burden of proof may fall to either side. For platform purposes, therefore, it is sensible to think of both sides as having an equal obligation to give convincing positive arguments.

A difficulty which sometimes arises is that the different speakers on each side do not have enough opportunity to confer with each other beforehand. As a result, they may duplicate each other's material. Or, at the other extreme, they may present such different lines of argument that there is little tie-up between them.

In the latter case, such serious inconsistencies may arise that the other side spends too much of its speaking time asking where their opponents really stand. So make every possible effort to get each set of speakers together before the event.

A generally accepted rule is that you should not try to develop essentially new constructive arguments in refutation speeches. You should concentrate, rather, on rebuttal and rejoinder.

Rebuttal is your criticism of the arguments made by your opponents in presentation.

Rejoinder is your renewed explanation and defence of your own previous arguments after rebuttal by your opponents.

The general plan of a constructive argumentative speech has already been discussed in Chapter Four. But something should be added here on refutation technique.

While preparing your own presentation you will have become fairly well acquainted with the more common arguments for the other side. It is a good idea to jot these down on separate cards as you go along, with notes as to how you would answer them if you had to.

Then, as the opposition speakers present their case, you can pick out already prepared notes on many of their points. And you can use these for most of your refutation speech, which you would otherwise have to pull together on the spur of the moment.

Be careful, however, not to let yourself be distracted by obvious errors which they make on minor points. Concentrate, rather, on possible major fallacies.

Check first to see whether your opponents' arguments are consistent with each other. Do they all fit together logically? Or do some contentions contradict others?

Check next to see whether your opponents' arguments are adequate in their overall structure. Even if you were to agree with all they contend, would you then be compelled to join their side? Or, could you accept what they say, as far as it goes, and still reasonably maintain your own conclusion?

Nothing is so devastating to an opponent's platform position as a rebuttal in which you can accept his premises but show that they serve your purposes.

This was the embarrassing position of one speaker against the proposition that teachers taking part in violent demonstrations be dismissed. He made a major issue of figures to show that there are actually fewer such teachers in our schools and universities than there are bank employees in prison for embezzlement.

His opponent accepted the statistics, but pointed out that, if there were fewer embezzling bank clerks than there were rioting teachers, the same line of reasoning would lead to the conclusion that we should retain embezzlers in banking jobs merely because there would then be so few of them. Since that was obviously ridiculous, the admittedly striking statistics were shown to be beside the point.

This kind of refutation penetrates to the underlying errors in the other fellow's thinking. Attend to it first. You can always put the commas and decimal points in the right places later.

The usual time-table for a medium debate runs as follows:

Affirmative Speakers	Phase	Negative Speakers	Minutes
	Presentation		
First			10
		First	10
Second			10
		Second	10
	Interval		
			5 or 10
	Refutation		
		First	5
First			5
		Second	5
Second			5

Total 65 or 70

With a single speaker on each side there may be only one presentation speech of about 15 minutes, and only one refutation speech of about eight minutes for each side.

The chief shortcoming of platform debates from the audience point of view is failure on the part of the speakers to get down to brass tacks on basic issues. Both affirmative and negative usually attempt to include every major point. Thus, in their concern for comprehensiveness, they tend to distribute their time almost equally over all possible issues, leaving themselves relatively little time to discuss specific points of difference.

Whenever you are speaking in any kind of debate avoid dwelling on points which are not seriously challenged. Concentrate your attention on the main issues of actual contention on that particular occasion. And fill in the details of the overall argument only to put these points in perspective.

(6) Platform Discussions

If your membership finds debates too formal, you may wish to try arranging a more informal kind of platform discussion in which a number of speakers—usually three to five—state their attitudes on a common question.

Propositions such as are necessary for debating will not do then because they allow for only two approaches—affirmative or negative.

The question must be posed in an *open* form which allows any kind of approach. For example:

- 'What should our national defence policy be?'
- 'How can we best deal with the problem of juvenile delinquency?'
- 'If I were Prime Minister . . .'
- 'What's right with British cooking?'
- 'How to domesticate a husband.'

From the above list it is clear that subjects may be as serious or as light as you wish. One of the main advantages of a discussion is its broad adaptability to almost any sort of theme.

In a platform discussion you may also feel free to express the most personal aspects of your way of thinking. Clear reasoning and sound substance are of course as desirable here as anywhere, but you need not limit yourself to weighing evidence as much as in a debate. The main purpose is to stimulate thinking by refracting the common theme through the prisms of the different personalities of the speakers.

Approach the occasion as an opportunity to get audience reactions to some of your more novel ideas. A platform discussion is sometimes called a *symposium*, from the Greek word meaning 'a drinking together'. That hardly places you under an obligation to be grimly sober.

(7) Forums

A *forum* is a discussion event in which the audience takes part. It may follow a single guest speaker, a debate in any form, or a platform discussion; or it may be a special event in itself.

From a programme point of view, you will generally find it wise never to arrange platform speaking without a *forum period*. A verbal exchange of ideas strikes sparks in the minds of listeners. They feel frustrated without the chance to have their own say. Some even regard saying their own bit afterwards as the main reason for coming. So do not let them down.

There is the danger, of course, of having such a period monopolized by cranks and bores. And there is a limit to what the most tactful chairman can do about this if others do not ask for the floor. So don't make the mistake of assuming you must plan only the platform part of the programme. You should also have a few prepared questioners in the audience.

One might be assigned, for example, to start off the forum period with a provocative question. For example:

'Mr. X, what would you do in your defence policy about our present stockpiles of obsolete weapons?'

Or:

'Mrs. Y, after all you have said about what is right with British cooking, could you now add a good word about our coffee-making?'

Never interrupt good, spontaneous discussion from the unrehearsed audience. But be prepared to supply leads or cues if they are needed. Then you may feel sure that you have done all you possibly can to make the event succeed.

(8) Informal Group Discussion

In some conference situations you may feel confident of your own conclusions, and you may be in a position of authority to command a hearing for them.

Let us suppose you are a sales manager and believe that your marketing campaign is falling flat because your salesmen are using the wrong approach to their customers, or are not keeping up with new developments in the field. In that case, you may call them in for a talk to point out their faults, show them what they could do if they went about it in the right way, and encourage them to try to do better with a fresh start.

But often, in a small discussion group, no one has such authority. If you are, for example, a member of the Entertainments Committee of a Residents' Association, you are in no position to take the others to task on the basis of your ideas of what should be done.

Sometimes, too, you may have more questions than answers in your own mind. All present may be looking for possible solutions to common problems. Then it is important for you to realize that group meetings need not be a backdrop for contention. Discussion can also be a method of inquiry and discovery.

It is as well to remember this even when you believe you know the answers, and even when you have the authority to call the tune.

(9) Discussion as Group Thinking

Perhaps you, as Sales Manager, are the most experienced member of your staff. In your time you have seen many salespeople come and go. When you were out in the field yourself, you booked record orders. That is how you came to be Sales Manager. And that proves you know how your product can be sold.

But wait. When you take *all* the responsibility for thinking things out, the entire sales programme is going to be limited by your ability, as a single individual, to foresee everything. That is a lot to expect, even of a genius.

Nobody really knows all the answers. Times change. And there is more than one way to do the same job. A tried-and-proven method for Jim may not work for Henry at all.

And what about *motivation*?

When the ideas themselves are all yours, you have to charge others with the enthusiasm which goes with your creative planning. That will be hard if you are the sole powerhouse for all you hope to get done.

Suppose, however, you take a different approach to the conference situation. Suppose you discuss the falling sales figures with your staff, not as a matter of reproach, but as a mutual problem. Suppose, instead of 'bawling them out', you take them into your confidence. Very briefly:

'As you see, we haven't been doing as well as we had hoped to. What do *you* think is the trouble? And what are your ideas as to what *we* can do about it?'

This is the only approach you can take when membership of your group is purely voluntary, and it may also be used to advantage in other cases. The results of recent research suggest that you can get the most out of a discussion by regarding its members as human resources in dealing with a problem.

Every participant, after all, is a potential source of information and ideas. Even the least informed may possess some useful bit of special knowledge. Even the least acute may have some insight which has escaped the thinking of the others.

Moreover, by letting them participate, you give all members of the group a stake in the outcome. Since they have had a part in making whatever decisions are reached, they feel a more personal responsibility for the results. They are no longer just following orders like sheep. They are thinking for themselves. The project is theirs just as much as it is yours. Its defeat would also be their personal defeat, so they are more likely to do everything possible to ensure its success.

Thus, by facing the problem *with* the group, you can tap abilities and energies which you might otherwise have to contend with as opposition in trying to make your solo-thinking prevail.

This sort of approach to discussion is sometimes referred to as the *group dynamics* theory. Behind it is a metaphor—a figure of speech which pictures each participant as a bundle of human energies that can generate social forces in different directions.

What the domineering discussion leader attempts, according to this theory, is to counteract those forces which oppose him, and to reinforce those which have the same direction as his. Thus, he must be a *forceful* speaker in a more literal sense than usual. But what the *dynamic* leader does is to draw upon all the energies of the group, to determine in what direction they may be most effectively applied together.

Do not take this figure of speech too literally. The problems of how best to talk things over are much too subtle to be explained by a simple physical analogy. But bearing it in mind may help you to visualize an important truth.

Discussion can be a way of making many minds better than one by enabling them to think things over together.

In any event, regardless of the theory by which it is explained, many responsible organizations are giving the approach a serious trial today. Some of the largest companies in America are testing it in their administrative meetings and in their relations with the public.

The armed services are usually regarded as a rigid set up with a chain-of-command from top to bottom. As Tennyson wrote in his *Charge of the Light Brigade*:

> 'Theirs not to make reply,
> Theirs not to reason why,
> Theirs but to do or die.'

Yet today the Army, the Navy and the Air Force are training their officers in the use of such conference techniques, wherever they can be practically applied, to give a broader base to military decision.

(10) Requirements for Co-operative Discussion

Thinking together in any way, however, requires a reasonably like-minded group.

People who are over-enthusiastic about discussion techniques seem to think these are ways of ironing out really basic differences of view. That is an illusion.

As Sales Manager you may be able to confer to advantage with members of your sales staff. But you can hardly expect to get helpful advice from a competitor by inviting him to your sales conference.

At a crime-prevention meeting, you may confidently discuss ways to improve law enforcement with representatives of your Local Authority and the police. But you are foolish indeed if you think you can sit down and reach an acceptable deal on such matters with criminals.

When some people get to 'understand each other better' they find all the more reason to disagree. Techniques of mutual understanding only serve to drive them further apart.

This does not mean that the members of your discussion group must be entirely of one mind—for in that case conference would be pointless. But all who take part do need to have *common ends in view*.

They may differ, within reason, over what they think is wrong. Or they may differ, within reason, over how to go about setting things right. But they must all want to see the sales campaign succeed, they must all want to see the forces of law and order prevail, and so on.

No mere discussion technique can reconcile the irreconcilable. So first do your best to make sure you have a reasonable basis for sitting down at the conference table.

Beyond that, the important thing is to encourage the right *social attitudes*. An atmosphere of courteous consideration is absolutely necessary. A spirit of positive friendliness is ideal.

The general rule is to avoid any form of expression which would sound a sour note in ordinary conversation.

Some sharpness of tongue, tempered with ironical wit, may be effective in a lively debate against aggressive opponents. But if you are serious about co-operation, and if only those who should be are present, you should have no 'opponents' in this situation.

There is no magic merely in calling a discussion 'co-operative'. Even when there is a good basis for it in the more fundamental convictions of the participants, you may still need considerable tact to keep the exchange from becoming a verbal free-for-all.

Even when something is said with which you violently disagree, avoid saying so too emphatically. If the matter is one you feel it is imperative to straighten out, explain why you 'cannot agree' with it.

Do not rush in to refute. Instead, explain what 'troubles' you when you 'try to see the point' of such statements. For example, do not say:

'I wish you people would stop talking about holding our annual dance at the Ritzworth Ballroom. Anyone with any sense ought to realize we couldn't afford it!'

Rather, deliver your message like this:

'It certainly would be wonderful if we could hold our dance at the Ritzworth. But do we know exactly what it would cost? And have the members been asked if they would be willing to pay that much?'

The best way to appear open-minded is really to keep your mind open. It could be that *you* have overlooked a few important points.

Try thinking of your part in discussion as *an exercise in objectivity*. Take your ideas out for an airing. Set them out before the group. Then try to see them yourself as though they belonged to somebody else. It is surprising how they sometimes begin to take on a new look.

(11) Pointers on Agenda

Since informal group discussion has no set order of business, there is always the danger that it will wander aimlessly.

One speaker after another may digress on a point in the previous speaker's remarks. Before you know it, you are all far from the subject and getting rapidly nowhere.

After a number of such experiences, some people become cynical about group discussion. There is a story that after Lindbergh's first trans-Atlantic flight, a young woman gushed to a well-known wit: 'Don't you think it wonderful that he did that *all by himself*!' The terse reply was: 'Well frankly, Miss Blank, I'd be much more impressed if he had flown the Atlantic with the help of a committee.'

The first step in dealing with this general problem is to set up an **agenda**—a list of the items you hope to cover, in the order you'd like to have them covered. Then you will at least have landmarks by which to plot your progress and tell when you are getting off the course.

The Chairman can draw up the agenda in advance and announce it at the outset of the meeting. But this procedure fails to get everyone into the planning.

'We are perfectly free to speak our minds,' the others may think, 'just as long as we talk only about what you tell us to.'

A more tactful start is for you to announce only the subject at the outset, and then ask: 'How do you feel we could best go about talking this over?'

If someone suggests more or less what you had in mind, your task is then simple.

But if impractical suggestions are offered, you can ask appropriate questions to bring out better ones.

If the group obviously prefers to have you take the initiative, by all means be prepared to 'propose an agenda for their approval'.

There need be no formal voting or show of hands for this or for any other decision. Put the question by asking: 'How would that be?' or 'Is that agreeable?'

Any member of the group should feel free to suggest possible changes. When none does, that is taken to be tacit approval.

What items should such an agenda include?

A common mistake is to assume there is a universal basic pattern to follow. But the content of the agenda will depend upon the circumstances in each case. Items which would be of key importance in some cases, would be quite pointless in others.

Here are a number of possibilities from which to choose to suit your purposes on different occasions.

Clarification of the Question

A conference on ways to promote sales of Sudsy Soap is not likely to have any real problems of definition. Everybody present knows very well what Sudsy Soap is. They know equally well why they want the public to buy more of it.

Suppose, however, that your problem is how to persuade people to make more constructive use of their leisure. Just what is meant by 'more constructive'? Coming to an understanding about such terms sooner rather than later may avoid wasting a lot of time speaking at cross-purposes.

This does not imply you must get unanimous consent on a water-tight definition of so elusive an idea as that of 'constructiveness'.

It is silly to suppose there is a single 'correct answer' to such a question. And pretending so results in quibbling—needless bickering about the meaning of words—which can break up a discussion before it even gets properly started.

It will serve your purposes simply to know, by a few concrete examples, what each of you has in mind when he uses such terms. Then you will not mistakenly think you differ in opinion only because you are using different words for the same thing. And you will not mistakenly think you agree only because you are using the same word for different things.

Surveying the Facts of the Problem

You have doubtless come across discussions which have no point because the facts are the exact opposite of what they are assumed to be —rather like the family conference on how to marry off the eldest daughter, when in fact she had just eloped.

But even when there *is* a sound factual basis for discussion, it helps to have a clear picture of the details of what you are talking about.

For example, it is announced that sales of Sudsy Soap are 'not up to quota this year'. How you react to that statement, and what you can intelligently say about it, depends upon the answers to a number of factual questions.

Sales could actually be better than ever. They may not be 'up to quota' only because the sales target was unreasonably high. Or sales could indeed be falling off, but not nearly so much as in the rest of the industry and in other industries.

How large *is* the quota for this year? How does this quota compare with the quotas for the past ten years? How do all those quotas compare with sales during the past ten years. What have sales been for the entire industry over the same period of time? And what are the corresponding trends in other industries?

Since no really practical discussion can take place without such facts, you should bring them up as soon as possible. This not only promotes clear thinking, but it also helps to sound a good keynote for what is to follow.

Even a review of familiar facts helps to give ballast to a discussion. Your more fuzzy-minded members are then less likely to speak on a vague 'it-rather-seems-to-me' basis. And others are encouraged to offer the more solid sort of contributions of which they are capable.

Diagnosing Possible Causes, Suggesting Possible Solutions

If your idea for improving the sales of Sudsy Soap is to change the product itself, this implies a corresponding belief as to what is causing its sales to lag. In the back of your mind must be the conviction that the public does not like its packaging, its texture, its smell, its size, its shape or its lather.

If your idea is to lower the price, in the back of your mind must be the conviction that the public is buying a cheaper competitive brand.

These two related points—possible cause and possible solution—are hard to separate in discussion. Is there any need to do so artificially when they come together naturally as in the above examples?

Yet, in preparing for your own participation, and in keeping a score of how the discussion is actually getting along, there are several good reasons for noting these two kinds of points separately.

A single effect may have several causes. These causes may admit of different solutions. Not all causes may be equally easy to deal with. Different possible solutions may have different degrees of practicability. And all may be inter-related with each other in complicated ways.

It is therefore sometimes difficult to keep track of interweaving lines of discussion. They may run, for example, something like this:

Speaker A suggests that lowering the price of Sudsy Soap will attract so many more buyers that the increased turnover will easily offset the slightly reduced profit per tablet of soap.

Speaker B, from the Production Department, reveals that the price is already so low that it could only be cut further by changing the product.

Speakers C and *D* thereupon suggest changes in the product which might increase its appeal.

While these are being questioned, *Speaker E* mentions the tie-up between product and advertising.

But then *you* may be able to point out that there is also a link between advertising appeal and the previously dropped subject of price. For example:

'We are advertising this product in our ads as "More Suds for Your

Money". The appeal is an economy appeal. Yet people who are attracted by an economy appeal, shop around and find they can do better. Perhaps what we need to do is change the advertising angle: "Here is a soap of distinction. It may cost a little more. But it's worth a lot more to those who insist on the best." For people who respond to so-called "snob appeal" the present price may seem a bargain for a quality product.'

As chairman, or even as one of the other participants, you are more likely to be able to see the possibility of such remarks if you have made notes in the form of a diagram something like this:

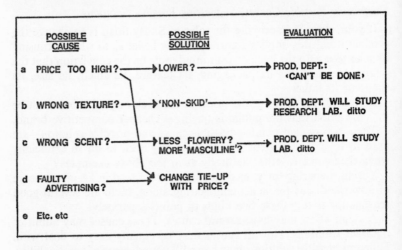

	POSSIBLE CAUSE	POSSIBLE SOLUTION	EVALUATION
a	PRICE TOO HIGH?	→ LOWER?	→ PROD. DEPT.: ‹CAN'T BE DONE›
b	WRONG TEXTURE?	→ 'NON–SKID'	→ PROD. DEPT. WILL STUDY RESEARCH LAB. ditto
c	WRONG SCENT?	→ LESS FLOWERY? MORE 'MASCULINE'?	→ PROD. DEPT. WILL STUDY LAB. ditto
d	FAULTY ADVERTISING?	→ CHANGE TIE-UP WITH PRICE?	
e	Etc. etc		

With your own abbreviations and other such short cuts, you can do this for quite a complicated discussion, on a small sheet of notepaper. It will give you a bird's eye view of what is being said when others find themselves getting lost.

Evaluation

It is one thing to suggest an idea in plausible general terms. It is quite another to examine it for what it is really worth. The latter is what is meant by *evaluation*.

Perhaps your group has been talking about the problem of juvenile delinquency just for the sake of exchanging ideas on the subject. They plan to take no immediate action on the outcome. Reliable statistics and the opinions of authorities in the field may then enable you to agree, for example, that more public playgrounds might help prevent juvenile delinquency.

But, in practical situations, you need to decide further how to go about *checking* what you think *may* be the answers to your problem.

A conference among the sales staff of Sudsy Soap is not likely to change the Company's marketing policy at once. But it may lead to a request that the Production Department estimate the costs of certain changes in the product. And it may lead to a market-research study of potential consumer reactions to such changes, or to different advertising appeals.

It is well to recognize, therefore, that evaluation is still another phase of group deliberation. Live discussion will also cut across this distinction at almost every stage. In the above example, for instance, the impossibility of price-cutting is pointed out as soon as the suggestion is made.

But to keep the several threads of discussion clearly in view, you should carefully note such points separately as on the above diagram.

Summarizing

Having thus kept track of major points that have been covered, a good discussion leader will be able to *sum up* from time to time.

The best opportunities for this are when the talk is about to shift from one phase of the agenda to another, or when there appears to be uncertainty as to just where it has arrived. This helps to clarify the sense of what has been said, in case it was not fully clear to all the group. It also helps those who have lost sight of the various trends of the discussion to get their bearings again.

But whether or not partial summaries are given earlier, a good complete summary is always needed at the very end. For then it serves, like the minutes of a formal business meeting, to confirm what has been agreed upon. For example:

'Well, gentlemen, we have faced the fact that sales of Sudsy Soap are down ten per cent this year. And we have recognized that our loss of sales compares with a two per cent increase in the rest of the industry and a five per cent average increase in other industries.

'We thought our trouble might be that our price was too high. But the Production Department tells us present costs will not allow a price cut.

'Mr. C reported customers as saying that our soap was too slippery, and suggested a "non-skid" texture.

'Mr. D reported customers as saying the scent was too "cloying", and proposed giving it a less flowery, more "masculine" scent.

'We are asking the Production Department to make a study of costs of both those changes. And we are asking the Consumer Research Department to try to find out how the general public would be likely to accept them.

'Lastly, Mr. E suggested that our price trouble might be due to its tie-up with an economy appeal in our advertising. That is another point we are putting to the Consumer Research Department. And I gather you want me to take it up also with the Advertising Department and the Executive Board.

'Am I correct in these understandings? If so, are there any important points to be added?'

Note that even in summing up, the discussion leader does not take his own understanding for granted. Neither does he ask for an actual vote on his version of the outcome. That would be artificially formal. But he does ask the group for additions or corrections. And lack of either can reasonably be taken as common consent.

Thus, the informal, co-operative spirit of the discussion is maintained to the very end.

CHAPTER SEVEN

DEVELOPING THE VOICE

The voice you now have depends upon many factors, including:

- the *physical make-up* of your voice mechanism, such as the size and shape of your mouth, nasal passages, etc.;
- your *general health*, and the consequent *physical tone* of your muscles;
- your *temperament* and *personality*—your outlook and the way you respond to the happenings of daily life;
- the *social influence* of family, friends, colleagues and others you speak with;
- the *vocal habits* you formed in early childhood and adolescence.

Developing your voice may involve doing something about any or all of these. Your physical make-up cannot usually be changed, but you can keep yourself physically fit, you can adopt a more positive attitude towards life, you can choose what social factors you will allow to influence you, and you can retrain your muscular habits.

In other words, you can improve and develop your present voice. Be confident of that.

Do not expect miracles, however. Do not expect to improve overnight. Above all, do not expect that mere wishing will bring improvement.

Many speakers before you have improved their voices. But it has taken time, patience, and the knowledge of how to go about it.

Voice development and speech training takes intelligent practice.

(1) Principles of Practice

Set aside regular practice periods each day, but choose times when you are not likely to be interrupted.

In addition, try to use spare moments to advantage. Certain simple voice exercises can be done while taking a bath, dressing, walking or driving.

Approach the practice periods willingly and with enthusiasm. No relaxed voice ever resulted from a feeling of constraint. No lively, vital one ever developed from a dull, formalized approach.

Practise one thing at a time. Split a big problem into parts and take up each separately. At the start, work on small, easy projects whose success will give you confidence and spur you on.

Make the transition from practice to performance gradually. Confine your new skills to your practice periods until you feel them well established. Then try them out in conversation at home, and after that with friends. Put off any public test till the last.

If you must deliver a talk during your early training, avoid trying to judge how you are doing while speaking. Concentrate on what you want to say. Save appraisal of your performance till afterwards.

(2) Ear Training

Begin by training your ear. Cultivate sensitivity to sounds and voices and their characteristics. It will prove an invaluable tool for guiding your progress.

Every sound we hear has four characteristics: *pitch, volume, quality*, and *duration* (or rate).

Pitch is the highness or lowness of a sound. On the musical scale, C is higher than B and lower than D.

Volume (or intensity) is the loudness of a sound. We speak of a *loud* clap of thunder, a *soft* whisper.

Quality (or timbre) is the identifying character of a sound. It is that characteristic by which we distinguish the sound of a violin from the sound of a trumpet, the vowel EE from the vowel OO, the voice of Jim from the voice of Joe.

Duration is the length of time a sound lasts. In voice-training, the term *rate* is used. Whether one's rate of talking is fast or slow depends on the duration of the individual sounds of which words are made up, the length of the phrases used and the duration of the pauses between phrases.

To train your ear, that is, to cultivate your sensitivity to these four characteristics of sounds and voices, you must *develop the habit of alert, varied and discriminating listening*.

Exercise No. 31

(*a*) In a bus or train, close your eyes and listen to the noises about you. Which are loudest? Which farthest away? Which is highest in pitch? Which lowest? Which do you find pleasant? Which unpleasant?

(*b*) Compare the use of the voice in different situations: football fans encouraging their team; a secretary reading the minutes; conversation at a reception.

(*c*) Notice how a good speaker varies his voice to fit his material: a preacher making announcements, reading from the Bible, delivering his sermon; an announcer reading the news, sports commentaries or introducing a symphony concert. Notice how actors use voice for characterization. Notice how voices change with mood, how they reflect personality.

(*d*) Collect a list of pronunciations which differ from yours. On the radio or television, note varying dialects or types of speech. Try to identify what makes the difference: the sounds, the speech melody, the quality of voice.

Exercise No. 32

(*a*) Listen to radio and television programmes of the same type as your favourites. Compare styles and techniques.

(*b*) Listen to programmes of a different type from your favourites. Attend meetings and discussions in your community. Note the various kinds of talking you hear.

Exercise No. 33

(*a*) Compare speakers you consider good with those you think poor. Try to account for your likes, dislikes.

Do you have difficulty hearing the speaker? Does he bellow? Does he adjust volume?

Is he too fast, too slow? Is his rate fast, but fitting? Is he slow, but impressively so?

Does the speaker sound whining, apologetic, vital; muffled, clear; vigorous, weak; harsh, colourless, pleasant?

Is the speaker's pitch high, too high; low, too low; monotonous, varied; stiff, flexible?

Does the speaker sound sincere, or is the voice used for its own sake? What impression of his personality do you get from his voice? Does the voice fit the occasion, the auditorium, the topic?

(*b*) Ask your friends what speakers they consider good, poor. Compare your list with theirs. Discuss your agreements and disagreements. Listen together to those speakers you disagree about. Try to understand your friends' reactions. Can you arrive at some generalizations about voice and its use?

Combine the above suggestions until you have fixed the habit of alert, varied and discriminating listening.

(3) Analysing Your Voice

When you think you have trained your ear to analyse the voices of others, begin analysing your own in the following ways.

Exercise No. 34

(*a*) Listen critically to your own voice: in conversation, reading aloud in a small and a large room. You will not hear it as others do, for this is physically impossible. But make mental notes as to your pitch, volume, quality, rate.

(*b*) Have a tape-recording of your voice made. Record both talking and reading aloud. Include such details as your name, the date, the place. Decide beforehand what topic you will discuss, jot down some of your ideas about it, but don't memorize. For reading, choose material with some dialogue.

You probably will not recognize your voice when you play back a recording of it. You will say, 'Is that me?' disbelievingly. But the recording will probably be fairly close to your voice as others hear you.

If you like what you hear, good. If not, do not be discouraged. Play the recording several times and, as objectively as possible, analyse your voice as you analysed the voices of others in your ear-training exercises above.

F

Write down your decisions about your rate, flexibility, pleasantness, vitality, expressiveness, intelligibility.

Ask your family and friends to give their opinions on your voice. (Do not expect them all to agree.) Compare their reactions with your own. Balancing the various judgements, you should get a good idea of what to aim at in practice.

When you have done this, study the following sections on *Basic Concepts*, *The Voice Mechanism* and *Good Phonation*, and practise all the exercises. Then skim through the remainder of the chapter, selecting for particular study those sections which, according to your voice analysis, will most repay careful practice.

Try to make recordings at regular intervals so that you can modify your original judgements and determine progress.

(4) Basic Concepts in Developing the Voice

Begin practice with the following exercises. They embody certain *basic concepts* for developing your voice and expression which you will use throughout all your later practice.

Free the Voice

You used your voice freely enough as a child. But with maturity your vocal habits may have become fixed, and you may no longer realize the extraordinary variety the voice is capable of.

Revive the sense of freedom in using your voice. Exercise your imagination. Experiment. Have fun with your voice.

EXERCISE No. 35

(*a*) Try imitating animals. Moo like a cow, crow like a cock, quack, caw, meow.

(*b*) Imitate musical sounds. Hear the sound inside you before you voice it.

Imitate a bell. Say *Ding-dong*, *Ding-dong*. (Concentrate on the *ng*; let the sound die out very slowly.)

Imitate a drum. Say *Boomlay*, *boomlay*, *boom*. (Try for a sharp, percussive effect with your lips.)

Imitate a bugle. Say *Blow*, *bugle*. *Blow*. *Ta*. . . *ta-ra* . . . *ta-ta*. (Try for a clear, free tone.)

(*c*) Get your arms, face, voice, your whole body into the exclamations below. Imagine a variety of situations; try to respond as you would in those situations.

Hurray!	*Hush!*
Come on, let's go!	*Hold on there!*
So!	*See! They're coming!*
So what?	*Ouch!*
I'm soaked!	*Isn't it hot!*
Stop thief!	*I'm so tired!*

(*d*) See in how many ways you can say these simple words. Be hearty, then perfunctory; show dislike, then conceal dislike; act surprised, then casual. Say one thing, but imply something else.

Good morning!	*Yes*
Hello!	*No*

Concentrate on Meaning

In reading aloud, always analyse your material beforehand for its meaning. Then try to communicate, to project, that meaning clearly. In talking, too, think what you say, and think hard. Your brain will help control your voice.

EXERCISE No. 36

In the selections below, concentrate on making the meaning crystal clear. Stress the basic thoughts, its development, the balance of ideas, the contrasts.

(i) Liberty and Union, now and for ever, one and inseparable.

(ii) 'Beauty is truth, truth beauty,'—that is all
Ye know on earth, and all ye need to know.

(iii) The evil that men do lives after them;
The good is oft interred with their bones.

(iv) Never in the field of human conflict was so much owed by so many to so few.

(v) Now faith is the substance of things hoped for, the evidence of things not seen.

(vi) To strive, to seek, to find, and not to yield.

(vii) I never could believe that Providence had sent a few men into the world, ready booted and spurred to ride, and millions ready saddled and bridled to be ridden.

(viii) That which hath been is that which shall be; and that which hath been done is that which shall be done; and there is no new thing under the sun.

(ix) If we spoke as we write we should find no one to listen; if we wrote as we speak we should find no one to read.

Let Emotion Help You

The aroused state of the body which accompanies (or is) emotion will help you to vocalize.

EXERCISE No. 37

Say the lines below, trying to feel the emotions asked for. As an aid, recall situations in which you have had similar feelings.

Feel the angry scorn of the tribune, Marullus, in the play *Julius Caesar*, as he seeks to curb the mob:
You blocks, you stones, you worse than senseless things!

Feel the loneliness of the Ancient Mariner as, gazing at the waste about him, he says:
Alone, alone, all, all alone,
Alone on a wide wide sea.

Feel the exuberant, physical joy of:
How good is man's life, the mere living!

Feel the terror of Hamlet, on first seeing the ghost of his murdered father:
Angels and ministers of grace defend us!

Feel the lover's affirmation of love eternal:
And I will love thee still, my dear,
Till a' the seas gang dry.

Just as a pianist practises scales, arpeggios and finger exercises as the essential mechanics of his playing, so practice in vocal mechanics will help to develop the strength and dexterity with which you control your voice.

The exercises below introduce types of voice routines used throughout this chapter:

Exercise No. 38

(a) Say a low-pitched *OO*. Glide smoothly up in pitch about an octave on the *OO*. Glide smoothly down.

(b) Prolong an *OO* on any pitch. Prolong *OO* on several other pitches. Do the same for *AH, OH, EE*.

(c) Prolong an *OO*, starting softly and gradually increasing the volume. Then let the sound die away. Similarly swell to loud and then die away to soft on *AH, OH, EE*.

(d) Say *MU, mu, mu, mu, mu*
　　　　　mu, MU, mu, mu, mu, etc.,
separating the syllables and shifting the accent to the third, fourth and fifth syllables. Repeat the exercise, joining the syllables as if you were saying a long word of five syllables: *MUmumumumu, muMUmumumu*, etc. Do it first fast and then slow.

(5) The Voice Mechanism

In further developing the voice, it will help to know a few simple facts about its mechanism.

All sound-making devices have at least two elements: a **vibrator** and a **motor.** The *vibrator* may be anything that vibrates readily—a taut rubber band for example. The *motor* may be any force that will set it in motion —the finger that plucks the rubber band, thus making it vibrate and produce a sound.

Most musical instruments have a third element: a **resonator,** which amplifies and enriches the original tone. In a violin the strings are the vibrator, the moving bow is the motor, and the body of the violin and its enclosed cavity form the resonator.

The voice also has **articulators,** which modify the amplified tone into the vowels and consonants of speech.

Thus, the voice mechanism has four parts:

The *vibrator* is the **vocal cords.** The production of sound by the vibration of the vocal cords is called **phonation.** (The root *phon-* is the same as that in the word 'gramophone', and comes from the Greek for *voice, sound.*)

The *motor* is the exhaled breath stream.

The *resonator* is chiefly the system of cavities above the vocal cords: the throat, the mouth and the nose.

The *articulators* are the lips, tongue, teeth, and the hard and soft palates. Articulation is discussed in Chapter Nine.

The Vocal Cords and Phonation

The vocal cords are situated in the larynx, or voice-box. (What we call the Adam's apple is the top-front edge of the larynx.) They are wedge-shaped folds of muscle, covered with mucous membrane. They project from the inner walls of the larynx, extending along the sides from front to rear.

During breathing, the cords are close together in front, apart in the rear. The triangular opening between them is called the **glottis.**

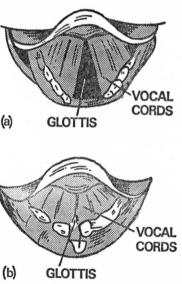

Fig. 1. The vocal cords seen from above: (*a*) during breathing; (*b*) during phonation

For phonation, that is, the production of voice, the cords are pivoted together, closing the glottis. The exhaled breath stream, building up pressure from below, forces the cords apart and causes them to vibrate.

The vocal cords are tensed or relaxed, lengthened or shortened, separated or closed, and moved upward or downward by the **intrinsic muscles** of the larynx: those pairs of muscles *within* the voice-box. The larynx itself is moved up and down and tilted by its **extrinsic muscles:** those which are attached to adjoining parts of the body, such as the jaw and the breast-bone. These movements are related to pitch, and phonation.

Phonation is essentially an automatic process. Start to speak, and immediately all the activities of phonation are co-ordinated to produce tone.

This does not imply that phonation may not be faulty. Developing good phonation, that is, the production of a good basic tone, is discussed below.

The Breath

Normally, we breathe in and out with no conscious effort. When the oxygen of the blood-stream is low and the carbon dioxide content high, the chest walls rise and expand, the dome-shaped diaphragm flattens downward. Air pours into the lungs to equalize the lowered pressure in the expanded chest cavity with that of the outside air. Air is pushed out as the diaphragm rises and the chest walls fall.

This automatic process will serve most of us for voice and speech as well as for sustaining life. Many of the breathing muscles, however, are voluntary, in other words we can control them. For some persons, conscious control of breathing is helpful.

Resonance

Resonance, the reinforcing and enriching of the original tone, is achieved in several ways. For example:

(i) The sound produced by the vocal cords is reflected from the walls of the throat, mouth and nose.

(ii) The air in the cavities of the mouth, throat and nose vibrates with, and thereby amplifies, the sound coming from the vocal cords.

(iii) Possibly the head and chest act as sounding-boards.

It will easily be appreciated that the ways in which the chief resonators (the mouth, throat and nose) are used will have an important effect on the voice. This is particularly so for developing volume and quality.

(6) Phonation—The Production of the Basic Tone

When the vocal cords vibrate freely and at maximum efficiency, producing a tone easily and without strain or unnecessary effort, you have good phonation.

Good tone begins smoothly, is clear and not 'breathy,' and can be sustained clearly and easily over a considerable period of time.

Essential conditions for good phonation are:

(i) Good posture, standing or sitting, so that the mechanism is not cramped.

(ii) A feeling of aliveness, of alert readiness from the toes up, so that the whole body 'supports' the tone.

(iii) Concentration on what you are saying, so that the mechanism is properly directed.

(iv) Absence of strain or constriction in the throat and neck (the extrinsic muscles of the larynx) so that the vocal cords may vibrate freely and the larynx move easily.

EXERCISE No. 39

Stand erect, with the feet comfortably apart. Hold the chest high. Don't stiffen the shoulders or over-arch the back. Be sure you are comfortably balanced. Say a long, sustained *AH*.

If your posture feels too stiff, bend forward from the hips, and let the arms and head hang limp. Then slowly uncurl, straightening first the small of the back, the upper back, the neck, before vocalizing. Don't adjust the shoulders at any time.

If you tend to slouch, lift your arms high above your head. Stretch upward, rising on your toes. Feel the tingling in your fingers, your whole body. Then sink back to normal posture and vocalize on *AH, OO, EE*.

EXERCISE No. 40

Letting breath escape with the voice (half-voice, half-whisper), say: *I am now talking with a very breathy voice.*

Straining hard, say: *I am now talking with a tight, hard, straining voice.*

With as easy and relaxed a tone as you can, say: *I am now trying to talk with as easy and relaxed a voice as I possibly can.*

Listen to the difference between the three versions. Feel the difference in your muscles as you say the sentences.

EXERCISE No. 41

(*a*) Yawn widely, with an open throat. To start a yawn, close the lips and drop the jaw. Softly and lazily, say a prolonged *AH, OH, OO*.

(*b*) Breathe in easily, feeling that you have an open throat. Softly, easily, and in a deep voice, say *one*, holding the tone for a silent count of three. Breathe in, count aloud *one, two*, holding each word for three silent counts. Similarly, count aloud to *three, four*. Very slowly and in a deep voice, say: *who are you; how now; a yellow, mellow moon.*

(*c*) Say *AH, AH, AH*, lightly and quickly, several times over. Try for a clear, sharp tone.

Prolong an *OO* for as long as you can without strain. Keep the tone clear and strong.

(*d*) Before and while phonating, imagine you are drinking very slowly from a glass of water. Concentrate on feeling the water slip down your throat as you vocalize on *OO, AW, AH*. Though this may seem contradictory, it helps counteract a tendency to force the voice.

EXERCISE NO. 42

Read the opening of Gray's *Elegy* in a clear, soft tone:

> The curfew tolls the knell of parting day,
> The lowing herd winds slowly o'er the lea,
> The ploughman homeward plods his weary way,
> And leaves the world to darkness and to me.

Achieving Relaxation

Tonicity is that state of the muscles in which they are ready to act. They are neither too tense nor too relaxed.

If, while doing the preceding exercises, you found your neck muscles too tense, or if you are too tense generally while talking, the following exercises will help you to relax.

EXERCISE NO. 43

(*a*) Stand at exaggerated 'Attention!', your legs, arms, fingers tense. Hold this stiff posture a moment. Then relax, sag, droop. Feel the difference in the muscles. Repeat, to make yourself more conscious of the difference. Learn to recognize this difference in other situations and while speaking.

(*b*) Stand at exaggerated 'Attention!' for a few moments. Then sink into an easy chair. Lean back, let your arms and head lie limp, close the eyes, think of dozing off. When you feel relaxed, try to recall the earlier feeling of tension. Compare the two muscle sensations. Try to carry the relaxed feeling into voice exercises.

EXERCISE NO. 44

(*a*) Stand erect and tense. Then bend forward at the waist, letting arms and head hang down. Jiggle the fingers, the hands, the arms, the head. Swing them slowly back and forth. Feel the limpness.

(*b*) In front of a mirror, grit the teeth, tense the neck muscles. See the cords tighten, the neck swell. Let the jaw drop, the neck muscles relax. *See* the relaxation.

Put your fingers lightly on your neck. Repeat the above exercise. *Feel* the tension, then the relaxation with your fingers.

(*c*) Let the head fall forward, the jaw sagging open and touching the chest. Slowly roll the head around, avoiding any stiffness or jerkiness of movement. Vocalize on *AH* while letting the head roll around.

Toning Sluggish Lax Muscles

Debilitating illness or a depressed state of mind will produce sluggish, lax muscles. If your muscles lack proper tonicity for good phonation, if your body slouches or droops, if your voice sounds dull and lifeless, the following exercises will prove helpful.

EXERCISE NO. 45

(*a*) Carry out physical actions which are accompanied by vocal effects:
Pull on a rope in a tug-of-war. Strain, grunt.

Be your own cricket team. Bowl a fast ball. Hit a six. Fling your arm wide. Call 'Owzat'.

Call the cows home. Cup your hands to your mouth. Call 'Come up, come up!'

Feed the chickens. Walk about scattering corn, calling, 'Here, chick, chick, chick, chick!'

Devise similar exercises of your own.

(*b*) Act out a situation where speech is accompanied by vigorous physical action:

Invite an audience to rise and sing the national anthem. Swing the arms wide.

Say, 'No, no, no!' pounding a desk.

Say, 'From Heaven above, to Hell beneath,' swinging your arm high, low.

Act out: 'So he came at me, and I punched him on the nose.'

Be an emotional Prosecuting Counsel. Wag your finger at the jury, with 'Now, gentlemen.' Point to the learned judge with one hand, 'As His Honour has told you,' and the cowering defendant with the other, 'Can you believe what this man has told you?'

EXERCISE No. 46

(*a*) Practise exclamations and sharp commands: *OH! SHHH!* Halt! Forward march!

(*b*) Let your imagination and feeling help you to achieve tonicity. Imagine yourself to be:

Macbeth, with shuddering suddenness, catching sight of his blood-stained hands: 'This is a sorry sight.'

Henry V, exhorting his army to battle: 'God for Harry, England, and St. George!'

(*c*) Practise the exercises for achieving relaxation (in the preceding section) in reverse, trying to achieve the feeling of muscle tension.

Faulty Phonation

Faulty phonation produces, or is partly responsible for, several unpleasant vocal effects: *breathiness* and *glottal shock; huskiness* and *hoarseness; pinched* or *strident tone*.

Breathiness occurs when unvocalized breath is allowed to escape along with the voice. The glottis, the space between the vocal cords, does not close completely during sound production. Slight breathiness is not objectionable, but the voice lacks strength and may tire quickly. The following exercises are designed to correct breathiness.

EXERCISE No. 47

(*a*) Prolong a whispered *AH*. Gradually add phonation, making the tone less and less breathy, more and more clear. Repeat until you achieve a completely clear, non-breathy tone.

(*b*) Start to say *AH, OO, EE* with a sharp, staccato click. Break off the tone immediately. Start the vowels with a sharp, but somewhat slighter click. Sustain the tone, keeping it clear. Start the vowels with a sharp, clean-cut attack. Make sure there is neither breathiness nor glottal shock (see below). Sustain the clear tone.

EXERCISE No. 48

Read the following paired words. Blow out hard on the *h* of the first words of the pairs, and allow the breathiness to carry over into the vowel; start the second word of the pairs with a sharp click:

hall	all	hill	ill	hive	I've
hone	own	hale	ale	whose	ooze
harm	arm	hand	and	hurl	Earl
heave	eve	hem	em	howl	owl

Read the pairs again. But this time say the *h* of the first words very lightly, without much breath, and try to begin phonation as quickly as possible. Begin the second words of the pairs without breathiness or click. This, of course, is the way the words should be said.

EXERCISE No. 49

Read this paragraph very loudly, and without breathiness. Read it again, and again, each time less loudly, until you are reading it very, very softly and without breathiness.

Glottal shock is the use of a sharp, staccato click to begin a sound. It usually occurs on words beginning with a vowel, such as *and, open*. In glottal shock the closure of the vocal cords is too tense, and the cords are blasted or coughed apart by breath pressure. The following exercises should help to correct glottal shock.

EXERCISE No. 50

(*a*) While whispering a prolonged *AH*, begin phonation with the softest tone you can. Do not sustain this tone, but repeat the exercise several times, each time trying to make the beginning of the tone easier, gentler, softer.

(*b*) Sustain a whispered *AH* and, as above, begin to phonate with the softest tone you can. Gradually let it swell out until the tone is firm and strong.

(*c*) Begin a tone so softly you can barely hear it yourself. If you are satisfied that you began without a click, gradually increase the volume.

EXERCISE No. 51

Glottal shock is often associated with the too-frequent breaking off of tone. Say these phrases as if each was one word:

(*a*) onanoldocean   (*d*) onaneveninginApril
(*b*) airisallIown   (*e*) nowIamalone
(*c*) nomanisanisland   (*f*) everyoneIknow
            (*g*) everywhereyougo

Practise linking words together in this way in your talking and reading aloud. Also, it will help if you whisper words beginning with vowels. Let the breath glide easily from word to word. When this has been achieved, say the words aloud. Try these sentences:

Aunt Emily always eats eggs and apples.
Uncle Arthur's apartment is in Eastern Avenue, Epping.

Huskiness is excessive breathiness of tone. It may result from abuse of the voice, such as shouting or talking for a long time with a strained throat; swelling of the vocal cords during a cold or chronic laryngitis; growths on the vocal cords; or from certain other diseased conditions. If you suffer from persistent huskiness you should seek medical advice.

Hoarseness resembles huskiness except that the tone is harsh, with added raspy noises from the throat. Like huskiness, it may result from abuse or misuse of the voice, or from disease.

Assuming that no medical treatment is required for huskiness or hoarseness, or *after* medical or surgical care, the next steps are careful practice of relaxation and controlled breathing exercises, easy phonation on soft tones, and the gradual development of volume. Shouting, throat-strain and over-use of the voice must be avoided, and a period of rest for the voice is often suggested.

Huskiness may be due to an improper, usually a too-high *pitch level*, discussed later in this chapter.

Pinched (or *strident*) **tone** results when a person talks as if trying to be heard over noise. He seems to talk only from the throat, as if the breath and the body had no part in speech. The larynx is held so tightly that it up-tilts to an abnormal position. The term *strident* is used when the tone is excessively loud and strained, with the throat walls excessively constricted.

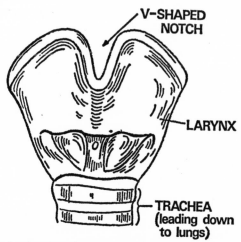

Fig. 2. Diagram showing the larynx from the front. The V-shaped notch at the top may be felt by lightly touching the Adam's apple with the finger-tips.

The following exercises are designed to correct pinched or strident tone.

EXERCISE No. 52

During normal breathing, feel the V-shaped notch at the top of your Adam's apple. Phonate on a moderately low pitch. You should be able to feel this V-notch. If you cannot, if the larynx has up-tilted so that you can feel only its front edge, you must bring the larynx back to its normal position for phonation. With the neck muscles relaxed, feel the notch with your index finger. Phonate on *AH* as softly as possible and with such little effort that you can still feel the V-notch. Your tone should be much less pinched. Repeat on other vowels.

EXERCISE No. 53

(*a*) Yawn audibly, enjoying your yawn. After the last sound has died away, take an easy breath and begin to phonate on *AH* with the same relaxation.

(*b*) Sigh deeply. Trying to keep the relaxed throat feeling that followed the sigh, phonate on *OH, OO, AH*.

(*c*) Massage the neck muscles during vocalization. Try to get them feeling relaxed.

(*d*) Chant *AH, OW, OY*, on very low notes. Drop the jaw well down. Feel that you are using a wide, open throat.

(*e*) Practise the routines for developing oral and pharyngeal resonance given later in this chapter.

EXERCISE No. 54

If you are a chairman, instead of banging the gavel and shouting to get order, rap once, wait for order and then talk quietly.

If you must talk in a noisy room, instead of trying to talk *over* and *louder* than the noise, listen for the approximate pitch of the noise, and talk quietly while trying to pitch your voice *under* the noise.

(7) Controlled Breathing

Learning to control the usually automatic process of breathing helps to develop a feeling of 'support' for the voice. It also helps to reduce strain and tension in the neck and throat during phonation. By concentrating on the chest and diaphragm, one tends to forget the region of the vocal cords and so to relax the neck muscles.

Many methods to control breathing have been taught. Probably there is only one *bad* method: raising the shoulder blades for inhalation, and dropping them for exhalation.

Possible Methods of Breath Control

Upper-chest breathing. The breast-bone is raised during inhalation, lowered for exhalation. This method of breathing is usually associated with moments of action (e.g. panting after running) and is not recommended as a method of breathing for voice.

Middle-chest breathing. The lower ribs are moved out and up for inhalation, in and down for exhalation. The abdomen moves only slightly.

Lower-chest and abdominal breathing. The lower ribs are moved out and the abdominal wall is relaxed for inhalation. For exhalation, the abdominal wall is pulled in sharply to help the diaphragm in its rise, and the lower ribs are drawn in (see Fig. 3).

To learn this method: lie down, placing the right hand on the abdomen, the left on the left lower ribs. Inhale, forcing the right hand up, the left to the side. Exhale, pulling in and down.

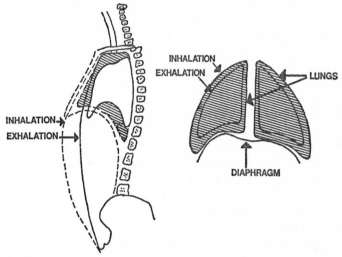

Fig. 3. Diagrams showing the chest, lungs, diaphragm and abdominal wall in inhalation and exhalation. For controlled breathing, concentrate on moving the upper chest, the lower chest, or the lower chest and abdominal wall

Stand up, hold a book against the abdomen with the hands. Breathe as you did while lying down.

Try these various methods of breath control to decide which you prefer, but remember, do not raise the shoulders when breathing in. There must be no tension of any kind around the top of the body, and the breathing must appear to be as effortless as possible.

The following exercises are designed to co-ordinate controlled breathing and phonation.

EXERCISE No. 55

(*a*) Breathe in to the silent count of *one*, out to the silent count of *one-two*. Breathe in to the silent count of *one*. Breathe out to the silent count of *one-two-three*. Increase the count until you are breathing out to the silent count of *ten*.

(*b*) Breathe in to the silent count of *one*. Say *AH*, while silently counting *two*. Breathe in, silently counting *one*. Say *AH*, while silently counting *three*. Continue till you are prolonging *AH* for a count of *ten*. Keep the tone steady.

(*c*) Count aloud in march time: 1, 2, 3, –; 1, 2, 3, –; 1, 2, 3, –; keeping silent for the fourth beat. Do the three groups on one breath.

(*d*) Count loudly in march time, 1, 2, 3, 4; 1, 2, 3, 4; 1, 2, 3, 4; taking a short catch-breath after each count of 4.

EXERCISE No. 56

(*a*) Say the following sentence slowly, taking a small breath at each (|):
Now is the time | for all good men | to come to the aid of the party.
Say the sentence more quickly on one breath with a slight pause at each (|).

(*b*) Breathe in. Letting the breath flow out very smoothly, say the following, taking one breath to each group:

Now fades the glimmering landscape | on the sight, |
And all the air | a solemn stillness holds, |
Save where the beetle | wheels his droning flight, |
And drowsy tinklings | lull the distant folds.

(*c*) Breathe in. Let the air out sharply on:

'Forward, | the Light Brigade! |
Charge | for the guns' | he said.

(*d*) Deciding how you will control your exhaled breath, say:

Speech is silver, silence is golden.

The Owl and the Pussy-cat went to sea
In a beautiful pea-green boat.

God who made thee mighty, make thee mightier yet!

The earth is the Lord's, and the fullness thereof.

Ready! Steady! Go!

(*e*) Take a breath at each (|) as you read through the following passage, gradually extending the out-going breath:

'Ladies and gentlemen, | I'm going to speak to you tonight | on a very serious matter that concerns us all. | For many years our business has been decreasing. | Unless we act now, we are finished . . .' |

(8) Pitch

Changes in pitch are produced by changes in the tension, length and thickness of the vocal cords.

Male voices are lower in pitch than women's because men's vocal cords are somewhat longer.

The vocal cords of the average person allow a pitch range of almost two octaves.

Since the muscular adjustments for changes in pitch take place automatically, training in pitch is accomplished by thinking, by feeling, and by training the ear.

Pitch-training involves:

(*a*) The selection of the best pitch level for the voice, and

(*b*) The fuller use of the pitch range through the development of varied pitch levels, intonation and inflexion.

Each of us has a *habitual pitch level:* the pitch he uses most frequently in conversation, and around which the other pitches he uses cluster.

If this habitual pitch level is too high or too low, variety and flexibility are impaired, the voice sounds strained or affected, or does not seem to fit the personality. The voice mechanism itself may be so harmed that huskiness results.

To Find Your Habitual Pitch Level

Method (*a*). With a pitch pipe or piano at hand, read a passage of unemotional prose in a conversational tone. Listen for the pitches you think you use most often, and find them in the musical scale.

Try to determine your average pitch from the pitches you use most often, and read the passage several times again to confirm your judgement. The average pitch you finally decide on is probably your habitual pitch level.

Method (*b*). If you find the above procedure difficult, ask a friend to sit at the piano and pick out the various possible pitches lightly as you read. Together, work out your habitual pitch level.

The *optimum* pitch level is the pitch at which your voice sounds clearest and fullest or strongest.

To Find Your Optimum Pitch Level

Method (*a*). At the piano, determine your pitch range. Hum up as high as you can without strain; hum down as low as you can. Note the limits and determine the mid-point of your range.

Method (*b*). If you can sing a scale with ease, hum down to your lowest pitch. Taking this as *one* count up the scale, a number to each tone. Either *three, four* or *five* should be your best pitch. Say a simple sentence, such as, 'This is the house that Jack built,' on each of these pitches, and decide where your voice is fullest and clearest.

Method (*c*). Stopping up your ears with your fingers, hum up and down the scale. Your best pitch level is approximately the pitch at which your voice rings strongest in your head.

Once you have determined your optimum pitch level, compare it with what you judged to be your habitual pitch level. If they differ, try in as many ways as possible to shift to the optimum pitch level and make it a part of you.

Exercise No. 57

(*a*) Hum your best pitch level to yourself. At various times of the day, check at a piano to make sure you are keeping to the pitch.

(*b*) Read short sentences in a monotone on this pitch.

(*c*) Read prose paragraphs out loud in a conversational tone, using your optimum pitch level as a base.

(*d*) Finally, try to use the optimum pitch level in conversation.

Varied Pitch Levels

The use of varied pitch levels in emotional material will help develop variety in your use of voice.

While your best pitch level is the one used for conversation and general reading, a somewhat higher pitch level would be more suitable for excited emotional states, a lower pitch level for depressed or serious states.

EXERCISE NO. 58

(*a*) Use a fairly high pitch level for:

On with the dance! Let joy be unconfined!

The sea! The sea! The open sea!
The blue, the fresh, the ever free!
Sail on, and on, and on!

Hey diddle, diddle, the cat and the fiddle.

My heart leaps up when I behold
A rainbow in the sky.

(*b*) Use a fairly low pitch level for:

Now he belongs to the ages.

The day is cold, and dark, and dreary.

With malice towards none; with charity for all.

The sea is calm tonight,
The tide is full, the moon lies fair
Upon the straits.

Without a grave, unknelled, uncoffined, and unknown.

The church bell solemnly tolled the hour of midnight.

(*c*) Read the selections in (*a*) above with low pitch levels, in (*b*) with high. What happens to the meaning of the selections?

EXERCISE NO. 59

As you read these selections, notice how your pitch levels change to fit the meaning:

Exult, O shores, and ring O bells!
But I, with mournful tread,
Walk the deck my Captain lies,
Fallen cold and dead.

'A merry Christmas, uncle! God save you!' cried a cheerful voice . . .
'Bah!' said Scrooge. 'Humbug!'

There was a sound of revelry by night . . .
And all went merry as a marriage bell;
But hush! hark! a deep sound strikes like a rising knell!

Intonation

Intonation is the melody pattern of the voice in speech. It resembles the melody of song, except that in singing we usually leap from one tone to the next, whereas in speech we glide up or down towards the next tone (see *Inflexions*, below).

The most important words, those that carry the meaning, are usually lifted well above the pitch level, less important words not quite so high. For example:

```
                    MONEY.
He gave me the
HE
        gave me the money.
            ME
        gave
He              the money
```

The faults of intonation are usually (*a*) talking almost in a monotone with few and relatively small changes in pitch, and (*b*) using stereotyped intonation patterns.

Example of stereotyped intonation:

```
off-        col-        use     fine    lec-
    ered        lege    of              tion
He      the     the     his     col-    of prints.
```

The following exercises are designed to help develop variety of intonation:

EXERCISE NO. 60

(*a*) Change the meaning of the first sentence used above by lifting still other words well above the pitch level:

He GAVE me the money.
He gave me THE money.
HE gave me the *money*.
He *gave* me the MONEY.

(*b*) Try saying the following sentences with different meanings, first lifting one word well above the pitch level, then another:

This is the spot.
Who did you say it was?
I'm very sorry about the whole matter.

EXERCISE No. 61

Analyse the following sentences for meaning. Decide which words should be emphasized. Say these words louder and longer than the rest, but try especially to lift them above the pitch level:

(a) I come to bury Caesar not to praise him.

(b) Cowards die many times before their death,
   The valiant never taste of death but once.

(c) Our birth is but a sleep and a forgetting.

(d) He who knows, and knows he knows,
   He is wise—follow him.
   He who knows, and knows not he knows,
   He is asleep—wake him.
   He who knows not, and knows not he knows not,
   He is a fool—shun him.
   He who knows not, and knows he knows not,
   He is a child—teach him.

(see key to this exercise in the answer section on page 250)

EXERCISE No. 62

Use pitch (and quality and rate) changes on the adjectives below to characterize the rats:

Great rats, small rats, lean rats, brawny rats,
Brown rats, black rats, grey rats, tawny rats,
Grave old plodders, gay young friskers.

EXERCISE No. 63

Read the selections in the exercises above (i) in a monotone, (ii) with only slight pitch changes, (iii) with moderate pitch changes, (iv) with as wide pitch changes as you can achieve. Check the last readings at the piano to see if you are using a good portion of your range. Do not feel that you must avail yourself of the whole range in every selection, for this would sound artificial.

Inflexions

Inflexions are the glides in pitch on single words. We are chiefly interested in the inflexions on words that end sentences and phrases.

A *rising inflexion* (/) generally indicates that the thought is incomplete and so connects one idea to the next. It is used in questions which do not begin with question-words. It also implies doubt and uncertainty. For example:

We bought apples, / peaches, / bananas, / . . . (incompleteness)
Are you going? / (question without question-word)
Perhaps / (doubt)

A *falling inflexion* (\) indicates that the thought is complete, and so it serves to disconnect ideas. It is used in questions which begin with question-words. It also implies certainty and finality. For example:

We bought the apples. \ (completeness)
Where are you going? \ (question with question-word)
Yes! \ (certainty)

A *falling-rising inflexion* (Ⅴ) is used at the end of a phrase when the sense is not grammatically complete. For example:

As I was saying, Ⅴ
One day, Ⅴ as he was driving by, Ⅴ

Circumflex inflexions (⎞ and ⎛) are associated both with spontaneous emotional reactions (surprise, delight) and with calculated implications and double-meaning (suspicion, irony). They may range from the heaviest sarcasm to the subtlest nuances of feeling. For example:

You say you arrived home at 12 ⎛ o'clock? (implying 'I don't believe it.')
He's a splendid ⎞ chap. (Far from it.)

Faults associated with inflexions are (*a*) a lack of inflexion or (*b*) overuse of one type. Too many falling inflexions make for dullness. Too many rising inflexions give an impression of light-headedness.

The following exercises are designed to help develop variety of inflexion:

Exercise No. 64

(*a*) Say *AH* on a low pitch. Glide swiftly up about a half-octave. Glide down. Glide up about an octave. Glide down.

(*b*) Clearly distinguish between rising and falling inflexions in the following:

A, / B, / C, / D. \
Are you going? / No! \
I've information vegetable, / animal, / and mineral. \
Bold, / cautious, / true, / and my loving comrade. \

(*c*) Speak as if to a very large audience, slowly, with short phrases, and with long inflexions:

A friend of the poor, / of the aged, / of the ill, / of all who are in need. \
He speaks to us as a businessman, / as a citizen, / and as a parent. \

(*d*) Say with falling-rising inflections:

That Ⅴ I need hardly tell you, Ⅴ
Once before, Ⅴ when he came here, Ⅴ
Never, Ⅴ to my knowledge, Ⅴ

Exercise No. 65

(*a*) Say the following words with falling, rising and circumflex inflexions. What do the several inflexions imply?

Go	Where	See
Please	When	Stop
Oh	I am	Never

(*b*) Imagine a variety of situations, of emotions, in which the above words might be used. Say them, then analyse to see what types of inflexions you used.

(9) Volume

Volume, the loudness of the voice, is dependent on the strength of the original tone and the degree of reinforcement of that tone by resonance.

A voice has good volume (*a*) when it can be heard, (*b*) when it is adjusted readily to varying physical conditions, such as the size of a hall—a voice can be too loud, (*c*) when changes in volume are used effectively for emphasis, and (*d*) when the voice, whatever its loudness or softness, is produced efficiently and without strain.

Training in volume involves training the ear to become sensitive to changes in loudness, the development of better habits of phonation, and the better use of the resonators: the mouth, throat and nose. Therefore, look again at the material and exercises on ear-training and phonation, and study this section in conjunction with that on *Quality* (below).

To Strengthen a Weak Voice

Your vocal equipment is probably adequate to produce the degree of volume needed in almost any situation. If your voice sounds weak to your friends, the fault may be due to a variety of causes, psychological or physical. Try all the types of exercises below to see which of them best helps to strengthen your voice.

Exercise No. 66

You may be talking absent-mindedly, i.e. with little attention to your listeners. Remember that speech is communication *to* an *audience*, and try to develop a lively sense of communication.

In conversation, look directly at the person you are talking to.

In talking to a group, let your eyes move from person to person.

In reading aloud to your family, try to *share* the information, the experience, with them.

When next you talk to an audience, let your eyes swing from section to section, side to side, forward and back.

Exercise No. 67

You may lack a sense of, or may have forgotten, the varying degrees of energy with which you can produce tone.

Imagine you are conducting a meeting. Say, 'The meeting will please come to order,' to an audience of (*a*) 10, (*b*) 100, (*c*) 1,000.

Say, 'Go all the way down' to a person (*a*) 10 feet away, (*b*) 50 feet away, (*c*) 100 feet away. Avoid straining the throat, or raising the pitch.

EXERCISE NO. 68

You may have fallen into the habit of talking only to the person nearest to you.

In an auditorium, talk (*a*) to the person half-way back, (*b*) to the person in the last row. Try to make your voice bounce off the back wall.

EXERCISE NO. 69

You may not be using the resonators sufficiently.

In talking, open the mouth more. Use wide-swinging action for the vowels. Focus the tone forward. Round the lips well on *oh, oo, oh, aw*. Make strong, firm *m, n, ng* and *l* sounds.

EXERCISE NO. 70

You may be talking too fast, clipping off sounds or letting them die away. Prolong vowels with good support from the body and the breath.

Say *all, nine, awning, maim, calm, mean, tedium*, prolonging both the vowels and the consonants.

Read a paragraph aloud slowly, concentrating on holding your tone strongly to the ends of the sentences.

EXERCISE NO. 71

Call out with an open throat:

Apples, peaches, ripe bananas!

Roll up! Roll up!

Ship ahoy! Ship ahoy!

Awake! Awake!

Ring the alarm bell! Murder and treason!

EXERCISE NO. 72

(*a*) Say, with varying volume:

Squad, HALT!
Squad, by the right, quick MARCH!
ONE, two, three, four. ONE, two, three, four.

(*b*) Just as in pitch training you changed meaning by lifting words above the pitch level, now emphasize by saying single words much louder than the rest.

HE said she wanted you to go.
He said SHE wanted you to go.
He said she wanted YOU to go.
He said she wanted you to GO.

(*c*) In this selection from Mark Twain, vary the volume to fit the description and the characters:

When (the mate) gave even the simplest order, he discharged it like a blast of lightning, and sent a long, reverberating peal of profanity thundering after it . . . If a landsman should wish the gangplank moved a foot farther forward, he would probably say: 'James, or William, one of you push that plank forward, please'; but put the mate in his place, and he would roar out: 'Here now, start that gangplank for'ard. Lively, now! *What*'re you about! Snatch it! *snatch* it! There! there! Aft again! aft again! Don't you hear me? Dash it to dash! are you going to *sleep* over it? . . . WHERE're you going with that barrel! *for'ard* with it, 'fore I make you swallow it, you dash-dash-dash-*dashed* split between a tired mud-turtle and a crippled hearse-horse!'

Exercise No. 73

Talk or read in a medium-sized room. As you say the first few words, listen for your voice to be reflected back from the walls. Experiment with larger and smaller degrees of volume to hear the effect of each.

Do the same in a small room, a large room, in an empty auditorium. When next you talk to a large group, let the sound of your first few words tell you how loudly you must talk.

(10) Quality

There are many pleasing qualities of voice. We enjoy brilliant sopranos, mellow contraltos, heroic tenors, basso profundos. We use such different words as velvety, flute-like, vibrant, pure, to describe qualities we like.

Quality will be improved if we focus the tone, so that the resonators—the mouth, throat and nose—may operate freely together as a well-balanced unit. It will also be improved if we develop the individual resonances of the mouth, nose and throat.

To Focus the Tone

The tone will be well focused if the throat is open and the voice is 'placed' forward in the mouth.

Exercise No. 74

(a) Hold a pencil about 18 inches in front of the mouth. Focusing on the pencil point, prolong *AH, OO, EE*. Try to feel that lines drawn from the lips would all converge on the pencil point.

(b) With the tip of the tongue behind the lower teeth, inhale lightly, feeling as if you were going to yawn. Prolong the *AH*, rolling the head around and feeling the openness of the throat. Repeat for *OO, EE*.

(c) With tongue-tip behind the lower teeth, say *we* half a dozen times, focusing the tone well forward in the mouth. Similarly, say *be, pea, me*. Move from *we* to *wah*, from *be* to *bah*, etc., still thinking of sending the tone against the gums.

Say *tea, dee, lee*. Move the tongue-tip quickly forward from the *t* and *d*-positions on the upper gum to the rest-position behind the lower teeth. Let the movement help you to 'place' the tone forward in the mouth.

(d) With open throat and a forward-focused tone, say:

Over the hills and far away.

Where are the snows of yesteryear?

Little Tommy Tucker, sing for your supper.

Build thee more stately mansions, O my soul.

To Develop Nasal Resonance

By nasal resonance is meant the reinforcement of the original tone in the nose cavity.

EXERCISE No. 75

(a) Hum a strong *mmm*. Feel the vibration in your lips, on the bridge of your nose, at the base of your cheek bones. Prolong *n* and *ng* with ringing quality.

(b) Chant with strong nasal consonants: *meem, maim, mime, mohm; neen, nain, nine, nohn*. Try to 'tie' the vowels onto the nasal resonance, keeping the tone as vibrant for the vowels as for the *m* and *n*.

(c) Say with ringing nasal resonance:

Mumbo Jumbo, god of the Congo.

Five miles meandering with a mazy motion.

The moon never beams without bringing me dreams.

The moanings of the homeless sea.

To the noise of the mourning of a mighty nation.

O Wind, if winter comes can spring be far behind?

O wind, a-blowing all day long,

O wind, that sings so loud a song.

Faulty Nasal Resonance

Nasality is a dull, smothered quality. It occurs when a lazy soft palate drops during the production of vowels so that too much sound is allowed to reverberate in the nose.

A test for the presence of nasality is to say a sentence without any nasal consonants, such as 'This is the house that Jack built', first in the ordinary way and then holding the nose tight shut. There should be no appreciable difference in the sound of the two sentences. If there is a difference, nasality is present.

To correct nasality: try to develop an active soft palate, one which drops low for the nasal consonants, and is held high against the back wall of the throat for the vowels and the other voiced consonants. Focus the sound forward, round the lips well, move the jaw actively (see Chapter Nine).

EXERCISE No. 76

Holding a mirror in front of your wide-open mouth, say: ung-ah-ung-ah-ung-ah. Let the soft palate drop down for the *ung*. Lift it up high for the *ah*. Keep the jaw stiff throughout the exercise.

Nasal twang is a hard, metallic, whining quality, as much due to tight pharyngeal resonance as to too much nasal resonance. It occurs when, with the jaw tight, the mouth opening very small, and the throat tense, the voice is forced through the nose.

To help correct nasal twang: in all talking and reading aloud, move the jaw actively, use a wider-open mouth than before, exaggerate lip movements, keep an open relaxed throat, and focus the tone forward.

Denasalization is the dull, 'cold-id-the-dose' quality. It results from a severe cold, enlarged adenoids or other nasal obstructions, or a soft palate held so high and tense that the nasal consonants, *m, n* and *ng* become *b, d* and *g*, and the voice lacks nasal resonance.

To help correct denasality (after medical or surgical care, if necessary): practise a free-swinging soft palate, low for the nasal consonants, high, but not too tight and tense, for the vowels and the other consonants. Try for strong, vigorous nasal consonants. Practise carefully the exercises for nasal resonance.

Assimilation nasality is the substitution of a nasalized vowel for a vowel plus a nasal consonant in such words as *my, time, find*. (Assimilation is the term used for the changing of one sound to another through the influence of a neighbouring sound. In this case, the *n* changes the vowel, but itself disappears.) The following exercise is designed to help correct assimilation nasality.

Exercise No. 77

In words with nasal consonants, sharply separate the vowels from the nasals. Say *time* as *tie-, tie-, tie-tie-m*. Keep the vowel free from nasal resonance all four times you say *tie*, but after the fourth *tie-* quickly press the lips together for a firm, strong *m*. In a similar way, practice all the words with nasals in part (*c*) of Exercise 75.

To Develop Oral Resonance

By oral resonance is meant the reinforcement of the original tone in the mouth cavity.

Exercise No. 78

(*a*) Say *woo, woh, waw*, exaggerating the rounding of the lips. Say each of these syllables rapidly several times with agile lip movement.

(*b*) Say *hoh, poh, boh* strongly with well-rounded lips. Hold the tone a moment, keeping the lips rounded.

(*c*) Open the mouth wide, round the lips, concentrate on projecting the voice through the mouth on:

Oh, what a beautiful day!

Who are you?

How do you do?

So all day long the noise of battle rolled.

Gold! Gold! Gold! Gold!
Bright and yellow, hard and cold.

Guard against trying too hard for oral resonance, for this will merely make you sound affected. You do not want 'pear-shaped' tones, too mellow and too beautiful.

To Develop Throat Resonance

By throat or pharyngeal resonance is meant the reinforcement of the original sound in the throat cavity.

EXERCISE No. 79

(*a*) With open throat, wide-swinging jaw, say: *wah, wow, woy; hah, how, hoy.*

(*b*) Yawn. On a low pitch and very slowly, say the syllables above.

(*c*) With low pitch and open throat, say:

And yonder all before us lie
Deserts of vast eternity.

The barge she sat in, like a burnished throne
Burned on the water.

Earth has not anything to show more fair.

(*d*) With very low pitch, and almost as if the voice came from the chest, say:

I am thy father's spirit:
Doom'd for a certain term to walk the night.
And for the day confined to fast in fires
Till the foul crimes done in my days of Nature
Are burnt and purged away.

Now o'er the one-half world
Nature seems dead, and wicked dreams abuse
The curtain's sleep.

The gaudy, blabbing and remorseful day
Is crept into the bosom of the sea,
And now loud-howling wolves arouse the jades
That drag the tragic melancholy night.

Loud from its rocky caverns, the deep-voiced neighbouring ocean
Speaks, and in accents disconsolate answers the wail of the forest.

Faulty pharyngeal resonance is part of stridency. The voice sounds pinched (see *Faulty Phonation*, page 157), the walls of the pharynx are held tight and tense.

To correct this faulty resonance: repeat Exercises 52–54, and practise vocalizing with relaxed throat and low pitch.

(11) Rate

The normal rate for speaking in public is about 125 words per minute. Radio talking averages about 150 words per minute.

EXERCISE NO. 80

With your normal rate, read the following paragraphs adapted from Samuel Butler's *Erewhon*. Have someone time you to see the place you reach in one minute, and measure the length of time you take to read the whole selection:

When I talked about originality and genius to some gentlemen whom I met at a supper party given by Mr. Thims in my honour, and said that original thought ought to be encouraged, I had to eat my words at once. A man's business, they hold, is to think as his neighbours do, for Heaven help him if he thinks good what they count bad. And really it is hard to see how their theory differs from our own, for the word 'Idiot' only means a person who forms his opinions for himself.

The venerable Professor of Worldly Wisdom, a man verging on eighty but still hale, spoke to me very seriously on this subject in consequence of the few words that I had imprudently let fall in defence of genius. He was one of those who carried most weight in the university, and had the reputation of having done more perhaps than any other living man to supress any kind of originality.

'It is not our business,' he said, 'to help students to think for themselves. Surely this is the very last thing which one who wishes them well should encourage them to do. Our duty is to ensure that they shall think as we do, or at any rate as we hold it expedient to say we do.' In some respects, however, he was thought to hold somewhat radical opinions, for he was President of the Society for the Suppression of Useless Knowledge, and for the Completer Obliteration of the Past.

(There are 93 words in the first paragraph. The 125th word is *imprudently* in the second paragraph; the 150th is *done* in the next sentence. There are 253 words in all.)

A good rate for you may well be somewhat above or below the average rates mentioned. It is the rate that is both comfortable for you, and easy for listeners to understand.

Read the paragraph above for several listeners to get their reactions to your rate.

If you decide, with their help, that your rate is too fast, too slow, or too jerky, go over the paragraph from *Erewhon* once again to see whether the fault lies with the length of the individual sounds, the number of pauses—that is, the way you *phrase* the selection—or the length of your pauses. After making this analysis, study the section below on *Phrasing* and practise the appropriate selections which follow.

Phrasing

We do not talk in single words, but in groups of words. In speech, such a group of related words is called a **phrase**. The phrase is said as if it were one long word.

An article is attached to a noun. We say:

not, *The book*	But, *Thebook*
not, *An apple*	But, *Anapple*
not, *A road*	But, *Aroad*

Adjectives are joined to nouns, adverbs to verbs. We say:

The open book as *Theopenbook*
Ride quickly as *Ridequickly*

A prepositional phrase is said without a break or pause: *totheend; ofthelastchapter.* Or two *prepositional phrases may be joined: totheendofthelastchapter.*

A short sentence may be said as a phrase: *Hewentaway.*

Where, then, do we break the tone? Where do we pause? Where does one phrase end and another begin? The answer depends upon several factors.

From the point of view of ideas and grammatical relationships, note the following:

We usually pause, of course, at the end of a sentence.

When a sentence is of some length, the subject-portion will be separated from the verb-portion: *ThemanIhopedtoseeelected | madeaverypoorshowing.*

An interpolated phrase will be set off by pauses: *Butsuddenly asIpeereddown | Isawawhiteformrising.*

If we talk in a very large hall, we must shorten our phrases, use more and longer pauses. The prizefight announcer calls: *Inthiscorner | inblacktights . . .*

A very serious subject, a very dignified occasion, will also cause us to use many short pauses and a generally slow rate.

And we may pause, break a phrase even, for special emphasis: *Isawawhiteform | rising.*

Finally, personal taste enters into phrasing and rate. One person might read the opening of the *Erewhon* passage above as: *WhenItalked | aboutoriginalityandgenius.* Another might say this as: *WhenItalkedaboutoriginalityandgenius.*

Mark the selections below for phrasing before you practise them, and then do the same for the *Erewhon* passage.

EXERCISE No. 81

(a) With long-held vowels, and many and long pauses, say:

Lord God of Hosts, be with us yet,
Lest we forget, lest we forget!

The quality of mercy is not strain'd;
It droppeth as the gentle rain from heaven
Upon the place beneath.

Tomorrow, and tomorrow and tomorrow,
Creeps in this petty pace from day to day
To the last syllable of recorded time;
And all our yesterdays have lighted fools
The way to dusty death. Out, out, brief candle!
Life's but a walking shadow, a poor player
That struts and frets his hour upon the stage
And then is heard no more. It is a tale
Told by an idiot, full of sound and fury,
Signifying nothing.

(*b*) With a fairly rapid rate (short vowels, and few and short pauses) say:

The year's at the spring
And day's at the morn;
Morning's at seven;
The hillside's dew-pearled;
The lark's on the wing;
The snail's on the thorn:
God's in his heaven—
All's right with the world.

I am the very model of a modern Major-General,
I've information vegetable, animal and mineral,
I know the kings of England, and I quote the fights historical,
From Marathon to Waterloo, in order categorical.

(*c*) Experiment with the selections in exercises (*a*) and (*b*) above, keeping the meaning clear, yet varying somewhat the length of vowels, and number and length of pauses.

(*d*) Say, as smoothly as possible:

On either side the river lie
Long fields of barley and of rye.

Far from the madding crowd's ignoble strife,
Their sober wishes never learn'd to stray;
Along the cool sequester'd vale of life
They kept the noiseless tenor of their way.

Earth has not anything to show more fair:
Dull would be he of soul who could pass by
A sight so touching in its majesty:
This City now doth like a garment wear
The beauty of the morning . . .

CHAPTER EIGHT

PRONUNCIATION

Those of us who wish to improve our speech want to use correct pronunciations. We want to be considered careful, not careless, in our speech habits; we want to avoid being caught in simple mistakes. We seek the assurance and confidence that comes from knowing we are doing something the right way.

In English, however, there is no such thing as a 'correct' pronunciation, in the sense that the answer to a problem in arithmetic is correct. There is no *one* right way to say a word. English-speaking peoples have no national academy to determine matters of pronunciation.

Therefore, it is better to think of pronunciations as being acceptable or unacceptable, that is, in good usage or not.

(1) Acceptable English Pronunciation

A pronunciation is acceptable if it meets the following requirements:

(*a*) If it is native, not foreign. Good English is not spoken with a foreign accent.

(*b*) If it is characteristic of some region of the British Isles, not some small locality, such as a particular town.

(*c*) If it is used by educated and cultured people. We should take as guides those who know something about the language and treat it with respect. We can get little help from those whose vocabulary is meagre and who do not care how they say the words they do know.

(*d*) If it is modern. Pronunciations change, and there isn't much sense in adopting a pronunciation last heard 500 years ago or one we think will be popular 25 years hence.

A corollary here is that while one need not use the pronunciations of one's grandmother, one should not criticize her for using those she was taught.

From these criteria it is clear that more than one pronunciation of a word may be acceptable, that is, in good usage.

A pronunciation may be unacceptable because it is foreign, provincial, pedantic, affected or obsolete.

(2) The Dictionary

The best aid in finding and selecting acceptable pronunciations is a good dictionary. The type of pronunciation given in most dictionaries is what is known as 'Standard English'; that is, the type of pronunciation most acceptable at all times in all parts of the British Isles and in other countries. It is the type of pronunciation most easily understood by all and has been made familiar by the voices of the news-readers on B.B.C. radio and on television. It is usually devoid of any regional accent and can be described as 'educated' speech—that of the public schools and the universities.

Of the dictionaries which pay special attention to the subject of pronunciation, perhaps the best known is *Everyman's English Pronouncing Dictionary* (twelfth edition) by Daniel Jones, published by Dent. The entries in this dictionary are written in international phonetic transcription, and the key provided makes it possible to check the *exact* pronunciation of over 58,000 words in regular usage.

Most other dictionaries provide a guide to the pronunciation of words. Though not as exact as a pronouncing dictionary, they can be very useful, particularly for checking the correct stresses in a word.

(3) How to Use a Dictionary

A dictionary will generally give alternative pronunciations where these are applicable. The first pronunciation given is the one most in use, and the following ones (sometimes presented in brackets) are less common but also acceptable.

In learning to use a dictionary you should:

(*a*) Familiarize yourself with its symbols indicating pronunciation. These are listed in a *Pronunciation Key* or *Guide to Pronunciation* at the beginning of the volume. You must realize, in following the various symbols and markings, that your pronunciation will only be as accurate as your interpretation of them. If you mistake the meaning of the marks and symbols, your pronunciation will be equally mistaken. Dictionaries help to guard against this by printing several key-words for each 'diacritical' mark in the full key at the beginning of the volume. Refer to these whenever you are in doubt about any sounds.

(*b*) Make sure you are looking up the right word, the one you want.

Sometimes words are spelt in the same way but have such different meanings that they are printed as separate entries. The word *primer* is an example.

One word may be used as several different parts of speech with possibly different pronunciations (for example, *perfect* as an adjective and as a verb). These may be listed together or separately.

In all dictionaries, check the meaning of the word and its part of speech before you look at its pronunciation.

(*c*) Examine all the pronunciations given for a word. Two, three or more may be offered. The word *alternate* has seven acceptable pronunciations (four as a verb, three as an adjective).

The first listing is usually the most widespread and therefore the preferred pronunciation. Pronunciations may be called local, colloquial, provincial, popular or poetic. In some dictionaries the phrases 'older', 'formerly' and 'less often' are also used.

(*d*) Finally, if the dictionary offers a choice of pronunciations, you should ask your friends for their vote. In general, you should try to conform to the pronunciations of your region.

The remainder of this chapter is devoted largely to **pronunciation lists.**

These are not intended to be a substitute for a dictionary. Rather, their purpose is to point out common types of mistakes in pronunciation, to show how these mistakes may be corrected, and to illustrate or emphasize certain principles that will be a help in improving your pronunciation generally.

Practise the lists only in conjunction with, and as illustrations for, the observations which precede them. Take up one list at a time. Read through it, saying aloud both the acceptable and the unacceptable forms. Note particularly those words which you have been mispronouncing. Say the correct pronunciation over several times, trying to fix it in your mind. Say the word in a short sentence. Keep a notebook of such words, and each week try to work three or four into your conversation.

(4) Pronunciation Key

In the lists that follow, the pronunciations are indicated by a simple system of re-spelling.

Vowels

SYMBOL	KEY-WORD	RE-SPELLING
EE	seem	SEEM
AY	say	SAY
Y	buy	BY
OH	no	NOH
OO	ooze	OOZ
AW	taught	TAWT
AH	farm	FAHM
UR	burn	BURN
OY	toy	TOY
OW	now	NOW
YOO	use	YOOZ
AYR	air	AYR

The remaining vowels are usually indicated by a vowel plus two consonants.

VOWEL	EXAMPLE	RE-SPELLING
I	ill	ILL
A	bat	BATT
E	end	ENND
O	hot	HOTT
U	cup	KUPP

The vowel of *push, pull* is usually indicated by U, and a key-word is supplied. In Chapter Nine (*Articulation*), the symbol UU is used for this vowel.

The vowels of unaccented syllables are weak, and have only a part of the quality of the original or else are completely blurred or indeterminate in quality. For these, the original spellings are usually retained: alone (a-LOHN), system (SISS-tem), easily (EE-zi-lee), honour (ONN--or), campus (KAMM-pus).

Consonants

The following letters have their usual value: **b, d, f, h, k, l, m, n, p, r, s, t, v, w, y** (before vowels, as in *yes*), **z**. The remaining consonants are indicated like this:

SYMBOL	KEY-WORD	RE-SPELLING
G	gay	GAY
J	jay	JAY
TCH	chief	TCHEEF
NG	sing	SING
SH	shoe	SHOO
ZH	measure	MEZH-ur
TH	thin	THINN
~~TH~~	than	~~TH~~ANN

NOTE: *W* is used for words spelled with *wh*, since this sound may be a *W*, a voiceless *W*, or an *HW*. *C* is not used, since it may have the sound of *S* or *K*. *Q* is not used, since its sound is *KW*. *X* is not used, since its sound is either *KS* or *GZ*.

In Chapter Nine (*Articulation*), the symbol *TSH* is used in place of *TCH*, and the symbol *DZH* is used in place of *J*. There, TCHEEF is TSHEEF, and JAY is DZHAY.

Syllables

Syllables are separated by dashes: *finger* (FING-ger). It should be remembered that syllables can be indicated only roughly in English.

Accent

Only the primary accent of a word is given and this is indicated by capitals: *going* (GOH-ing), *demoniacal* (dee-mo-NY-a-kal). The secondary accent is not indicated because it usually does not present a problem.

Exercise No. 82

Test yourself on the pronunciation of the following words.

WORD	SHOULD ONE SAY	OR
1. *women*	WIMM-in	WOH-men
2. *culinary*	KULL-i-ner-ee	KYOO-li-ner-ee
3. *awry*	a-RY	AW-ree

WORD	SHOULD ONE SAY	OR
4. *orgy*	AW-ji	AW-gi
5. *grievous*	GREEV-us	GREEV-ee-us
6. *ignoramus*	ig-no-RAY-mus	ig-no-RAM-us
7. *museum*	myoo-ZEE-um	MYOO-zee-um
8. *verbatim*	vur-BAY-tim	vur-BATT-im
9. *flaccid*	FLAKK-sid	FLASS-id
10. *suite*	SWEET	SOOT

(5) Common Mistakes in Pronunciation

Spelling Pronunciations

Certain mistakes in pronunciation are made because the speaker follows spellings too closely.

Sometimes there is good reason for this sort of mistake. Simple, old words may decline in use, or words common to one region may not be used in another. We may never have seen these words, yet we consider them too simple to look up in a dictionary. These very ordinary words, however, deserve to be correctly pronounced:

WORD	SAY	NOT
ague	AY-gyoo	AYG
awry	a-RY	AW-ree
blackguard	BLAG-ard	BLAKK-GAHRD
breeches	BRITCH-iz	BREETCH-iz
comely	KUMM-lee	KOHM-lee
orgy	AW-ji	AWR-guee (*g* as in *get*)
quay	KEE	KWAY
victuals	VITT-'lz	VIKK-tchoo-'lz

Sometimes the mispronounced words, while not literary, are a bit out of the ordinary. A careful speaker would have looked them up in a dictionary rather than guessed at their pronunciation from the spelling. In the word *misled*, the spelling pronunciation MIZZ-'ld probably occurs only when the word is read aloud.

WORD	SAY	NOT
comptroller	kon-TROH-ler	komp-TROH-ler
dishevelled	di-SHEVV-eld	diss-HEVV-eld
doughty	DOW-tee	DOH-tee
indict (to charge with a crime)	in-DYT	in-DIKT
longevity	lon-JEV-i-tee	long-GEV-i-tee
misled	miss-LED	MIZZ-'ld
parliamentary	pahr-li-MEN-ter-ee	pahr-lee-a-MEN-ter-ee
piquant	PEE-k'nt	PEE-kwant
solace	SOLL-iss	SOH-liss
subtle	SUTT-'l	SUBB-tel
vehement	VEE-e-mint	VEE-hem-ent
zoology	zoo-OLL-o-jee	ZOO-lo-jee

On the other hand, people occasionally mispronounce ordinary words that they must hear very frequently indeed. It is an extraordinary

G

tribute to the power of the printed word that a warning must be issued
about these curious spelling pronunciations.

WORD	SAY	NOT
comfort	KUMM-fort	KOMM-fort
cupboard	KUBB-'rd	KUPP-BOHRD
forehead	FORR-id	FOHR-HEDD
heroine	HERR-o-in	HERR-oyn
hiccough	HIK-up	HIK-koff
often	OFF-'n	OFF-ten
raspberry	RAZZ-berr-ee	RASP-berr-ee
said	SEDD	SAYD
says	SEZZ	SAYZ
whooping cough	HOOP-ing KOFF	WOOP-ing KOFF
women	WIMM-in	WOH-men

The *spelling CH* so often has the sound of TCH, as in *chin*, that
a common mistake is to tend to pronounce it always this way. But CH
especially in words taken from Greek, may also have the sound of K:

WORD	SAY	NOT
archives	AHR-kyvz	AHR-tchyvz
archipelago	ahr-ki-PELL-a-go	ahr-tchi-PELL-a-go
archangel	AHRK-ayn-jel	AHRTCH-ayn-jel
chasm	KAZZ-m	TCHAZZ-'m
chimera	ky-MIRR-a, ki-	tchy-MIRR-a
chiropodist	ki-ROPP-o-dist	tchi-ROPP-o-dist
choreographer	KORR-i-yog-raffer	TCHORR-i-yog-raffer
machinations	mak-i-NAY-sh'nz	mach-i-NAY-sh'nz
schizophrenic	skizz-o-FRENN-ik	———

But notice:

archbishop	ahtch-BISH-op	ahk-BISH-op
archdeacon	ahtch-DEE-k'n	ahk-DEE-k'n
schism	SIZZ'm	SKIZZ'm

The *spelling CH*, especially in words taken from French, may also
have the sound of SH:

WORD	SAY	NOT
cache	KASH	KATCH
chaise	SHAYZ, or SHEZZ	TCHAYZ
chamois (leather)	SHAM-ee	TCHAM-ee
chassis	SHASS-ee	TCHASS-ee
chic	SHEEK	TCHIK
chicanery	shi-KAYN-er-ee	tchi-KAYN-er-ee

The *spelling G* is troublesome because it has three pronunciations.
The hard G of *get*, the J of *jet*, and the ZH sound as in *pleasure* may
be confused in the following words:

WORD	SAY	NOT
beige	BAYZH	BAYJ
garage	ga-RAHZH	ga-RAHJ
gesture	JESS-tcher	guess-tcher
gesticulate	jess-TIK-yoo-layt	guess-TIK-yoo-layt
gibbet	JIB-et	GIB-et
mirage	mi-RAHZH	mi-RAHJ
regime	ray-ZHEEM	ray-JEEM
rouge	ROOZH	ROOJ

Reversing the Order of Sounds

If spelling is not looked at carefully enough, mispronunciations may occur because the order of certain sounds is reversed:

WORD	SAY	NOT
bronchial	BRONG-kee-al	BRONN-i-kal
cavalry	KAVV-al-ri	KAL-va-ri
irrelevant	ir-RELL-e-vant	ir-REVV-e-lant
larynx	LARR-ingks	LAHR-niks
pharynx	FARR-ingks	FAHR-niks
relevant	RELL-e-vant	REVV-e-lant

The sound R is particularly troublesome in this respect:

WORD	SAY	NOT
children	TCHILL-dren	TCHILL-dern
hundred	HUN-dred	HUN-derd
modern	MODD-en	MODD-ren
incongruous	in-KONG-groo-us	in-KONG-ger-us
pattern	PATT-en	PATT-ren
perspiration	pur-spir-AY-shun	press-pir-AY-shun

Added Sounds

In uneducated speech, sounds may be added to words because of their similarity to other words or because of a mistaken idea of their spelling. (Sounds added to ease the saying of difficult sound-combinations are discussed in Chapter Nine.)

WORD	SAY	NOT
across	a-KROSS	a-KROST
attack	a-TAKK	a-TAKT
attacked	a-TAKT	a-TAKK-ted
aureomycin	aw-ree-o-MY-sin	aw-ree-o-MY-o-sin
column	KOLL-um	KOLL-yum
drowned	DROWND	DROWN-ded
escape	es-KAYP	eks-KAYP
grievous	GREEV-us	GREEV-ee-us

WORD	SAY	NOT
mischievous	MISS-tchiv-us	miss-TCHEEV-ee-us
once	WUNSS	WUNST
streptomycin	strep-to-MY-sin	strep-to-MY-o-sin
help	HELP	HELL-up
film	FILLM	FILL-um

Sounds Left Out

Where two vowels occur together in a word, one is sometimes left out so that a syllable is lost. This sounds careless.

WORD	SAY	NOT
cruel	KROO-el	KROOL
diary	DY-a-ree	DY-ree
jewel	JOO-el	JOOL
poem	POH-em	POHM
ruin	ROO-in	ROON
violet	VY-o-let	VY-let

The mistake of leaving out a syllable may occur in other types of words:

WORD	SAY	NOT
president	PREZZ-i-dent	PREZZ-dent
probably	PROBB-a-blee	PROBB-lee
regularly	REGG-yoo-lar-lee	REGG-yu-lee
valuable	VALL-yoo-a-b'l	VALL-a-b'l

In careless speech, consonants are often left out. Be sure to say the consonants in these words:

WORD	SAY	NOT
all right	AWL RYT	AW RYT
Arctic	AHRK-tik	AHR-tik
district	DISS-trikt	DISS-trik
exactly	eg-ZAKT-lee	eg-ZAK-lee
flaccid	FLAKK-sid	FLASS-id
gentlemen	JENN-tel-man	JENN-l-man
help	HELP	HEPP
hound	HOWND	HOWN
hundred	HUNN-dred	HUNN-ed
recognize	REKK-og-nyz	REKK-o-nyz
succinct	sukk-SINGT	su-SINGT
thousand	THOW-zand	THOW-zan
told	TOHLD	TOHL

Substitution of One Sound for Another

One sound is sometimes mistakenly substituted for another. This may be a 'foreignism' or a spelling pronunciation.

WORD	SAY	NOT
average	AVV-er-ij	AVV-er-itch
because	bi-KOZ	bi-KOSS, bi-KAWSS
college	KOLL-ej	KOLL-itch
electricity	e-lekk-TRISS-i-tee	e-lekk-TRIZZ-i-tee
gas	GASS	GAZZ

Sound-substitutions also occur in uneducated or provincial speech. Some of the pronunciations may once have been acceptable, but are now considered archaic.

WORD	SAY	NOT
deaf	DEFF	DEEF
genuine	JENN-yoo-in	JENN-yoo-wyn
ignoramus	ig-no-RAY-mus	ig-no-RAM-us
length	LENGTH, LENGKTH	LENTH
pincers	PINN-surz	PINCH-urz
radiator	RAY-dee-ay-tor	RADD-ee-ay-tor
radio	RAY-dee-o	RADD-ee-o
rather	RAHTH-er	RUTH-er
strength	STRENGTH	STRENTH
tremendous	tre-MENN-dus	tre-MENN-jus
wrestle	RESS-'l	RASS-'l

The letter *X* may cause confusion because it has two pronunciations, KS and GZ. In words beginning with *ex-* which have the accent on the first syllable, the *ex* is pronounced EKS (*exodus*, EKS-o-dus). This is also the case if the accent falls on the second syllable and the second syllable begins with a consonant (*expect*, eks-PEKT). But if the second and accented syllable begins with a vowel, the sound is either EGZ or IGZ, *exalt* (egz-AWLT, igz-AWLT). Note, however:

exit	either EKS-it or EGZ-it
exile	either EKS-yl or EGZ-yl
luxury	LUKK-shu-ree
luxurious	either lukk-SHUR-i-us or lugg-ZHUR-i-us

Confusing Words with Similar Spelling

Words of different meaning but similar spelling are sometimes confused in pronunciation:

WORD AND MEANING	SAY
adjoin, to lie next to	a-JOYN
adjourn, to suspend a session	a-JURN
coral, skeleton of a sea animal	KORR-al
corral, pen for horses	ko-RAL
crochet, kind of needlework	kro-SHAY
crotchet, a perverse fancy	KROTCH-et
croquet, a lawn game	kro-KAY
croquette, crumbed, fried minced meat	kro-KETT
era, period of time	EE-ra, IRR-a
err, to be mistaken	UR
error, a mistake	ERR-a
lineament, feature of the face	LINN-ee-a-ment
liniment, liquid for sprains	LINN-i-ment
precedence, priority in order or rank	pre-SEE-dens
precedents, cases which serve as examples	PRESS-e-dens
slough, n., soft muddy place; condition of degradation; v., to plod through mud	SLOW (OW as in HOW)
slough, to cast off skin	SLUFF
viola, a stringed instrument	ve-OH-la, vy-OH-la
Viola a girl's name	VY-o-la, VEE-o-la, ve-OH-la, vy-OH-la

Accenting the Wrong Syllable

The accenting of certain syllables is an important feature of English pronunciation. Mistakes in placing the accent are either wrong guesses made by persons who have not yet acquired the habit of looking up pronunciations in a dictionary, or are relics of older pronunciations now too infrequently used to be considered acceptable. The list below gives both the acceptable and the unacceptable forms of words in which the accent is frequently misplaced.

WORD	SAY	NOT
alias	AY-lee-as	a-LY-as
brigand	BRIG-and	bri-GAND
cabal	ka-BAL (as in *cat*)	KABB-al
cement	si-MENT	SEE-ment
condolence	konn-DOH-lens	KONN-do-lens
consider	konn-SID-er	KONN-sidder
contribute	konn-TRIBB-yoot	KONN-tri-byoot
decade	DEKK-ayd	de-KAYD
demonstrate	DEMM-on-strayt	de-MONN-strayt

WORD	SAY	NOT
disciple	di-SY-p'l	DISS-i-p'l
elixir	i-LIKK-sur	ELL-ik-sur
episcopal	e-PIS-ko-pal	ep-i-SKAH-pal
exponent	ek-SPOH-nent	EKS-poh-nent
gondola	GONN-do-la	gon-DOH-la
grimace	gri-MAYSS	GRIMM-as
horizon	ho-RY-z'n	HORR-i-zon
hyperbole	hy-PUR-bo-lee	HY-pur-bohl
incognito	in-KOGG-ni-toh	in-kogg-NEE-toh
influence	IN-floo-enss	in-FLOO-enss
lyceum	ly-SEE-um	LY-see-um
municipal	myoo-NISS-a-p'l	myoo-ni-SIPP-'l
museum	myoo-ZEE-um	MYOO-zee-um
police	po-LEESS	POH-leess
robust	roh-BUST	ROH-bust
sepulchre	SEPP-ul-kur	se-PULL-kurr (as in *cut*)
theatre	THEE-a-tur (*th* as in *thin*)	thi-YITT-ur, the-AY-tur

Notice that a root may cause a misplaced accent:

impious	IMM-pee-us	imm-PY-us
impotent	IMM-po-tent	imm-POH-tent

The four-syllable adjectives ending in -*able* (*admirable*) are frequently mispronounced. The mistaken tendency is to accent them on the second syllable, usually on the analogy of the word from which they have been formed (*admire*). These adjectives are correctly accented on the first syllable.

WORD	SAY	NOT
amicable	AMM-i-ka-b'l	a-MIKK-a-b'l
admirable	ADD-mir-a-b'l	ad-MY-ra-b'l
applicable	APP-li-ka-b'l	a-PLIKK-a-b'l (2nd pronunciation)
comparable	KOMM-pa-ra-b'l	komm-PAYR-a-b'l
despicable	DESS-pik-a-b'l	de-SPIKK-a-b'l
equitable	EKK-wit-a-b'l	e-KWITT-a-b'l
formidable	FAWR-mid-a-b'l	fawr-MIDD-a-b'l (2nd pronunciation)
hospitable	HOSS-pit-a-b'l	hoss-PITT-a-b'l (2nd pronunciation)
lamentable	LAMM-en-ta-b'l	la-MENT-a-b'l
preferable	PREFF-ur-a-b'l	pre-FUR-a-b'l
reputable	REPP-yoo-ta-b'l	re-PYOO-ta-b'l

Notice also:

indefatigable	in-de-FATT-i-ga-b'l	(do not accent the 2nd or 4th syllable)
irreparable	i-REPP-a-ra-b'l	i-re-PAYR-a-b'l
irrevocable	i-REVV-o-ka-b'l	i-re-VOH-ka-b'l

Affectations

Certain persons go out of their way to pronounce words differently from their acquaintances or from the educated persons of their part of the country. They seek out poetic or archaic pronunciations and seem to put quotation marks around each of these whenever they say them.

Avoid such affectation. Let the pronunciations of the educated people of your region be good enough for you.

WORD	SAY	NOT
aerial	AYR-ee-al	ay-IRR-ee-al
aeroplane	AYR-o-playn	AY-e-ro-playn
again	a-GENN	a-GAYN
coupon	KOO-pon	KYOO-pon
either	Y-ther	EE-ther
		(2nd pronunciation)
hearth	HAHRTH	HURTH
hygiene	HY-jeen	HY-ji-een
issue	ISS-yoo	ISH-oo
		(2nd pronunciation)
laboratory	LABB-o-ra-toh-ree	LABB-ra-tree
nature	NAYTCH-er	NAYT-yoor
neither	NY-ther	NEE-ther
rabies	RAY-beez	RAY-bi-eez
stature	STATCH-er	STATT-yoor
vase	VAHZ	VAYSS (American)

Some people who are not trying to act in a superior way but are merely trying to be careful, try too hard, and succeed in *sounding affected.* (See also Chapter Nine.)

One instance of this is saying the ending *-ness* as if it were an accented syllable, NESS. The ending is always unaccented and should be said with an indeterminate vowel, resembling NISS.

EXAMPLE	SAY	NOT
madness	MADD-niss	MADD-ness

Another instance is saying the ending *-or* as AWR. This ending is also unaccented and should be said with an indeterminate vowel, resembling ER.

EXAMPLE	SAY	NOT
actor	AKK-ter	AKK-tawr

EXERCISE No. 83

This exercise is based on the words in the preceding section, *Common Mistakes in Pronunciation.*

WORD	SHOULD YOU SAY	OR
1. *ague*	AY-gyoo	AYG
2. *piquant*	PEE-kwant	PEE-k'nt
3. *cupboard*	KUBB-'rd	KUPP-BOHRD
4. *archangel*	AHRTCH-ayn-jel	AHRK-ayn-jel
5. *gibbet*	GIB-et	JIB-et
6. *poem*	POH-em	POHM
7. *succinct*	su-SINGT	sukk-SINGT
8. *luxury*	LUKK-shu-ree	LUGG-zhu-ree
9. *umbrella*	UM-ber-ella	um-BRELL-a
10. *incognito*	in-KOGG-ni-toh	in-kogg-NEE-toh
11. *formidable*	fawr-MIDD-a-b'l	FAWR-mid-a-b'l
12. *coupon*	KYOO-pon	KOO-pon

(6) Aids to Better Pronunciation

Influence of Part of Speech on Pronunciation

Certain words are accented on the first syllable when used as nouns or adjectives, on the second when used as verbs.

EXAMPLE	NOUN OR ADJ.	VERB
absent	ABB-sent	ab-SENT
addict	ADD-ikt	a-DIKT
annexe	ANN-eks	a-NEKS
perfect	PUR-fekt	per-FEKT

Other words which shift accent in this way are:

collect	digest	permit	record
combat	escort	prefix	reject
combine	export	present	subject
compound	import	produce	survey
conduct	imprint	progress	suspect
contract	incense	project	transfer
convert	increase	rebel	transport
desert			

Notice, however:

WORD	NOUN OR ADJ.	VERB
attribute	ATT-ri-byoot	a-TRIBB-yoot
consummate	kon-SUMM-it	KONN-su-mayt
perfume	PUR-fyoom, per-FYOOM	per-FYOOM
refuse	REFF-yooss	re-FYOOZ

The word *adept* is pronounced ADD-ept when used as a noun, a-DEPT when used as an adjective.

The word *compact* is pronounced KOMM-pakt when used as a noun, kom-PAKT when used as a verb, and either KOMM-pakt or kom-PAKT when used as an adjective.

The word *cleanly* is pronounced KLENN-lee when used as an adjective, KLEEN-lee when used as an adverb.

When certain words ending in *-ate* are used as verbs, this last syllable is pronounced AYT. But when they are used as adjectives or nouns, the final vowel is indeterminate in quality and the syllable resembles -IT.

EXAMPLES	NOUN OR ADJ.	VERB
advocate	ADD-vo-kit	ADD-vo-kayt
aggregate	AGG-re-git	AGG-re-gayt

Other words which shift pronunciation in this way are:

alternate	delegate	duplicate	moderate
appropriate	deliberate	estimate	predicate
approximate	designate	graduate	prostrate
associate	desolate	intimate	separate
degenerate			

Words We Read but Seldom Say

Writing tends to be formal, to use learned (LURN-ed) words. In talking, we try for informality, directness, simplicity.

There are many words which we read and know the meaning of, but which we seldom hear and seldom say. Consequently, when we do have to say them, as when we read aloud to our family or friends from a newspaper or magazine, we are frequently at a loss as to how to pronounce them.

The list below contains a sampling of such words. Read them. Say them out loud. Memorize their pronunciation. Check them in your dictionary. Make a habit of looking up the pronunciation of other 'hard' words when you come across them.

Only a few mispronunciations are given below, for the simple reason that the words are not said often enough to acquire any common mispronunciations.

WORD AND MEANING	PRONOUNCED
aborigines, primitive inhabitants	ab-o-RIJ-i-neez
abstemious, sparing in diet	ab-STEE-mee-us
aggrandizement, enlargement in size or power	a-GRANN-diz-ment
bestial, brutal, inhuman	BESS-tchel, BEST-yal
congeries, collection of particles in a mass	kon-JIRR-eez kon-JIRR-i-eez
Deity, the; God	DEE-i-tee (not DAY-i-tee)
demise, death	di-MYZ
demoniacal, possessed by an evil spirit	dee-mo-NY-a-kal
egregious, remarkably flagrant: *an egregious lie*	e-GREE-jus, e-GREE-ji-us
epitome, a summary	e-PITT-o-mee (not EPP-i-tohm)
harbinger, a forerunner	HAHR-bin-jer
heinous, hateful, odious	HAY-nus
inveigle, to win over by guile	in-VEE-g'l, in-VAY-g'l
lugubrious, ridiculously mournful	loo-GYOO-bri-us
malinger, to feign sickness to avoid work	ma-LING-ger
phlegmatic, not easily excited	flegg-MATT-ik
promulgate, to proclaim formally	PROM-ull-gayt
recluse, a person who lives in seclusion	ri-KLOOSS
spontaneity, action proceeding from an inner impulse	spon-ta-NEE-i-tee (not NAY-i-tee)
squalor, foulness	SKWOLL-or
unguent, a salve or ointment	UNG-gwent
zealot, one showing excess of zeal	ZELL-ot

Choice of Pronunciation

Sometimes persons dispute about the pronunciation of a word, not realizing that two (or even more) pronunciations of that word are equally acceptable. The unabridged dictionaries carry a special section devoted to such words.

Below is a list of fairly common words for which a choice of pronunciation is allowed. Of the pronunciations given, try to use the one you hear most frequently among your friends or in your part of the country. Follow the same practice when you find two or more pronunciations give in a dictionary.

WORD	SAY EITHER	OR
abdomen	ABB-do-men	ab-DOH-men
adult	ADD-ult	a-DULT
alternate (verb)	AWL-ter-nayt	AL-ter-nayt
aspirant	a-SPYR-ant	ASS-pirant
banal	ba-NAHL	BAY-nal
brusque	BRUSK	BRUUSK (as in *soon*)
chauffeur	SHOW-fer	sho-FUR
coadjutor	ko-AJJ-u-tor	koh-a-JOO-tor
defect	di-FEKT	DEE-fekt
exquisite	EKS-kwizz-it	eks-KWIZZ-it (used for special emphasis)
extraordinary	ek-STRAW-din-ri	eks-tra-AW-di-nerr-i
finance	fi-NANS	FY-nans
financier	fy-NAN-seer	fi-NAN-seer
gala	GAH-la	GAY-la
grovel	GROVV-'l	GRUVV-'l
hovel	HOVV-'l	HUVV-'l
indissolubly	in-di-SOLL-yoo-bli	in-DISS-o-lyoo-bli
jocund	jokk-und	JOH-kund
obligatory	o-BLIGG-a-toh-ri	OBB-li-gay-toh-ri
photograph	FOH-te-grahf	FOH-te-graf
pianist	PEE-a-nist	pi-ANN-ist
provost	PROVV-ost	PROVV-OH (military use)
quinine	kwi-NEEN	KWI-neen
reservoir	REZZ-er-vwah	REZZ-er-vwaw
route	ROOT	ROWT (military use)
sacrilegious	sak-ri-LIJJ-us	sakk-ri-LEE-jus

EXERCISE No. 84

This exercise is based on the preceding section, *Aids to Better Pronunciation.*

	WORD	SHOULD ONE SAY	OR
1.	*consummate,* adj.	kon-SUMM-it	KONN-su-mayt
2.	*consummate,* verb	kon-SUMM-it	KONN-su-mayt
3.	*advocate,* noun	ADD-vo-kayt	ADD-vo-kit
4.	*advocate,* verb	ADD-vo-kit	ADD-vo-kayt
5.	*epitome*	e-PITT-o-mee	EPP-i-tohm
6.	*inveigle*	in-VEE-g'l	in-VAY-g'l
7.	*zealot*	ZEE-lot	ZELL-ot
8.	*extant*	EKS-tant	eks-TANT
9.	*patronize*	PAY-tro-nyz	PATT-ro-nyz
10.	*profile*	PROH-fyl	PROH-fill

(7) Foreign Words and Phrases

Latin Words and Phrases

The following words and phrases taken from Latin are fairly often encountered in English. They are heard in business, law, logic, politics, the arts, and in conversation generally.

A brief definition accompanies each entry.

WORD AND MEANING	SAY
a fortiori; with the greater force, said of one conclusion as compared with another	AY fawr-shi-AW-ry
ad infinitum; without limit	ADD in-fi-NY-tum
ad libitum (ad lib.); as one wishes	ADD LIBB-i-tum
alma mater; fostering mother; hence, one's school	AHL-ma MAH-ter, AL-ma MAY-ter
alumnus, /i, /a, /ae; graduate of a school	masc. a-LUMM-nus, pl. -ny; fem. -na. pl. -nee
anno Domini; in the year of the Christian era	ANN-oh DOMM-i-ny
a posteriori; known afterwards; hence, through experience	AY poss-tirr-i-OH-ree
a priori; known beforehand; hence, through reasoning	AY pri-OH-ry, pry-OH-ry; AH pri-OH-ree
bona fide; in good faith	BOH-na FY-de; as adj., BOH-na FYD, BONN-a
carpe diem; enjoy the day	KAHR-pe DY-em
corpus delicti; in a murder case, the actual death of the one alleged to have been murdered	KAWR-pus di-LIKK-ty
data: things given, esp. facts on which an inference is based	DAY-ta
de facto; actually, in fact	DEE FAKK-toh
de jure; by right or lawful title	DEE JOO-ree
dramatis personae; characters in a drama	DRAMM-a-tiss pur-SOH-nee (or -ny)
ex cathedra; by virtue of one's office	EKS ka-THEE-dra
ex officio; by virtue of an office	EKS o-FISH-i-oh
ex post facto; done afterwards but retroactive	EKS POHST FAKK-toh
extempore; without preparation	eks-TEMM-po-ree
finis; end	FY-niss
gratis; for nothing	GRAY-tiss, GRATT-iss
habeus corpus; a writ to bring a person before a court	HAY-be-us KAWR-pus
imprimatur; licence to publish a book	imm-pri-MAY-tur, -pry—
in absentia; in absence	IN abb-SENN-she-a
in extremis; near death	IN eks-TREE-miss
in toto; entirely	IN TOH-toh
non sequitur; a conclusion which does not follow from the premises	NONN SEKK-wi-tur
obiter dictum, -a; incidental remark or observation	OBB-i-ter DIKK-tum
per diem; by the day	PUR DY-em
persona non grata; an unacceptable person	pur-SOH-na NONN GRAH-ta
prima facie; at first view	PRY-ma FAY-shi-ee, FAY-shi
pro rata; according to share	PROH RAY-ta, RAH-ta
pro tempore (pro tem); for the time being	PROH TEMM-po-ree
quasi; as if, seeming	KWAY-sy, KWAH-see
re; with reference to	REE
sine die; without naming a day to meet again	SY-ni DY-ee
status; state of a person or affairs	STAY-tus, STATT-us
status quo; the state existing	STAY-tus KWOH, STATT-us

WORD AND MEANING	SAY
stratum, -a; a layer or level	STRAY-tum, STRAH-tum
subpoena; a writ commanding appearance in court	su-PEE-na, sub-
ultimatum; a final proposition	ull-ti-MAY-tum
verbatim; word for word	vur-BAY-tum
via; by way of	VY-a, VEE-a
viva voce; orally	VY-va VOH-see
vox populi; voice of the people	VOKKS POPP-yoo-ly

French Words and Phrases

The French words and phrases in the lists below occur fairly frequently in English. They have been grouped in several categories, but of course they may be used in other fields.

When we say these words and phrases we usually tend only to approximate the French pronunciation, to give them a slightly French flavour, as it were. Sometimes we Anglicize them entirely, saying them as if they were native words.

When an N is italicized below as in *en* (AH*N*), it means that the preceding vowel is nasalized (with the soft palate dropped slightly and the tone allowed to resonate in the nose) while the N itself is silent.

French syllables are more evenly stressed than English syllables, with a slight stress on the last syllable of the word or phrase. This is frequently carried over into English, as in **à la carte** (ah la KAHRT).

Food and Restaurant Words

WORD AND MEANING	SAY
à la carte; dish by dish, with a stated price for each	ah la KAHRT
à la mode; (i) dessert served with ice cream, (ii) stewed or braised with vegetables and served with gravy, (iii) fashionable	ah la MOHD, AL a mohd
cuisine; style of cooking	kwe-ZEEN
entrée; (i) main course of a meal, (ii) the dish before the main course, (iii) right of entry	AHN-tray
filet mignon; round fillet of beef	fee-lay-mee-NYAWN, fe-LAY MEEN-yonn
garçon; waiter, boy	gahr-SAWN
gourmand; a lover of good eating	GOOR-mand, goor-MAHN
gourmet; one who shows taste in appreciating good food	GOOR-may, goor-MAY
hors-d'œuvre; appetizer	AWR DU(R)VR (like an UR without R)
menu; bill of fare	MENN-yoo, MAY-nyoo
pièce de résistance; main dish	PYESS de ray-zees-TAHNSS
table d'hôte; meal for which one pays a fixed price	TAH-b'l DOHT, TABB-'l

Military Words

WORD AND MEANING	SAY
aide de camp; officer-assistant to a general	AYD de KAMP, EDD-de-KAHN

WORD AND MEANING	SAY
camouflage; disguise of a camp, and so any disguise expedient	KAMM-o-flahzh (zh, like *s* in pleasure)
corps; body of persons under common direction	KOHR (not KAWRPSS) plur. KOHRZ
coup de grâce; a finishing stroke	KOO de GRAHSS
hors de combat; disabled and so out of the combat	awr de kaw*n*-BA (part-way between c*a*t and c*a*lm)

Words from the Arts

WORD AND MEANING	SAY
bas-relief; sculpture in low relief	bah re-LEEF, BAH re-leef, BASS (as in c*a*t)
baton: conductor's stick, staff of office	BATT-aw*n*, BATT-on
belles-lettres; aesthetic, rather than informational, literature	bell LETT'r
connoisseur; one competent as a critic of art	konn-i-SUR
façade; face of a building, front of anything	fa-SAHD
nom de plume; pen name	NOMM de ploom
protégé; one under protection of another	PROH-te-zhay
tour de force: feat of strength or skill	toor de FAWRSS

Political Words and Phrases

WORD AND MEANING	SAY
bourgeois; middle class	boor-ZHWAH, BOOR-zhwah
bourgeoisie; people of the middle class	boor-zhwah-ZEE
cause célèbre; legal case of great interest	kohz se-LEBB'r
entente cordiale; cordial understanding between two governments	ah*n*-TAH*N*T kawr-DYAL
laissez faire; non-interference	LESS-ay FAYR

Social and General Words

WORD AND MEANING	SAY
au revoir; goodbye till we meet again	oh re-VWAHR
beau geste; ingratiating act or gesture	boh ZHEST
bête noire; bugbear	bett NWAHR, bayt
billet doux; love letter	BILL-i doo, BILL-ay, plur. dooz
bon vivant; lover of good living	baw*n* vee-VAH*N*
carte blanche; unconditional power	KAHRT BLAHNSH
château; (i) castle, (ii) large country house	sha-TOH
cortège: (i) procession, (ii) train of attendants	kawr-TEZH, -TAYZH
crèche; representation of the figures at Bethlehem	KRESH, KRAYSH
cul-de-sac; a blind alley or deadlock	KULL de sakk (or *u* as in p*u*ll)
début; entrance on a career or into society	DAY-byoo, de-BYOO
débutante; one making a debut	debb-yoo-TAHNT, DEBB-yoo-tant
{deshabille; loose or careless style of dress / **dishabille;**	dezz-a-BEEL / diss-a-BEEL
élite; the choice part, as of a group	i-LEET, ay-LEET
enfant terrible; child whose remarks cause embarrassment	ah*n*-fah*n* te-REEB'l
en route; on the way	ahn ROOT
faux pas; false step, offence against social convention	foh PAH, plur. PAHZ

WORD AND MEANING	SAY
gauche; awkward	GOHSH
gendarme; policeman	ZHAHN-dahrm
joie de vivre; keen enjoyment of life	zhwa de VEE'vr (*a* between c*a*t and c*a*lm)
loge; box in a theatre	LOHZH
mal-de-mer; seasickness	mal de MERR
qui vive, on the; on the alert	kee VEEV
sang-froid; coolness in any circumstance	sah*n* FRWA
savoir faire; social ease and grace	SAVV-wahr FAYR
suite; (i) set, (ii) retinue, (iii) instrumental composition	SWEET
tête-à-tête; conversion for two alone	tett a TETT, tayt a TAYT
vis-à-vis; face to face	vee-za-VEE

German Words and Phrases

A few German words have gained acceptance in English speech.

WORD AND MEANING	SAY
auf Wiedersehen; till we meet again	owff VEE-der-ZAYN
ersatz; substitute	err-ZAHTSS
Gesundheit; to your health	ge-ZUUNT-hyt (UU as in p*u*t)
Lebensraum; territory desired by a nation for expansion	LAY-benss-ROWM (OW as in h*ow*)
Leitmotif; theme associated with a person or idea	LYT-moh-teef
Reichstag; Germ. legislative assembly	RYKS-tahg
verboten; forbidden	fer-BOH-ten
Wanderlust; strong impulse to wander	WONN-der-lust, VAHN-der-lust
Weltanschauung; world-view	VELT AHN-show-ung (ow as in h*ow*)
Weltschmerz; sadness from a pessimistic world-view	VELT-shmerrts
Zeitgeist; spirit of the times	TSYT-gyst

Italian Words

A great many Italian words are used by musicians and artists. Below are a few words which present special pronunciation problems:

WORD AND MEANING	SAY
adagio; slowly	a-DAH-joh, -zhoh (*zh* like *s* in pleasure)
concerto; composition for one or several instruments and orchestra	kon-TCHERR-toh
crescendo; gradual increase in volume	kre-SHENN-doh
plazza; veranda	pi-ATT-sa
pizzicato: plucked	pitt-si-KAH-toh
vivace; lively	vee-VAH-tchee

Exercise No. 85

This exercise is based on the words in the preceding section, *Foreign Words and Phrases*.

WORD	SHOULD ONE SAY	OR
1. *finis*	FINN-is	FY-niss
2. *per diem*	pur DEE-em	pur DY-em

WORD	SHOULD ONE SAY	OR
3. *ultimatum*	ull-ti-MATT-um	ull-ti-MAY-tum
4. *coup de grâce*	KOO de GRAHSS	KOO de GRAYSS
5. *au revoir*	oh re-VWAHR	oh re-VAWR
6. *ersatz*	ERR-zahtss	err-ZAHTSS
7. *loge*	LOHZH	LOHJ
8. *pizzicato*	pitt-si-KAH-toh	pizz-i-KAH-toh
9. *baton*	BATT-aw*n*	BATT-on
10. *gratis*	GRAY-tiss	GRATT-iss

(8) Names of Persons and Places

Names of Persons

The names of persons are often a troublesome problem in pronunciation. For family names, the family itself decides how its name is to be pronounced.

The following lists contain examples of choices in the pronunciation of names, or of common mispronunciations.

Family Names

NAME	USUALLY PRONOUNCED
Beauchamp	BEE-tcham (not BOH-sha*n*)
Knopf	KNOPPF (not NOPPF)
MacLeod	ma-KLOWD (as in h*ow*)
McLean	ma-KLAYN (not mak-LEEN)
Monroe	munn-ROH (not MONN-roh)
Pierce	PIRRSS or PURRSS
Roosevelt	ROHZ-e-velt, or ROHZ-velt (not ROOZ-e-velt)
Van Wyck	vann WYK (not vann WIKK)
Xavier	ZAY-vi-er (not ekk-ZAY-vi-er)

Nationalities

Arab	AR-ab (not AY-rab)
Celtic	SELL-tik or KELL-tik
Czech	TCHEKK
Maori	MAH-o-ree, MOW-ree (ow as in h*ow*)
	MAH-ree
Italian	i-TAL-yan (not Y-TAL-yan)
Note also:	
Magi	MAY-jy (not MAGG-y)

Composers

Bartok	BAHR-tokk, -tohk
Beethoven	BAY-toh-ven
Berlioz	BERR-li-ohz
Chopin	SHOH-pann, shoh-PA*NN*
Debussy	de-BYOO-see, or Fr. de-bu-SEE (u as a lip-rounded EE)
de Falla	de FAHL-ya
Dvorak	DVAWR-zhakk, -zhahk
Haydn	HY-d'n
Purcell	PUR-sel (not pur-SELL)
Saint-Saëns	sa*n* SAH*NS*
Shostakovitch	shoss-tah-KOH-vitch
Villa-Lobos	VEE-lah LAW-bawss
Wagner	VAHG-ner

Authors

NAME	USUALLY PRONOUNCED
Balzac	BAL-zakk or BAWL-zakk
Boccaccio	boh-KAH-tchi-o
Cellini	tche-LEE-nee
Cervantes	ser-VANN-teez, ser-VAHN-tayss
Dostoevsky	dawss-to-YEFF-skee
Dumas	DYOO-mah, DOO-mah
Goethe	GOE-tuh (for OE, lips rounded as for OH, while trying to say AY), GU(R)-tuh
Maeterlinck	MAY-ter-lingk
Maugham	MAWM
Pepys	PEEPS, PEPS, PEP-iss
Yeats	YAYTS

Characters

Adonis	a-DOH-niss, a-DONN-iss
Aeschylus	EES-ki-lus
Don Juan	donn JOO-an, don HWAHN
Don Quixote	donn KWIKK-sit, don kee-HO-tay
Odysseus	oh-DISS-yoos, oh-DISS-i-us
Oedipus	EE-di-pus

British Place Names

The pronunciation of British place names is usually determined by the locality itself. Interesting differences occur, and the pronunciations of one part of the country often surprises those living elsewhere. The following list contains examples of some of the more outstanding pronunciations.

NAME	SAY
Cirencester	SY-ren-sest-er (SISS-it-er also correct, used by local county families)
Derby	DAH-bi (DUR-bi also used by local people)
Greenwich	GRIN-ij, or GREN-itch
Heysham	HEE-shum
Holborn	HOH-bn
Hougham	HUFF-um
Magdalen (Oxford)	MAWD-lin
Norwich	NORR-ij
Pall Mall	PEL-MEL or PAL-MAL
Salisbury	SAWLZ-bri
Shrewsbury	SHROWZ-bri (used by the school and by old county families)
	SHREWZ-bri (commonly used in the town and by outsiders)
Sidmouth	SID-muth
Teignmouth	TIN-muth, TING-muth
Towcester	TOHS-tu
Waltham	WAWL-tum (say WAWL-thum on the telephone to avoid confusion with Walton)
Woburn	WOO-burn (Beds.)
	WOH-burn, WOH-bun (Square in London)
Worcester	WUST-u
Wrotham	ROOT-um

The *English Pronouncing Dictionary* by Daniel Jones gives the correct pronunciations of all unusual place names in the British Isles.

Foreign Place Names

Foreign place names fall into two categories with regard to their pronunciation in English:

(*a*) The names of the larger, better-known cities and towns are completely Anglicized. We say mi-LANN for Milan, as if it were a native word, and with no thought of the fact that Italians call the place mee-LAH-noh.

(*b*) For the less well-known places, we tend to approximate the foreign pronunciation, partially Anglicizing it, and sometimes keeping only one element of the original pronunciation. *Nice* is said NEESS.

Choices are possible for fairly well-known places. Difficulties in pronunciation occur when, for some reason, places formerly obscure suddenly become well known. The following list contains some interesting examples of the pronunciation of foreign place names.

You may use the foreign pronunciation of a place name if you wish, but do so only if your command of the foreign language is good and if you find that your friends and acquaintances do not raise their eyebrows at such attempts. Of course, if you are going abroad, learn the foreign pronunciation of place names while you are studying the language.

NAME	SAY
Aix-la-Chapelle	AYKSS lah-shah-PELL, EKKS
Aachen (German name of above)	AH-ken
Bayreuth	BY-royt
Buenos Aires	BWAY-nos Y-rizz, BOH-nos AYR-eez
Caen (compare with *Cannes*)	KAH*N* (nasalized AH)
Cairo, Egypt	KY-roh
Calais	KAL-ay, KAL-is, ka-LAY
Cannes	KANN, KANNZ
Caribbean	kar-i-BEE-an, ka-RIB-ee-an
Delhi, India	DELL-ee
Guadalajara	gwah-dah-lah-HAH-rah
Himalaya	he-MAHL-ya, him-a-LAY-a
Hiroshima	hir-o-SHEE-ma
Kiev	KEE-eff
Lima, Peru	LEE-ma
Lourdes	LOORD
Lyons	LY-onz, lee-AW*N*
Madras	ma-DRASS, ma-DRAHSS
Marseilles	mahr-SAY, older, -SAYLZ
Milan	mi-LANN, MILL-an
Monte Video	MONN-te vi-DAY-oh, MONN-te VIDD-i-oh
Moscow	MOSS-kow, MOSS-koh
Nice	NEESS
Peiping	BAY-PING, formerly PEE-PING
Prague	PRAHG, older, PRAYG
Rheims	REEMZ
Rio de Janeiro	REE-oh de zha-NAYR-oh
Transvaal	trans-VAHL, tranz-
Trieste	tre-EST
Versailles	vayr-SY
Ypres	EE-pr

EXERCISE NO. 86

This exercise is based on the preceding section, *Names of Persons and Places*.

	WORD	SHOULD ONE SAY	OR
1.	*Van Wyck*	vann WYK	vann-WIKK
2.	*Dvorak*	DVAWR-zhakk	DVAWR-zhahk
3.	*Boccaccio*	boh-KAH-tchio-o	boh-KASS-i-o
4.	*Oedipus*	EDD-i-pus	EE-di-pus
5.	*Spokane*	spo-KAYN	spo-KANN
6.	*Bayreuth*	BAY-rooth	BY-royt
7.	*Ypres*	EE-pr	Y-pres
8.	*Milan*	MILL-an	mi-LANN
9.	*Rheims*	REEMZ	RAMMZ
10.	*Cairo*	KY-roh	KAYR-oh

EXERCISE NO. 87

This is a general exercise, based on the preceding sections and also containing some words not considered there.

	WORD	SHOULD ONE SAY	OR
1.	*chiropodist*	ki-ROPP-o-dist	tchi-ROPP-o-dist
2.	*chaise*	SHAYZ, SHEZZ	TCHAYZ
3.	*lamentable*	LAMM-en-ta-b'l	la-MENT-a-b'l
4.	*aye*, meaning yes	Y	AY
5.	*ay*, meaning *ever*	Y	AY
6.	*cerebral*	SERR-e-bral	se-REE-bral
7.	*re*	RAY	REE
8.	*Magi*	MAGG-y	MAY-jy
9.	*Cannes*	KANN	KANNZ
10.	*bestial*	BESS-tchel	BEEST-yal
11.	*vagary*	VAYG-a-ree	va-GAYR-ee

CHAPTER NINE

ARTICULATION

Articulation is the muscular process by means of which we modify voice or breath with tongue, teeth, lips, and other speech organs, to produce speech sounds.

Good articulation is important, first of all, because it enables one to speak with the least muscular effort. The people who are most skilled in any physical activity are those who have learned to use their muscles in so relaxed and efficient a manner that they do not tire quickly. If talking soon fatigues you physically, the likelihood is that you are not using your speech muscles efficiently. And the resulting drain on your energies impairs your total speech effectiveness.

Secondly, good articulation helps you to speak more distinctly. Better muscular skill in speaking means not only less exertion, but greater audibility. By producing the sounds of speech more accurately, it enables your listeners to hear you clearly even though you speak in quiet tones.

Thirdly, better articulation helps you to focus attention on your message. A manner of speaking which calls attention to itself is a serious obstacle to your speaking purpose. Sound-peculiarities such as whistling *S*'s will so distract some listeners that they do not take note of what is being said. Good articulation lets your listeners concentrate on the substance of your speech.

Lastly, poor articulation may be the cause of other speech trouble. Artificial pronunciations and shrill or husky voice qualities are often due to misguided efforts to make poor articulation more audible. In such cases, better articulation may be an important key to the improvement of other aspects of your speech personality.

(1) How Articulation Can Be Improved

The factors influencing our articulation are much the same as those which determine the kind of voice we have (discussed in Chapter Seven). The most important factors are:

(i) The physical make-up of our speech organs such as the tongue, teeth and lips.

(ii) The social influence of those with whom we speak.

(iii) The speech habits we have formed earlier in life.

More can usually be done about the physical factors which affect articulation than about those which affect voice quality. A skilled dentist can often straighten out tooth irregularities which interfere with such sounds as *F, V, TH, S* and *Z*.

But even though services of specialists are sometimes necessary, it is best to consult a general medical practitioner first. The same holds true of any other physiological impediment which seems to prevent you from forming speech sounds as described in this chapter.

Most of our articulation difficulties, however, are due to *muscular habits* formed under the *social influence* of those with whom we speak. Early in life we may have unconsciously imitated someone who mumbled his words, who spoke out of the corner of his mouth, who lisped, or who had a pronounced foreign or regional accent.

More likely still, we may have been influenced by examples which were not so much harmful to our speech as unhelpful to it. A large number of people who are quite meticulous about their grooming and dress are astonishingly unaware that they show the frayed edges of their articulation every time they talk. They would certainly throw away any garment that showed signs of wear and tear, yet they are content to go on using year after year shoddy speech patterns and never give any thought to how slovenly speaking affects their 'image'.

The main tendency against which we have to work is just plain slovenliness in articulation—and that takes more effort than is commonly realized.

To correct a pronunciation we need only to find out what the dictionary says about it. But to improve our articulation it is not enough merely to learn *what* should be done. We must also learn *how* to do it.

The difficulty is that our articulation is a set of habits so long established that we never give them conscious thought. Such habits can be changed only by *regular practice* over a considerable period of time.

Some people think they will improve their articulation merely by 'taking more care when speaking'. But that is as futile as it is absurd. To think about the movements of one's tongue while discussing the issues of the day or the affairs of one's friends, does not make for better speech any more than it makes for good conversation or naturalness of conduct.

The only effective care you can take is to take care to practise. The most important part of the rest of this chapter are the *exercises*. The *explanations* are mainly to help you practise these exercises in such a manner as to get the best result for the time spent.

There is little value in just going through the motions of the exercises. A ritualistic muttering of certain words to yourself may testify to your good intentions, but is not likely to do your articulation any good.

Notice that you are never advised in the exercises merely to say something 'carefully'. You are always given *specific suggestions as to what to be careful about in each case*. Even the order of the exercises is based upon principles of effective practice. So it is important, as you work through them, to make sure you do your utmost to apply the principles explained.

Where wide opening of the mouth or vigorous lip movement is recommended, do not be afraid to 'make faces'. That will be only temporary. A vigorous muscular approach is necessary from the beginning in order better to articulate the differences between similar speech sounds. It will also help to overcome any tendency towards the more common 'frozen-lip' appearance of many speakers. Once you are beyond the initial stages, you will find your facial appearance becoming one of natural expressiveness, with neither distortion nor the more common 'dead-pan' effect.

Social wits may poke fun at an earnest individual repeating 'How now brown cow' in front of a mirror. They may also jeer at an athlete jogging round a track, stop-watch in hand. But these are the training methods which produce results. More truly ludicrous is an articulation pattern which is muffled and blurred when it could be sharp and clear.

Let both the spirit and method of your articulation practice be athletic. Then, when you are later in a serious speaking situation, better muscular habits will help you. Your articulation will take care of itself, leaving you free to concentrate on the real issues of the occasion.

(2) The Organs of Speech

It will be helpful in understanding many of the explanations in this chapter to study first the accompanying diagram of the speech tract (Fig. 4).

Note that the blade of the tongue is the part just behind the tip.

The **palate** (PAL-et) is divided into two main parts—the **hard** palate which is forward towards the teeth, and the **soft** palate which is further back. By raising the tip of the tongue gradually up and back from the upper front teeth, you can feel that the roof of the mouth is hard, up to a point about midway, and softer from there back.

The **gum ridge**—also called the **alveolar** (al-VEE-o-lar) **ridge**—is that part of the hard palate which is about one-quarter of an inch behind the upper front teeth. Hardly used at all for the articulation of many languages, it is the most important single reference point for the articulation of English.

The **uvula** (YOO-vyoo-la) may be seen in a mirror if you open your mouth towards a source of light. It is a small finger-like projection down from the centre at the back of the mouth. Important in many languages for the articulation of the *R* sound, its use is to be *wholly avoided* in English.

Exercise No. 88

Sketch and label the diagram of the speech tract (Fig. 4) from memory. Check your work against the original in the text.

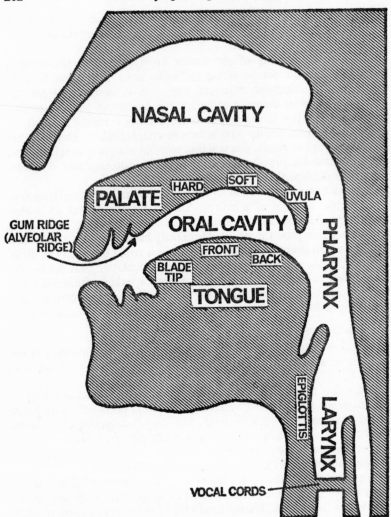

Fig. 4. Diagram of the Organs of Speech

Prepare a clear correct copy on a convenient card or sheet and keep it as a book-mark for reference during your work in the rest of this chapter.

(3) The Importance of Listening

One important organ of articulation is not shown on the diagram. Ordinarily it is not even considered an organ of speech. Yet, in some respects, this organ—the ear—is the most important of all for good articulation.

Have you ever heard the speech of a person who was born deaf? His tongue, teeth, lips and other such organs may be perfectly normal. Yet, unless he has been very carefully trained, his speech is difficult to understand. This is simply because he cannot hear either what his speech should sound like or what it does sound like.

Though our auditory nerves may be normal, all of us are partly 'deaf' to the extent that we do not ordinarily listen to many of the things we are able to hear. The ticking of a watch, the hum of traffic in the distance—these are sounds which our minds habitually ignore. If we listened to them all the time we should never be able to concentrate on anything else.

But if our present listening habits ignore differences in speech sounds, the first and most basic step in speech improvements is *to cultivate the sensitivity of our ears* in detecting shades of difference in them.

It is recommended, therefore, that you turn back to the exercises on ear-training given in Chapter Seven. Then, as individual sounds are explained in detail, and exercises are given for their practice, in the rest of this chapter, listen carefully to the way these sounds are articulated by others—your friends, people at work, speakers on radio and on television.

Note how each of these sounds is articulated by persons whom you otherwise consider to be well groomed, pleasant, competent and well educated. Note also how the same sounds are articulated by persons whom you otherwise consider to be careless, unpleasant, incompetent and poorly educated.

Observe how often the details of speech pattern are just another aspect of the same general type of personality. But also observe how articulation sometimes gives such a mistaken impression of the person that, if improved, it would allow him to present his other qualities to better advantage.

(4) Vowels and Diphthongs

All speech sounds may be classified as either *vowels* or *consonants*.

The **vowels** are those sounds which are relatively unobstructed in articulation by the tongue, teeth or lips. They are represented in spelling by the letters *a, e, i, o, u*, and sometimes *y*, or by some combination of these such as *ie, ei, ai, ou*, etc.

A **diphthong** (DIF-thong) is simply a combination of two vowel sounds articulated together in close succession in the same syllable.

Note, however, that the number of letters used in English spelling does not, in itself, indicate whether a sound is a simple vowel or a diphthong. In some words *two* letters are used to spell a diphthong, as in:

house	HO*W*SS
raise	RA*Y*Z
point	PO*Y*NT

In others, *two* letters may be used to spell a *single vowel* sound as in:

said	SED
tough	TUF
sieve	SIV

Also, some sounds which are really diphthongs are spelled in English with a single letter, as in:

late	LAYT
go	GOH
I	Y = AH plus EE

(For an explanation of how pronunciations such as the above are to be read, see the general explanation at the beginning of Chapter Eight.)

Exercise No. 89

Which of the following words contain single vowel sounds, and which contain diphthongs?

1. do	5. house	9. raise	12. sieve
2. day	6. late	10. I	13. seek
3. dog	7. lease	11. said	14. poet
4. go	8. point		

The Special Role of Vowels in Speech

Although there are only five vowel letters in our alphabet, most English-speaking people use at least 20 different vowel *sounds* in their speech. And a large number of the words we most commonly use differ from each other in sound only by relatively small shades of distinction in this wide range of possible vowels.

Consider, for example, how many different words can be formed by putting different single vowels or diphthongs between the first two consonants of the alphabet, B and D. Some are:

bead	bad	buoyed	beard
bid	bide	bawd	bared
bayed	bud	bowed	bard
bed	bode	booed	bird

These 16 different words all begin with the same split-second explosive sound *B*, and end with the similar explosive sound *D*: they are distinguishable by the ear only through a nuance of intervening vowel.

Exercise No. 90

What similar lists of different words can you form simply by placing different vowels or diphthongs between the following other pairs of consonant sounds?

(a) K and D	(c) M and N
(b) K and T	(d) T and N

(Note that we refer here only to *sounds*, and *not* to the *letters of ordinary spelling* which sometimes have nothing to do with sounds. When we refer to words beginning with the sound *K*, we do not mean such words as 'know' or 'knight' even though their spelling begins with the alphabet letter 'k'. But we do mean such words as 'car' or 'queen' even though there is no letter 'k' in their ordinary spelling.)

(5) Vowel Production

It follows from the foregoing that, in order to speak distinctly, we must fully articulate all the many subtle nuances of difference among the vowel sounds.

Since a vowel is the physical result of modifying the basic sound of the voice by a particular shape in the opening of the mouth, *the difference between any two vowels is due to differences in the positions of the jaw, tongue and lips.*

The jaw may be held relatively far *down* with the *mouth* more *open*, or relatively far *up* with the mouth more *closed*.

The arch of the tongue may be held in positions relatively far *forward* or *back*, *high* or *low*, in the mouth cavity.

The lips may be held so as to form a *larger* or a *smaller* opening with different shaped contours and different degrees of *protrusion* or *retraction*.

How all these muscular adjustments are variously combined can be seen most clearly in the case of those sounds which require them in the most extreme degree.

The Extreme Vowels

Consider for a moment the vowels in the following four *B-D* words taken from the list above:

bead (B*EE*D)	booed (B*OO*D)
bad (B*A*D)	bawd (B*AW*D)

In order to enunciate the *EE* sound in *bead* (BEED) very distinctly, you have to:

(*a*) Drop the jaw so that the mouth is open.

(*b*) Arch the front of the tongue to a position high and forward in the mouth cavity, with the tip of the tongue down behind the lower teeth and the sides of the tongue touching the upper teeth or gums (Fig. 5).

(*c*) Relax the lips completely—if there is tension in the lips or if they are stretched back the sound will be strained and pinched.

For good clear enunciation of the *A* sound in *bad*, you have to:

(*a*) Drop the jaw further open—you should be able to place two fingers between the teeth.

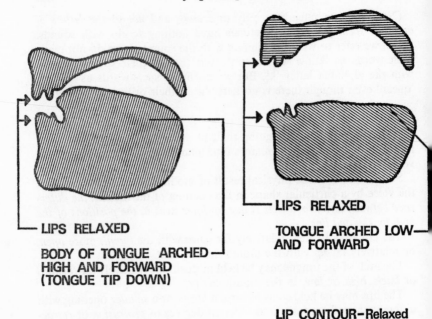

LIPS RELAXED

BODY OF TONGUE ARCHED HIGH AND FORWARD (TONGUE TIP DOWN)

LIPS RELAXED

TONGUE ARCHED LOW AND FORWARD

LIP CONTOUR—Relaxed

LIP CONTOUR—Relaxed

Fig. 5. Making the *EE* sound in the word 'bead'

Fig. 6. Making the *A* sound in the word 'bad'

(*b*) Flatten the arch of the tongue so that it is low and relaxed in the mouth cavity.

(*c*) Again relax the lips.

(*d*) Open the lips to a large circular shape (Fig. 6).

For the *AW* sound in *bawd*, you have to:

(*a*) Drop the jaw down so that the mouth is again wide open (Fig. 7).

(*b*) Flatten the tongue so that its arch is low and back in the mouth cavity.

(*c*) Protrude the lips to a position somewhat forward from the teeth.

(*d*) Narrow the opening of the lips to a tall oval shape.

For good clear enunciation of the *OO* sound in *booed*, you have to:

(*a*) Drop the jaw somewhat less, as for *EE*.

(*b*) Arch the back of the tongue to a position high and back in the mouth cavity.

(*c*) Again protrude the lips to a position somewhat forward from the teeth.

(*d*) Round the lips to a small circular contour (Fig. 8).

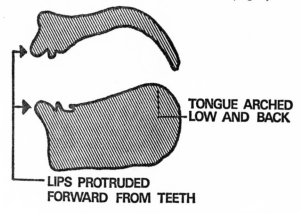

TONGUE ARCHED LOW AND BACK

LIPS PROTRUDED FORWARD FROM TEETH

LIP CONTOUR Tall and narrow

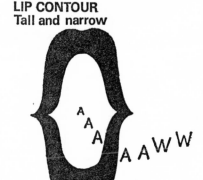

Fig. 7. Making the *AW* sound in the word 'bawd'

Consider now the following diagram (Fig. 9) of possible placements of the arch of the tongue in the mouth. The divisions *front*, *centre* and *back* indicate how far forward or back in the mouth the tongue is arched. The divisions *high*, *mid* and *low* indicate whether the tongue is arched very high with a relatively small jaw opening, moderately high with a medium jaw opening, or is allowed to drop very low with a wide jaw opening.

The four sounds we have just described are located at *the four extreme corners*.

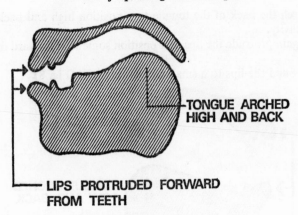

LIP CONTOUR
Small and round

Fig. 8. Making the *OO* sound in the word 'booed'

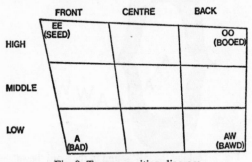

Fig. 9. Tongue-position diagram

EXERCISE NO. 91

Sketch the tongue-position diagram from memory.
Check your result against Fig. 9.
Prepare a corrected version to add to your place-marker for convenient reference during your work in the rest of this chapter.

Although everyone *tends* to make the above-described muscular adjustments in forming these vowels, many people do so only in a cramped, half-hearted way. With their jaw muscles too tense, their mouths too closed, or their lips held too rigid, they literally do not allow themselves room in which to articulate such sounds properly.

Remembering what was said earlier about an athletic approach to articulation practice, therefore, approach the following exercises in this manner:

(i) Let the jaw drop *freely* and low enough so that the movements of the tongue are not cramped.

(ii) Arch the tongue *accurately* in both directions of its prescribed movements, forward and back, up and down.

(iii) Make full use of the lips, *vigorously* protruding them in the various required contours, or relaxing them where necessary.

During practice, *consciously exaggerate* all these movements. Watch in a mirror that your mouth is really open wide enough, that your lips are really moving as you intend them to. The more accurately and energetically you go about it, the clearer your resulting articulation will be.

EXERCISE NO. 92

In the manner described in the text, practise making each vowel sound at the four corners of the above diagram (Fig. 9). Watching in your mirror, be sure that:

EE is made with the arch of the tongue forward and with the lips relaxed.

AW and *OO* are both made with the arch of the tongue back and with the lips protruded in narrow contours.

A and *AW* are both made with the jaw down, the teeth about two fingers' width apart. The lips are relaxed for *A* and forward for *AW*.

EE and *OO* are both made with the arch of the tongue raised: right forward for *EE* and lower for *OO*. The lips are relaxed for *EE* and forward to a small rounded shape for *OO*.

A and *EE* both have relaxed lips.

Articulate the same four sounds, one after the other, in different sequences, prolonging each for several seconds:

EE . . . A . . . AW . . . OO . . .
EE . . . OO . . . AW . . . A . . .
EE . . . A . . . EE . . . AW . . . EE . . . OO . . .
A . . . EE . . . A . . . OO . . . A . . . AW . . ., etc.

With similar attention to the clear articulation of the vowels, practise each of the following columns of words separately several times:

EE	A	AW	OO
bead	bad	bawd	booed
heed	had	hawed	who'd
heel	Hal	hawl	who'll
heat	hat	haughty	hoot
Keats	cat	caught	coot
mead	mad	Maude	mood
geese	gas	gauze	goose
lead	lad	laud	looed
she	shall	shawl	shoe
deed	dad	Daw	do

With the same precautions, work back and forth across the lines in the above columns. Vary the sequence, prolonging each sound for several seconds.

The Front Vowels

Again from our original list of *B-D* words, consider now the following:

    (1) *bead* (BEED)
    (2) *bid* (BID)
    (3) *bayed* (BAYD)
    (4) *bed* (BED)
    (5) *bad* (BAD)

With the words so arranged, their vowels are approximately in the same relative places as the corresponding tongue positions required to articulate them. On the front part of the tongue-position diagram for vowels, they would be placed as shown in Fig. 10.

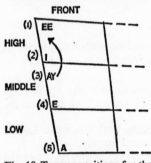

Fig. 10. Tongue positions for the 'front vowels'

Since *AY* is a diphthong, only the first part of it is in the position indicated above. Its second part is usually somewhere between *I* and *EE*, and for its articulation the arch of the tongue moves as is shown approximately by the arrow.

The most important thing to note in the above diagram, however, is that *there are five distinct vowels to be a articulated with the tongue at almost the same distance forward in the mouth.* The main difference in the production of all these sounds is in the dropping of the jaw, the height of the tongue positions, and the contours of the lips.

Obviously, if the jaw is held tight, the mouth nearly closed, and the lips rigid, all these sounds will be so 'jammed down' on each other that their differences will be difficult to hear distinctly.

Exercise No. 93

With the same precautions as in the preceding exercise on the corner vowels, practise positioning each of the above front vowels. Using your mirror, see that your mouth opens successively wider as you work from (1) *EE*, to (2) *I*, then to (3) *AY*, (4) *E* and (5) *A*.

Articulate all five sounds in varying sequences, prolonging each several seconds as in the preceding exercise, for *EE, A, AW* and *OO*.

Practise each of the following columns of words separately for distinct articulation of the vowels:

EE	I	AY	E	A
bead	bid	bayed	bed	bad
meet	mit	mate	met	mat
dean	din	Dane	den	Dan
teen	tin	Taine	ten	tan
keel	kill	kale	Kell	Cal
heed	hid	Hade	head	had
keet	kit	Kate	Kett	cat
peek	pick	opaque	peck	pack
keep	Kip	cape	kept	cap
week	wick	wake	Weck	whack

Work back and forth across the lines of the above columns, emphasizing articulation of the differences between the vowels.

The Low Vowels

Also from the original list of *B-D* words, consider next:

		U	AW
		(7) bud	(9) bawd
A	Y		AH
(5) bad	(6) bide		(8) bard

Once more, with the words so arranged, their vowels are approximately in the same relative places as the corresponding tongue positions required to articulate them. On the lower part of the tongue position diagram for vowels, they are situated as shown in Fig. 11.

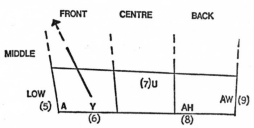

Fig. 11. Tongue positions for the 'low vowels'

As in the preceding case of *AY*, only the first part of the *Y* sound is strictly in the position indicated above. The second part of this diphthong is in the area of *EE* or *I*, and for its articulation the tongue moves as shown by the arrow.

The most important thing to note here, however, is that *there are five different vowels to be articulated with the jaw down and the tongue arched at almost the same distance from the roof of the mouth.* The principal difference in the formation of these sounds is in the degree to which the tongue is pushed forward or pulled back, and in the corresponding contours of the lips.

EXERCISE NO. 94

Apply the methods of the first two parts of the preceding exercise to the low-vowel sequence from (5), *A*, to (9), *AW*. Watch in your mirror that the lips gradually narrow their contour and protrude, in the movement from *A* to *AW*, and that the jaw remains down and relaxed for all of them.

As in the third part of the preceding exercise, practise the following, up and down the columns, and back and forth across the lines, emphasizing distinct articulation of the vowels.

(5) A	(6) I	(7) U	(8) AH	(9) AW
bad	bide	bud	bard	bawd
cat	kite	cut	cart	caught
tack	tike	tuck	stark	talk
Dan	dine	done	darn	dawn
hack	hike	Huck	hark	hawk
lack	like	luck	lark	law
gal	guile	gull	gala	gall
bat	bite	but	barter	bought
sad	side	sud	Sade	sawed
sat	site	Sutter	psalm	sought

The Back Vowels

Again from the list of *B-D* words, plus the additional word 'wood,' consider the following:

(12) *booed (OO)*
(11) *wood (UU)*
(10) *bode (OH)*
(9) *bawd (AW)*
(8) *bard (AH)*

The arrangement is again one in which the vowels are approximately in the same relative places as the corresponding tongue positions required to form the sounds. On the 'back' portion of the tongue-position diagram for vowels, they would be placed as shown in Fig. 12.

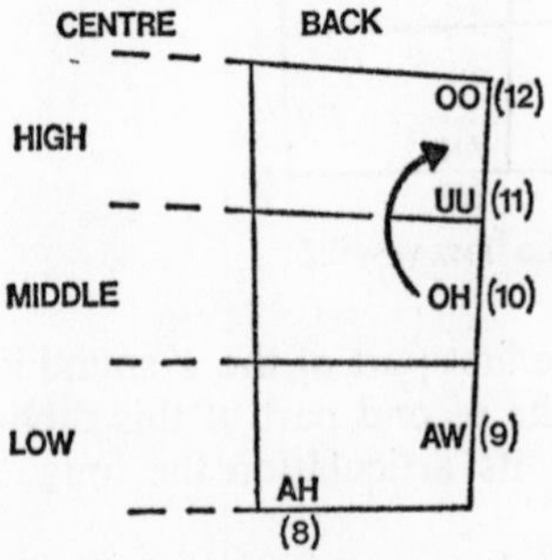

Fig. 12. Tongue positions for the 'back vowels'

As in the preceding cases of *AY* and *Y*, only the first part of the diphthong *OH* is in the indicated position, the second being in the area to which the arrow points.

Note, however, that once again *there are five distinct vowels to be articulated with the tongue at almost the same distance from the front of the mouth.* As with the front vowels, the main differences in the production of these sounds are in the dropping of the jaw, the height of the tongue positions, and the corresponding contours of the lips.

Once more your practice must emphasize the successively wider openings of the mouth from top to bottom of the chart, and the corresponding protruded formations of the lip contours.

EXERCISE No. 95

Apply the methods of the preceding exercises to the back vowels and to the following columns:

(8)	(9)	(10)	(11)	(12)
AH	**AW**	**OH**	**UU**	**OO**
bard	bawd	bode	wood	booed
hard	hawed	hoed	hood	who'd
tarka	talk	toe	took	too
bark	balk	beau	book	boo
lark	law	low	look	Lou
shark	Shaw	show	shook	shoe
hark	hawk	hoe	hook	who
card	cawed	code	could	cooed
Carl	caulk	coke	cook	coo
shah	pshaw	showed	should	shoo

The Central Vowels

Centred as to tongue position in the mouth are the vowels in the following words:

(13) bird (*UR*)

(14) *ago* (*a*)

(7) bud (*U*)

The relative positions in the tongue-position diagram are shown in Fig. 13.

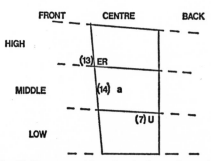

Fig. 13. Tongue positions for the 'central vowels'

Possibly because of its less extreme tongue position the vowel *UR* (13) is sometimes confused with *U* (7), as when *first* becomes FUSST. Thus we get the inelegant word, 'bust', or 'busted', from 'burst'.

The vowel *UR* is more commonly confused, however, with the diphthong *OY* which consists of *AW* followed by *I* or *EE*. Note that the movement of the tongue in saying *OY* must be from a position

H

below and behind that of *UR* for *AW*, to one above and in front of it for *EE*.

The remaining vowel, *a* as in fath*er*, pict*u*re etc., is called the neutral vowel because, while articulating it, the tongue remains in a relaxed neutral position—neither high nor low, front nor back. It is used only in unaccented syllables and unstressed words (see *Over-Articulation*, page 230).

EXERCISE NO. 96

Pushing the tongue deliberately up and forward for *UR* and pulling it deliberately back and down for *U*, practise the following, reversing order, etc., with strong vowel distinctions:

(13)	(7)		(13)	(7)
UR	**U**		**UR**	**U**
bird	bud		turn	ton
curd	cud		burn	bun
third	thud		fern	fun
lurk	luck		burst	bust
Turk	tuck		curl	cull

Holding the tongue as for *UR* in the first part of this exercise, and emphasizing the separate components *AW* and *EE* in the diphthong *OY*, practise the following, varying the order, etc.:

(13)	(15)	(13)	(15)
UR	**OY**	**UR**	**OY**
earl	oil	Berle	Boyle
bird	buoyed	hurl	Hoyle
curl	coil	learn	loin
furl	foil	Kern	coin
first	foist	adjourn	adjoin

Combine the two preceding practices with variations of:

(7)	(13)	(15)
U	**UR**	**OY**
cull	curl	coil
bud	bird	buoyed
tuck	Turk	toy
fun	fern	Foy
cud	curd	coy, etc.

All the vowel groups we have studied may be put together in a single diagram, as shown in Fig. 14.

As before, arrows point to the second part of sounds which are usually 'diphthongized'.

EXERCISE NO. 97

Sketch and label Fig. 14 from memory. Check your work against the original in the text. Then prepare a clean copy to add to your place marker for convenient reference elsewhere in this chapter.

Making a rough sketch of the nine-boxed plan of the diagram on page 215, write in the *B* . . . *D* words 'bead, bid, bad . . .' etc. so that their vowels are correctly placed as to tongue position. Do the same with the *K* . . . *D*, *K* . . . *T*,

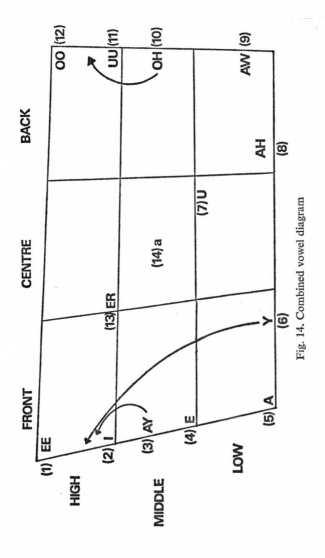

Fig. 14. Combined vowel diagram

M . . . N and *T . . . N* words given in answer to Exercise No. 90. Put an X where no word is supplied, as shown in Fig. 15.

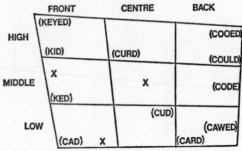

Fig. 15. Diagram for use with Exercise No. 90

In the manner of previous exercises on separate groups of vowels, practise distinguishing all the vowels on the above chart, varying sequence, etc.

Do the same for the word series used in the practices above on *B . . . D*, *K . . . D*, *M . . . N* and *T . . . N* words.

Do the same for the vowels in the following sentences:

    (i) He meets Steve three times each week.
    (ii) Little Kit bit the pit in his mitt.
    (iii) Lane and Jane stayed away all May.
    (iv) Let them set the rest of the mess on the deck.
    (v) Mack ran back after the bag and the basket.
    (vi) By and by the kite will fly high in the sky.
    (vii) The hunter cut up the unlucky duck for supper.
    (viii) Clark's dark pot is not on the hot spot.
    (ix) Claude sorted all, short and tall, along the wall.
    (x) Going home slowly, Joe stole the whole show.
    (xi) By hook or by crook, get a look at that book.
    (xii) Who will do for you what you won't do for Lou?
    (xiii) Her first words were pert, curt, and worldly.

Distortions

Now that the general pattern of all the basic vowels has been presented, we conclude our study of them with a look at certain distortions which cross lines of division between the groups so far considered separately.

Ea for A. If the mouth has been habitually held too closed, the *A* sounds in *bad* tends to become more like the diphthong in *bared.* Then a sentence like *The mAn put his hAnd on the bAnjo* sounds like *The mEan put his hEand on the bEanjo.*

A glance at the Vowel Chart (Fig. 14) should suggest why this happens. With the jaw placement too tight for proper *A* tongue placement, the nearby *E* sound is articulated instead and glides off into a neutral vowel to complete the substitution.

OY for Y. A similar explanation may be given for the tendency of the diphthong *O Y* sometimes to be substituted for *E YE*. When *I'll have a fine time* sounds more like *O Yll have a fOYn tOYm*, muscular tightness is probably keeping the back of the tongue humped too close to the roof of the mouth and the lips too close together.

AOW or EOW for OW. In the same type of tight-jawed articulation, *Brown is down town* sounds more like *BrAOWn is dAOWn tAOWn* or *BrEOWn is dEOWn tEOWn*.

EXERCISE No. 98

Go back to the front-vowel practices (Exercise No. 92). Then practise the words in the columns below, reinforcing the distinction between the *A* in the first column and the *Ea* in the third column by means of the intermediate *E* in the second column.

A	E	Ea
bad	bed	bared
tan	ten	tear
can	ken	care
ban	Ben	bare
man	men	mare
cad	Ked	cared
fan	fen	fare
than	then	there
ran	wren	rare
barrow	berry	bearing

Go back to the low-vowel practices (Exercise No. 93). Then practise the words below in the same manner as those above, ending with strong distinctions between the diphthongs in the first and last columns.

OY	AW	AH	Y
buoyed	bawd	bard	bide
soy	saw	Saar	sigh
toyed	tore	tar	tide
jo	jaw	jar	jibe
boy	bore	bar	by
Lloyd	law	lard	lied
poise	pause	pa's	pies
coy	caw	car	kite

Practise the sound distinctions between *E*, *A* and *AH* in the first three of the following columns. Then practise the fourth column, making sure the jaw is well down so that the first vowel in the diphthong is clearly the *AH* of the third column.

E	A	AH	OW
bed	bad	bard	bowed
den	Dan	Don	down
Ked	cad	card	cowed
net	gnat	not	knout
led	lad	lard	loud
let	Latt	lot	lout
hell	Hal	Harley	howl
sped	spat	Spartan	spout

Also:

How loud is the sound of mountain fountains!

Howard found no clowns in our sound town.

(6) The Consonants

Consonants are those speech sounds in which the voice or breath is partially hindered by some combination of the tongue, teeth, lips or other organs of articulation. They include all speech sounds other than the *vowels*.

The various kinds of consonants will be defined as their articulation is discussed.

The Alveolars

We are easily amused at the innocence of the small boy who thought that 'The people in China must be awfully clever to be able to speak so unusual and difficult a language as Chinese!' Yet, we are all a little like this lad.

We find it hard not to think of the language we have always spoken as 'natural', and the other languages as somehow 'out of the ordinary'. However, in the general pattern of articulation, it is English which is exceptional.

In most languages, the group of sounds which include the *T, D, N, L, S* and *Z*, are called **dentals** or **linguo-dentals.** That is because they are actually articulated by placing the tongue (Latin: *lingua*) on the teeth (Latin: *dentis*). People who speak some of those languages normally let the tongue lie on the lower jaw with the tip behind the lower teeth. They sound their dentals by lifting the jaw so that the blade of the tongue touches the upper teeth. The movement is much like that of biting.

In English, however, the true linguo-dentals are the *TH*'s—sounds which do not occur at all in most other languages. We more properly call our *T, N, S,* group **alveolars** (al-VEE-o-lahrz) because they are articulated on the **alveolar ridge** (gum ridge).

Moreover, although we have so far worked only on the vowels, *we cannot altogether separate our articulation of the vowels from that of the consonants.* No matter how much we practise such sounds as *E* or *AW* individually, we shall form them differently in words like 'dead' or 'taught' if our *D*'s and *T*'s are dentalized than if they are articulated on the alveolar ridge. In one respect, the vowels are merely voiced transitions from one consonant to another. As with any other movement, that of the tongue in forming vowels depends partly on where it starts from and where it goes to.

Work on this group of consonants, therefore, involves much more than the improvement of a few individual sounds. *How we articulate the alveolars affects almost the entire structure of our speech pattern.* By starting our consonant work with them we can accomplish more, from the outset, than by any other means.

In order to improve any of the alveolars, however, we must first strengthen the tongue muscle for high placements independent of the lower jaw.

EXERCISE NO. 99

Watching in a mirror, open your mouth wide as for *A*, and raise the tip of the tongue to the upper teeth.

Then gradually draw the tip of the tongue up along the centre of the hard palate as far as you can while keeping the jaw down and the lips relaxed.

You should be able to do this to a point at about the centre of the roof of the mouth, where the soft palate begins. But if your tongue has habitually been held too low, or left habitually lying on the lower jaw and lifted only with a biting motion of the jaw, you may not at first be able to reach so high. Do not, however, close the mouth in order to reach higher with the tongue. Keep the lower jaw down and proceed with the tongue tip at the highest point you can reach. Gradually, as the tongue muscles become stronger and more flexible with repeated practice, you will be able to raise the tip higher.

On the roof of the mouth, trace a small clockwise circle with the tip of the tongue. Then reverse direction to anti-clockwise, tracing numbers and other figures in the circle, etc.

Check in your mirror that the facial muscles are relaxed and that the jaw is not 'wagging' with the above routine. Movement should be localized in the tongue itself.

Of course, no actual sounds are made with the tongue in the positions of the above exercise. It is a basic routine for limbering, stretching and strengthening the tongue muscles. It cannot profitably be continued for more than a few minutes at a time. But you should return to it regularly at the beginning of each practice session.

The N sound. The easiest to articulate of all the alveolars is the *N*, so we shall start with it in order to be able, later, to transfer its placement to the others in the group.

EXERCISE NO. 100

Opening the mouth wide, sound the vowel *A* for three beats. Then, watching in your mirror that the jaw and lips remains relaxed in the *A* position, raise the tip of the tongue to the alveolar ridge and continue without a pause, sounding *N* for three beats. Still without a pause, return to *A* for three beats, thus:

A . . . A . . . A . . . N . . . N . . . N, etc.

Do the same for other low vowels:

AH . . . AH . . . AH . . . N . . . N . . . etc.

Watching in the mirror, practise each of the following columns with the mouth remaining open as for the vowels, and with both vowels and *N*'s prolonged:

-N	-N-	N-	N-N
an	Anna	knack	Nan
kine	Heine	nigh	nine
on	honour	knock	non-
own	owner	no	known
cane	caner	nay	inane
in	inner	nick	ninny

In the same manner, practise working across the lines in the above columns.

Since *N* is a nasal sound, we do not actually need to have the mouth open wide to articulate it alone. But we recommend practising it in this way because opening the mouth is relatively easy for the *N*, and because doing so *helps with the articulation of other sounds.*

The T and D sounds. When the tongue has been strengthened for high positions, and when the *N* has been well placed, we can use its placement to help 'anchor' other alveolars to the same ridge.

First will be the *T* and *D*. *Characteristically, in English these consonants have a light, delicately executed sound* which is difficult to obtain when the tongue gets on or near the teeth. Note the differences of tongue, jaw and lip positions in Figs. 16 and 17.

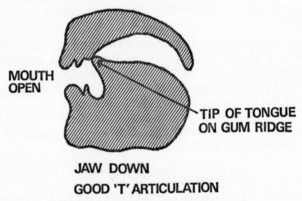

MOUTH OPEN

TIP OF TONGUE ON GUM RIDGE

JAW DOWN

GOOD 'T' ARTICULATION

Fig. 16. Correct articulation of letter 'T'

Exercise No. 101

Practise the following columns as in the preceding exercises, but at the end of each *N*, well positioned on the gum ridge, allow the *T* or *D* to explode lightly and delicately with a quick flick of the tip of the tongue.

Unless the tip of the tongue breaks its contact with the gum ridge sharply and abruptly, there is likely to be a noisy, scraping effect like *Tch*, even though the contact point is correct.

NT	ND	NT	ND
ant	and	went	wend
pint	pined	paint	pained
hunt	gunned	anti-	Andy
want	wand	hunter	under
haunt	yawned	Wanter	wander

Similarly practise expressions such as:

Untie Auntie.
The hunter wanted to hinder the panda.
Candy is dandy for Andy, etc.

After confirming that the *T* and *D* are well positioned by the *N* approach,

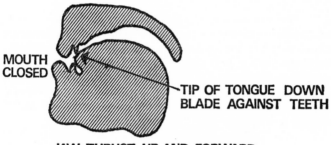

DENTALIZED 'T' ARTICULATION

Fig. 17. Bad (dentalized) articulation of letter 'T'

exercise on these sounds separately in 'tongue gymnastics'. Make sure that both tongue movements and sounds are executed lightly and delicately, thus:

T T T D D D T T T D D D, etc.
T T D D T T D D T T D D, etc.

Combine these tongue gymnastics with practise of the words in the following columns by preceding each with three practice sounds, thus:

T T T	TAHK	D D D	DAHK, etc.
T	**D**	**T**	**D**
tock	dock	at	add
tuck	duck	height	hide
tore	door	Ott	odd
ten	den	net	Ned
tear	dare	ate	aid
Taine	Dane	cat	cad
tone	Doane	tot	Dodd
tent	denned	tight	died
tint	dinned	Tut	dud
taunt	dawned	tat	dad

Practise the following, watching that the *T*'s, in the middle position do no tend to become voiced as *D*'s.

attar	better	ability
otter	bitter	electricity
butter	batter	scarcity

Revise all the above by practising such phrases and sentences as:

Taunted tot.

Tinted tent.

Take a turn at tic tac toe.

Dad aided the dude.

The otter shuddered at the adder.

Better butter makes better batter.

The bitter hatter's heart went pitter patter, pitter patter.

The L sound. *L* is also properly articulated with the tip of the tongue on the alveolar ridge, but the rest of the tongue is narrowed and lowered so that the sound of the voice escapes around it on both sides.

Some people say a sentence like *Please clean the blackboard quietly* more like *PWease queen the bWackboard quitWy*. This is a major speech defect called **lallation** (la-LAY-shn). Its *W*-like substitution for *L* is due to failure to place the tip of the tongue *anywhere* on the roof of the mouth.

Weakness or distortion of the *L*, however, is more commonly caused by failure to place the tip of the tongue high enough, or failure to bring the sides of the tongue low enough.

In the first case, the tip of the tongue is sometimes visible, protruding slightly under the biting edge of the upper teeth. The second case has no externally visible symptom, but the sound takes on the 'Continental' quality of a French or German *L* which is easily detected by the ear.

EXERCISE No. 102

Revise the preceding *N*, *T* and *D* exercises.

Practise the following slowly, being careful to place the *N*'s high on the alveolar ridge and to release only the sides of the tongue for the following *L*'s. Say the two-word expressions continuously as though they were one ('caN ... L ... ead', etc.):

NL	NL	NL
only	can-lead	Dan-lied
unlike	none-lit	Nan-led
inlay	tin-lamp	one-land
in-law	tan-light	fine-lawn

Practise the following in a similar manner, using the *T* and *D* this time to anchor the *L* to the alveolar ridge.

TL	DL
neatly	oddly
nightly	madly
went-late	maudlin
outlay	odd-lad

When followed by an alveolar, the *T* and *D* should not be allowed to explode as when followed by a vowel. This muffling of the explosion in the next sound is called **implosion** and the *T* or *D* is said to be **imploded**.

To check that the *L* sound *remains* positioned on the alveolar ridge throughout its duration, practise the following, with attention to the placement of the *N*'s, *T*'s and *D*'s.

LN	LT	LD
ill-now	all-tuned	all-day
all-night	I'll-talk	I'll-do
call-none	all-told	ill-done
I'll-need	ale-tank	tall-dam

The following is to help lower the sides of the tongue and so clarify the *L* sound. Sound a prolonged *A* vowel, watching jaw and lip positions in your mirror. Then alternate with prolonged *L*'s well positioned on the alveolar ridge. Do the same for all the other vowels on the vowel chart, beginning with the lower ones and working to the higher, thus:

A . . . L . . . A . . . L . . .,
AH . . . L . . . AH . . . L . . .,
E . . . L . . . E . . . L . . ., etc.

Apply the same precautions to practice of the following words:

-L	-L-	L-L
Al	alley	lall
aisle	tiling	lisle
owl	towelling	lull
ell	Ollie	loll
ill	tiller	Lil
Ole	holy	lowly

Since the *L* is more likely to cause difficulty after *P*, *B*, *K* or *G*, practise the words in the following columns in two stages, first without the preceding stopped sounds, then with them, thus:

L . . . ACK,   PL . . . ACK, etc.

PL	BL	KL	GL
plaque	black	clap	glass
ply	blithe	clam	glamour
pluck	blood	clot	glottis
plot	blot	clay	glaze
plea	bleed	clue	glue

Apply all the foregoing to practise of such expressions as:

Tra-la-la-la-la-la. Tra-la-la-la-la.
Lovely, lowly lily, etc.

The Sibilants. The last group of alveolars, *S*, *Z*, *SH* and *ZH*, are commonly called *sibilants* because of their hissing sound. They are perhaps the most commonly mis-articulated sounds in speech.

S and Z. Properly to form the *S*, the tongue should seal off the escape of air along the gum ridge except at the very centre where a single thin stream of air should be allowed to pass between the ridge and the tip of the tongue. If the lower lip is held a bit down, and the lower teeth are held slightly down and behind the upper teeth as when in position for a normal bite, there will be as little interference as possible with the escaping breath stream.

Sigmatism is a general name for the speech defects which occurs when this is not properly done.

In the extreme case where the tongue is pushed forward very bluntly on to the biting edge of the teeth, there is a *TH*-like substitution, as when *Sister Suzie* is made to sound like *THiTHter THuTHie*. Sometimes the sound is also *faked*, however, by bringing the lower lip to the upper teeth with a result more like *FSiFSter FSuFSie*, with *FS* used here to indicate a sort of hissing *F*-like sound. Both of these cases are more commonly called *lisping*.

Faulty tooth alignment or spacing, especially if it dates from childhood, sometimes encourages habitual tongue placement which allows the breath to escape at one side rather than at the centre of the tongue. This is technically known as *lateral emission*.

The most common trouble with *S* articulation, however, is due to low placement of the tongue. The resulting low S, as it is called, may be 'whistling' if the sound is worked into the groove between the two upper front teeth; or, it may be 'noisy' or 'sibilant' if the tongue placement is less firm and if the opening formed is too wide.

Exercise No. 103

Revise the *N* placement exercises and the *T* and *D* tongue gymnastics above.

As in the above exercises for *T* and *D*, make use of the easy placement of *N* to position *S* and *Z* in the following:

NSN	NZN
dance-now	Don's-not
once-new	one's-new
ounce-net	owns none
tense-neck	Dane's-net
wince-not	wins-now

Ensnare one's net on snow.
He wins not who earns not, etc.

Make similar use of *N*, *T* and *D* placements in practising:

NTST	NDZD
wants-to	pond's-dry
can't-stay	lands-down
Aunt-Stella	ends-day
won't-stop	bends-down
bent-stick	finds-Dad

With no further help from preceding *N*'s now make use of *T*, *D* and *L* placements alone to position *S* and *Z*. It is useful to combine this drill with tongue gymnastics in four steps as follows:

```
T T T HAT              D D D ADD
T T T HATS             D D D ADDS
T T T . . . TORE       D D D . . . DOWN
T T T HATSTORE, etc.   D D D ADDSDOWN, etc.
```

TST	DZD	ISL	IZL
hat-store	adds-down	will-slip	Will's lap
hot-stove	kneads-dough	fill-slowly	fills-lamp
meat-stew	kid's-doll	call-slyly	calls-lad
neat-sty	bird's-dead	tell-Slim	tells-Linda
let-stay	lad's-day	cool-slate	cools-lips

To avoid contracting *STS* to a mere prolonged *S*, practise the following, holding the first *S* for a moment, then saying the *TS* quickly and lightly, almost as if saying one sound: *cas-ts* for example.

casts	fists	coasts
lasts	mists	boasts, etc.

Apply all the above to step-by-step practice of such expressions as:

Suspicious circumstances
Lists of casts, etc.

SH and ZH. Articulation of the *SH* and *ZH* sounds is much like that of the *S* and *Z* except that the tongue is pulled up and back slightly to form a somewhat broader, slit-like opening between the gum ridge and the blade of the tongue just behind the tip.

Because their placement is higher, these sounds are sometimes weak, or lispy, even when the *S* and *Z* are relatively well articulated. Sometimes, too, the *S* tends to sound more like the *SH* when it precedes a *T*.

EXERCISE NO. 104

To strengthen the *SH* and *ZH* sounds, practise them in their common combination with a preceding *T* or *D* as in *chat* (TSHATT) or *jaw* (DZHAW). Work on the following columns may be combined with such tongue gymnastics as:

```
T T T TSH . . .        D D D DZH . . .
T T T TSHAT, etc.      D D D EDZH . . .
```

TSH-	DZH-	-TSH	-DZH
chat	jam	catch	badge
child	jibe	larch	large
chuck	jug	etch	edge
char	jar	'H'	age
Chet	jet	torch	George
chose	Joe's	church	judge

To sharpen the distinction between the *ST* and *SHT*, first practise the following three columns from left to right and from right to left. Then continue in a similar manner with the first and third, leaving out the centre one.

SH-	S-	ST-
shy	sigh	stye
shock	sock	stock
shuck	suck	stuck
Shaw	saw	store
shed	said	steady
shirr	sir	stir
Shay	say	stay

Miss Shaw makes delicious fish-sticks.
She also sells seashells on the seashore, etc.

The Linguo-Dentals

The *true linguo-dentals* of English are, as we have said, the *TH*'s. These may be *voiced* as in 'this' or *unvoiced* as in 'thing'.

The main difficulty with their articulation is due to tendencies to blunt them as dentalized *T*- or *D*-like sounds, or to lisp them as *S*- or *Z*-like sounds.

In either case, these consonants are most troublesome when they occur in combination with the sounds with which they tend to be confused.

EXERCISE No. 105

To strengthen the positioning of the *TH*'s, first *exaggerate* their articulation as follows: protruding the tongue from the mouth, press the blade against the upper teeth and expel the breath while drawing the surface of the tongue slowly back until the tip is just under the biting edge of the teeth. Prolong the sound *in this final position* for several seconds. Then do the same for the corresponding voiced *TH*.

With preliminary *TH*'s articulated as above, practise each of the words in the second column of each of the two groups of columns below. Then practise the words across the page, emphasizing the differences in the key sounds.

T	TH	S
tie	thigh	sigh
tun	thunder	sunder
tore	thaw	saw
tin	thin	sin
tick	thick	sick
pat	path	pass
mat	maths	mass
mit	myth	miss
mental	menthol	mensal
ought-to	author	hoarser

D	Th	S or Z
die	thy	sigh
Dow	thou	sow
den	then	Zenda
dough	though	Zoe
disc	this	Ziss

D	Th	S or Z
bade	bathe	bays
laid	lathe	lays
load	loathe	lows
muddy	mother	muzzle
weeder	either	easier

By breaking the articulation down into easy steps, practise the following until they can be said smoothly. The word *sixths*, for example, is broken down as:

SIK
SIKS
SIKS-TH
SIKS-THS

widths	depths	sixths
breadths	tenths	bathed
lengths	hundredths	loathed, etc.

Apply the same technique to such phrases and sentences as:

Hither and thither through thickets of thistles.
Neither their father nor mother was there.
They measured the depths in tenths and hundredths, etc.

The 'R' Sound

Next to *S*, the *R* is perhaps the most commonly mis-articulated sound.

In other languages this consonant is a trilled or scraping sound made either with the tip of the tongue near the teeth or with the back of the tongue near the uvula. The *R* in English should be formed by placing the sides of the tongue high against the gums at the sides of the mouth.

Most trouble with the sound is due to the high tongue position which it requires. Until their tongue muscles are strong enough and well enough under control to reach this position, most children tend to substitute a *W*-like lip movement for it. Thus, *railway* becomes *Wailway* or *rabbit* becomes *Wabbit*. And the replacement often remains to a greater or lesser degree throughout life.

Some side-mouthed articulation is a one-sided lip substitution for the true *R*.

The sound is also sometimes faultily made by the teeth with a biting movement, or by the lower lip against the upper teeth. In the latter case the substitution may approach the *V*-sound after a *B*, as when *Bring brown bread* becomes more like *BVing, bVown, bVead*.

EXERCISE No. 106

Watching in your mirror that the mouth is kept open as for *AH*, raise the sides of the tongue to a point of contact high on the gums of the back upper teeth, keeping the tip raised, and make a prolonged *R* sound. Then, without pausing between sounds, alternate *R*'s with *AH*'s, thus:

AH . . . R . . . AH . . . R . . . AH . . ., etc.

Do the same with the other vowel sounds in order, beginning with the lower ones. Check that your lips are not making movements as for *W*.

To emphasize tongue, rather than lip, movement, alternate the above exercise with *L's*, thus:

AH . . . L . . . AH . . . R . . . AH . . . L, etc.

Practise the pairs of words in the following columns, emphasizing the above-indicated difference in their articulation especially with regard to lip movement.

R-	W-
rag	wag
right	white
run	one
rod	wad
red	wed
ray	way
row	woe
reel	wheel
rue	woo
reed	weed

To strengthen the tongue in articulating the *R* in the more difficult position after *B* or *P*, practise the following in two steps, thus: ROW, PROW; ROW, BROW; etc.

PR	BR
prow	brow
pry	bright
pray	bray
probe	broke

Similarly, strengthen the first *R* in the following words of special difficulty:

lib*R*ary	(*not* li-berry)
lib*R*arian	(*not* li-berrian)
Feb*R*uary	(*not* Feb-you-ary)

Revise the preceding by careful practice of such phrases and sentences as:

Hurry, Harry, hurry.
Broken railroad tracks.
The arena's a horridly arid area.
The present librarian presided in February, etc.

(7) General Articulation Faults

Omissions

If all the sounds discussed above are well formed, you are not likely to have much difficulty with the others.

There are some common omissions of vowels and consonants which should be given further attention, however, because they give an impression of carelessness and may even result in misunderstanding.

EXERCISE NO. 107

Practise each of the following words carefully as they are indicated in the second column, never as in the third. (The pronunciations are re-spelled only enough to indicate correction of the faults.)

WORD	SAY	NOT
acts	AKTS	AKS
adopts	a-DOPTS	a-DOPS
kept	KEPT	KEP
help	HELP	HEP
didn't	DID'nt	DINT
didn't you	DID-nt you	DIN-tsha
wouldn't	WUD-nt	WUNT
shouldn't	SHUD-nt	SHUNT
going to	GO-ing to	GAWN-a
want to	WONT-to	WONN-a
picture	PIK-ture	PITSH-er
modern	MOD-ern	MOD-n
secretary	SEK-retary	SEK-itary
geometry	jee-OMMetry	JOMM-etry
government	GUV-ernment	GUV-mint
subject	SUB-ject	SUB-zhect

Additions

Sometimes the improper addition of sounds in words is due more to difficulty with their articulation than to actual error in their intended pronunciation.

Extra vowels may be added to words like *athlete* or *film* to make them sound like *A-tha-leet* or *FIL-um*, because the tongue has difficulty passing from the *TH* to the *L*, or because it has difficulty holding the *L* until the lips form the *M*.

Intrusive R's, as they are called, may be inserted into words where they do not belong, as when *idea of drawing* becomes *i-DI-Ruv-DRAW-Ring*. This is usually due to tightness in the jaw muscles which so cramps the movement of the tongue from vowel position to vowel position that *R* is unintentionally sounded during the transition.

Likewise, a *G* sound may be added to the NG between two vowels, as when *singer* is said as *SING-Ger*; but additions of this sort are discussed in more detail in Chapter Ten.

EXERCISE NO. 108

Practise the following as indicated.

WORD	SAY	NOT
athlete	ATH-lete	A-tha-lete
elm	ELM	ELL-um
film	FILM	FILL-um
umbrella	um-BREL-a	um-ber-EL-a
modern	MOD-ern	MOD-er-en
		MOD-ren
idea	i-DI-a	i-DIER
drawing	DRAW-ing	DRAW-Ring

ɪ

WORD	SAY	NOT
law	LAW	LAWR
Asia	AY-zha	AY-zher
India	IN-dia	IN-dieR
Nebraska	ne-BRAS-ka	ne-BRAS-keR

Over-Articulation

In most of this chapter we have stressed the need of clear, strong production of the sounds we have considered. That is because the more common faults are due to weakness or indistinctness of articulation.

At times, however, the opposite error is made: in trying to make their speech more distinct, some people emphasize the wrong sounds.

A common instance of this error is the articulation of *a* and *the* always as *AY* and *THEE*. Take, for example, the sentence:

A man and a woman walked across the Plaza.

Normally, this would be said:

a MAN and a WUU-man WAWKT a-KROSS the PLA-za.

Some misguided speech-improvers, however, deliberately try to say such a sentence as:

AY MAN AND AY WO-MAN WAWKT AY-KROSS THEE PLA-ZUH.

This is no improvement, whatsoever. By reminding the listener of the stumbling of a child reading his first primer aloud, this sort of *artificial over-articulation* is more distracting than helpful. And it sometimes gives the mistaken notion that better articulation is not to be desired.

A similar fault is theatrical *over-explosion* of *stopped sounds—K, G, T, D, P* and *B*—when they come at the end of a word. Consider the sentence:

Bert and Meg went back to the last stop.

Misguided attempts at speech improvement will sometimes deliberately make it sound like:

BerT anD MeG wenT bacK to the lasT stoP.

There is an excuse for something a *little* like this from an actor on the stage of a large theatre with such poor acoustics that it is hard to hear normal speech in the back rows of the balcony. But the actor does this only to make the final consonants sound *normal* in such an auditorium. The artificiality has no place in ordinary speech under ordinary conditions.

Finally, the vowels in unaccented syllables of long words are also sometimes over-emphasized. Consider the expression:

Constitutional convention.

This is reasonably well said as:

kon-sti-TYOO, shn-l kn-VEN-shn

Over-articulated, with stress on every syllable, it may sound like:

KONN-STI-TYOO-SHUN-AWL KUN-VEN-SHUN

But here again, artificial additions to normal articulation distort, rather than improve it.

Speech improvement does require regular, energetic practice. But at certain points it *also needs restraint and good judgement.*

Foreign Influence

If there is a possibility that your speech has been influenced by the speech patterns of a language other than English—you may have been brought up in another country—you should practise the exercises in Chapter Ten on *Foreign Accent,* considering the latter part of that chapter a continuation of this.

FOREIGN ACCENT

This chapter is devoted to special problems of speech commonly called 'foreign accent'. For convenience we will use this term to include also broad 'regional' dialects and the characteristic pronunciations of English-speaking countries overseas. Those who spoke another language before English should study first the sections below on *Stress, Linking* and *Falling and Rising Inflexions.* They should then study Chapter Nine (Articulation) in the light of the suggestions made in the remaining sections. Chapter Seven (Developing the Voice) and Chapter Eight (Pronunciation) should also be studied.

Anyone who feels that his speech contains 'foreignisms', should practise the exercises on those problems, such as the 'NG click' or cognate confusion, which are particularly his.

People with foreign accents sometimes try to *hide* faulty articulation rather than to *correct* it. They talk very softly, as if hoping that their mistakes will not be heard; or very fast, as if at such speed their mistakes will pass unnoticed; or very loud, as if the increase in volume will help them to be better understood.

Such notions and such devices will only make it harder for you to improve your speech.

Adopt a healthy approach. Talk slowly while you are learning, and neither louder nor softer than the people around you. You will make mistakes, of course, and people will notice them, but don't let this disturb you. Study the descriptions given here, practise the exercises, practise them many times, and your accent will gradually improve.

(1) Stress

Accent. English is a stress language. In words of two or more syllables, one is usually said *more loudly*, on a different *pitch*, and is held for a *longer time* than the other syllable or syllables. The stressed syllable is said to be *accented.*

Practise the following words, stressing or accenting those syllables which are printed in capital letters. *Prolong* these syllables, *change* your pitch for them, say them *forcefully*. Make the other syllables *weaker* and *shorter*. (The words have not been re-spelled to indicate pronunciation. Concentrate on *stress*, and do not concern yourself, for the present, with correct individual sounds. The words have been re-spelled for pronunciation in Exercise No. 112, but use that list only after you have practised these exercises.)

DOLL-ar	de-CEIVE	HAPP-i-ness
COW-ard	com-MIT	COW-ar-dice
YEAR-ly	a-BOUT	PAL-a-ces
AL-tar	a-MUSE	ME-te-or
A-ble	de-NY	CHOC-o-late
be-GINN-er	U-su-al-ly	e-CON-o-my
ac-COM-plice	PER-son-al-ly	ex-EC-u-tive
con-SU-mer	OB-stin-a-cy	a-lu-MIN-ium
de-CI-sive	FOR-mid-a-ble	ma-CHI-ne-ry
com-MER-cial	MIN-i-a-ture	la-BOR-i-ous
me-CHAN-i-cal-ly	in -EV-it-a-ble	in-COM-par-a-ble

Secondary Accent. In certain three-, four-, and five-syllabled words, one syllable is stressed *strongly*, and a second is given a somewhat *lighter* stress or accent, being held a little less long and being said with a little less force. Syllables with such *moderate*, or *secondary* stress are printed in *italics* in the list below. The remaining syllables are weak and unstressed.

OR-ga-*nize*	*pi*-o-NEER	ME-di-*a*-tor
MI-cro-*phone*	*per*-son-NEL	DIC-tion-*ar*-y
HOL-i-*day*	*con*-tra-DICT	AR-chi-*tec*-ture
DY-na-*mite*	*un*-der-NEATH	LEG-is-*la*-tive
O-ver-*tone*	*o*-ver-TAKE	MEM-o-*ri*-zing
a-CCOMM-o-*date*	*lo*-co-MO-tive	de-CLAM-a-*tor*-y
e-CON-o-*mize*	*e*-co-NOM-ic	a-POTH-e-*car*-y
con-SOL-i-*date*	*det*-o-NA-tion	au-THOR-i-*ta*-tive
per-SON-i-*fied*	*im*-po-SI-tion	pre-DOM-i-*na*-ting
ca-TAS-tro-*phe*	*pen*-i-CILL-in	con-TAM-i-*na*-ted

in-ge-NU-i-ty	com-*mu*-ni-CA-tion
in-ter-ME-di-ate	de-*ter*-mi-NA-tion
en-to-MOL-o-gy	pro-*nun*-ci-A-tion
math-e-MAT-i-cal	e-*lim*-i-NA-tion
ann-i-VER-sa-ry	en-*cy*-clo-PE-dic

Unstressed Syllables. In weak, *unstressed* syllables, the vowel usually has no very definite quality. It is neutral, indeterminate, the sort of tone one would make if one were simply vocalizing without trying to produce any particular vowel. This sort of sound is used especially when the spelling is *a, o* or *u*. When the spelling is *e* or *i*, the sound may be either the neutral-voice murmur, or a weak EE or I. For -*y* and -*ly* endings, the sound is between EE and I, but closer to EE.

EXERCISE No. 109

Say the lists above out loud once again, using indeterminate or only slightly definite vowels for the weak, unstressed syllables.

Stress in Speech

These stress patterns are part of the structure of the language. Thus, in the phrase, *the first of March,* if one wanted to emphasize the day, one would say:

First

of

the   *March*

But if one wanted to emphasize the month:

March

first

of

the

(See the section on *Intonation* in Chapter Seven.)

Strong and Weak Forms

The words that carry meaning—nouns, verbs, adjectives and adverbs —may have one or more acceptable pronunciations. If English is not your native tongue, when using the dictionary it would be best for you to use the first form listed there. Whatever pronunciation you select, however, say it in approximately the same way no matter how important it is in the sentence. Thus, whether you stress the first syllable strongly or moderately or comparatively lightly, you will always say *offer* as *OFF-er.*

But the small, connecting words of the language, the pronouns, the prepositions, the conjunctions, the auxiliary verb forms, and the articles, have *two* pronunciations. One, the **strong form,** the dictionary pronunciation, is used when we say the word by itself or emphasize it in a sentence. The other, the **weak form,** is used in unstressed positions. The vowels of the weak forms will be neutral and indeterminate. Sometimes they may not even be said. Compare: *That is MY book,* with *THAT is my book,* and *THAT'S my book.*

The following is a list of some of the most common connectives which have two pronunciations, strong and weak. They are arranged according to their use as *parts of speech* and roughly according to their *frequency of occurrence* in English.

Articles: the, a, an

Prepositions: of, to, in, for, with, on, by, at, from, up, into, upon

Conjunctions: and, that, for, as, but, or, than, nor

Auxiliary and Connecting Verbs: is, be, was, have, are, will, had, has, been, were, do, can, must, come, shall, should, am, does, could, would

Pronouns: it, you, he, we, his, our, their, my, him, them, her, your, she, us, some

Adverb: there

Read aloud any paragraph or any group of selections in this book, using indeterminate vowels in all the weak, unstressed words and syllables.

Underline these words and syllables beforehand, if you wish, but *do not re-stress the weak, unstressed syllables and words*. That is, do *not* prolong the indeterminate vowels, do *not* say them forcefully or lift them in pitch. Say them weakly, quickly, blurringly.

(2) Linking Words and Syllables

In English, one sound is *linked* closely to the next. The two-syllable word *seeing* is said with no break between the syllables, the EE flowing smoothly into the I.

An important aspect of this linking is revealed in the way we say the word *feeling*. For spelling purposes we would call *feel-* the first syllable and *-ing* the second. But in talking, the syllables are so linked that it is impossible to tell exactly when the first syllable ends and the second begins. The *l* is as much a part of the one syllable as the other. It is a *link* between the two syllables.

Say aloud one or two words from each group in the preceding lists, trying to link the syllables. Keep on saying them until you can do so without breaking the tone. (There will be minor breaks, of course, for voiceless consonants.)

Words are linked together as well as syllables. In conversation, it is as difficult to say where one word ends and the next begins as it is to separate the syllables.

Link the words in the phrases below, just as you link the syllables in the words above them. Syllable markings have been left out to emphasize the linking.

	SAY		SAY
shilling	SHILLing	**amuse**	aMUSE
He knows	HEknows	**by land**	byLAND
cowardice	COWardice	**beginner**	beGINNer
pulling it	PULLingit	**to find him**	toFINDhim
economy	eCONomy	**organize**	ORganize
The nerve of it	theNERVEofit	**Jim is here**	JIMishere
pioneer	pioNEER	**mediator**	MEdiator
Put it down	putitDOWN	**Spring is coming**	SPRINGiscoming
economize	eCONomize	**economic**	ecoNOMic
I saw the boy	iSAWtheboy	**I saw no one**	isawNOone

declamatory	deCLAMa*tory*
The horn is blowing	theHORNis*blow*ing
ingenuity	*inge*NUity
Who is Sylvia?	*who*isSYLvia
communication	com*muni*CAtion
They never caught him	they*never*CAUGHThim

The tone is broken eventually, of course, at the ends of sentences and phrases, to permit us to take a breath or to separate ideas; occasionally, also, for emphasis. The principles underlying the grouping of words are discussed in the section on *Phrasing* at the end of Chapter Seven. For the present it is much more important for you to learn principles of linking.

(3) Falling and Rising Inflexions

In English a statement ends with a *falling inflexion*. The voice slides down from the original pitch of the last syllable of the sentence, becoming softer until the voice stops.

Sometimes these slides are short and swift, as in saying, *Yes.* Sometimes longer and more gradual, as in saying, *No.* But their movement is always straight and directly downward, and involves a gradual weakening of tone.

Foreigners sometimes say the falling inflexion waveringly. The voice falls, but as if down a bumpy playground slide.

Another fault is to say the inflexion with *two* chief tones, instead of *one*. The foreigner starts on C, slides down to G, pauses briefly, and then continues his slide down.

Be sure that the last syllable of a sentence ending with a falling inflexion is said with only one peak, and that the voice slides down directly and unwaveringly from that tone.

Some words in which the slide would be short and swift are: *gift, bit, heat, type, lock*. Some words in which the slide would be slightly longer and more gradual are: *be, go, fall, tin, glad, now*. The difference depends on the *length of the vowel*, discussed in the section on *Vowels and Diphthongs*, below.

A *rising inflexion* is used to connect ideas, and at the end of questions which do not have a question-word: *apples,/ peaches,/ bananas,/* . . . *Has he gone?/* The important thing about this inflexion is that the voice glides up in pitch from a point at or near the pitch of the preceding syllable.

Foreigners reveal their lack of acquaintance with English by starting the glide up from a pitch which is well above that of the preceding syllable. Instead of *apples* and *he gone* being inflected as/, they are said with a leap in pitch ⌐.

In the following phrases, *glide*, do not leap, up the syllables before the commas:

'We service Fords, Minis, Hillmans . . .'
'of the people, by the people, . . .'
'He heard the bell, went to the door, opened it, . . .'

In the following questions, before saying the rising inflexion of the last syllable, think of the pitch of the syllable you have just said:
'Did he go?'
'Are they here?'
'Have you seen John's book?'

(See the section on *Inflexions* in Chapter Seven.)

EXERCISE No. 112

Practise the following list, which duplicates the material used in this section and the preceding sections of this chapter, with proper stress, linking and inflexion, and with greater care as to pronunciation. The words have been re-spelled to indicate pronunciation according to the scheme used in Chapter Eight.

Say some groups of words as single words with falling inflexions. Say others as words in series, the first four of a group with rising inflexions, the last with a falling inflexion. Go from word to word across the page as well as down.

Return to practise this list occasionally as you work through the chapters on *Articulation* and *Developing Your Voice*.

SHILL-ing	de-SEEV	HAPP-i-niss
KOW-ard	kom-MITT	KOW-ar-diss
YIRR-lee	a-BOWT	PAL-a-sizz
AWL-tar	a-MYOOZ	MEE-te-or
AY-b'l	de-NY	TCHOK-o-lit
be-GINN-er	YOO-zhoo-a-ly	e-KONN-o-mee
a-KOMM-pliss	PUR-son-a-lee	igg-ZEKK-yu-tiv
kon-SOO-mer	OBB-stin-a-see	a-lu-MIN-ium
de-SY-siv	FAWR-mid-a-b'l	ma-SHEE-ne-ree
kom-MUR-shal	MINN-i-a-tcher	la-BAWR-i-us
me-KANN-i-ka-lee	in-EVV-it-a-b'l	in-KOMM-per-a-b'l
AWR-ga-*nyz*	*py*-o-NIRR (NEER)	MEE-di-*ay*-tor
MY-kro-*fohn*	*pur*-so-NELL	DIKK-shon-*ayr*-ee
HOLL-i-*day*	*konn*-tra-DIKT	AHR-ki-*tekk*-tcher
DY-na-*myt*	*unn*-der-NEETH	LEJ-iss-*lay*-tiv
OH-ver-*tohn*	*oh*-ver-TAYK	MEMM-o-*ry*-zing
a-KOMM-o-*dayt*	*loh*-ko-MOH-tiv	de-KLAMM-a-*tohr*-ee
e-KONN-o-*myz*	*e*-ko-NOMM-ik	a-POTH-e-*kayr*-ee
kon-SOLL-i-*dayt*	*det*-o-NAY-shun	aw-THORR-i-*tay*-tiv
pur-SONN-i-*fyd*	*im*-po-ZISH-on	pre-DOMM-i-*nay*-ting
ka-TASS-tro-*fee*	*pen*-i-SILL-in	kon-TAMM-i-*nay*-ted

in-je-NYOO-i-tee	kom-*myoo*-ni-KAY-shon
in-ter-MEE-di-et	de-*tur*-mi-NAY-shon
en-to-MOLL-o-jee	pro-*nun*-si-AY-shon
math-e-MATT-i-kal	e-*lim*-i-NAY-shon
ann-i-VURR-sa-ree	en-*sy*-klo-PEE-dik

the FURST ov *mahrtch*; the furst ov MAHRTCH
that is MY buuk; THAT iz my buuk; THATS my buuk

HEE nohz; by LANND; PUULL-ing it; to FYND'm; the NURV ov it; JIMM is *hirr*; *putt* it DOWN; SPRING iz *kumm*-ing; y SAW the boy; y saw NOH wunn; the HAWRN iz *bloh*-ing; *hoo* is SILL-vi-a; thay *nevv*-er KAWT him

GIFT, BITT, HEET, TYP, LOKK
BEE, GOH, FAWL, TINN, GLADD, NOW

APP-'lz, PEETCH-iz, ba-NAN-az, . . .; hazz he GONN?

we *sur*-viss FAWRDZ, MINN-iz, HILL-manz . . .

UVV the *pee*-p'l. BY the pee-p'l. . . .; he HURD the *bell*, . . . WENNT to the *dawr*, OH-pend it, . . .

did he GOH? ahr thay HIRR?; havv you *seen* jonnz BUUK?

(4) Vowels and Diphthongs

English has both vowels and diphthongs (blends the two vowels). But the foreigner must remember that the English vowels are not 'pure' vowels, in the sense of staying *one* sound from beginning to end. Rather, all English vowels are slightly *diphthongized*, that is, we glide *into* the sound and *off* it. This gliding or diphthongizing cannot be indicated in spelling, but is, nevertheless, part of the essential character of English vowels.

Production of Vowels

In studying vowels in the appropriate section of Chapter Nine, the foreigner may practise individual vowels by holding them steadily for their entire length. But when he says the word lists, he should consciously try to glide *into* and *off* the vowel.

English vowels are squeezed into a narrower compass than those of many other languages. The foreigner has difficulty because some are so 'close' to each other. Thus, French has an equivalent for both the English *EE* and *AY*, but no equivalent for the English *I* which lies between them.

Follow carefully the directions given in Chapter Nine, for the production of vowels, listen to the quality of the vowels used by native-born speakers, and in your practice distinguish particularly between:

EE and *I*	*OO* and *UU*	*A*, *E* and *AH*
AY and *E*	*U* and *UU*	*U*, *AH* and *AW*
	A and *AW*	

Production of Diphthongs

Foreigners may think of diphthongs as two single vowels said separately, one after the other, with about equal value. But English diphthongs are not formed in this way. In English diphthongs one vowel shades into the other, and the first vowel is said strongly and the second very lightly. As a matter of fact, the foreigner should practise diphthongs by saying the first vowel and then gliding *towards* the second.

Practise the diphthongs and the vowels of which they are composed as demonstrated in Chapter Nine, keeping in mind the suggestion just made. Then strengthen your diphthongs by practising the following exercises. Pay particular attention to *AY* and *OH*, for these are not diphthongs but 'pure' or single vowels in the European languages.

EXERCISE No. 113

The final sound in *AY*, *Y* and *OY* should be close to that of *EE*. Read across the page.

EE	AY	Y	OY
he	hay	high	ahoy
be	bay	by	boy
Lee	lay	lie	alloy
see	say	sigh	soy
knee	nay	nigh	annoy

The final sound of *OH* and *OW* should be close to that of *OO*.

OO	OH	OW
who	hoe	how
do	dough	endow
to	toe	kowtow
Lou	low	allow
new	no	now

When followed by a consonant, the final sound in *AY*, *Y* and *OY* may be closer to that of *I*. Read across the page.

EE	I	AY	Y	OY
heat	hit	hate	height	Hoyt
meat	mit	mate	mite	moist
leak	lick	lake	like	———
delete	lit	late	light	loiter
keen	kin	cane	kine	coin

When followed by a consonant, the final sound in *OH* and *OW* may be closer to that of *UU*.

OO	UU	OH	OW
fool	full	foal	fowl
boon	book	bone	bound
noon	nook	known	noun
repute	put	potent	pout
cooed	could	code	cowed

Length of Vowels and Diphthongs

All English vowels and diphthongs may be held for longer or shorter periods of time. Vowels and diphthongs are comparatively long when final, or when followed by voiced consonants such as *b*, *l*, *z*. They are comparatively short when followed by voiceless consonants such as *p, f, s*. (See *Cognate Confusion* below.)

Long	Short	Long	Short
fee, feed	feet, feast	pull	put
bid	bit	rue, rude	root, roost
may, maze	make, mace	burr, bird	Bert, burst
led	let	cub	cup
tag, tanned	tack, tact	lie, lied	life
log, lard	lock	how, house, v.	house, n.
saw, sawed	sought	joy, joys	joist
roe, road	wrote, roast		

The vowel in such words as *half, past, laugh, dance, path* is the long sound *AH*.

Vowels in unstressed syllables are, of course, extremely short. The diphthongs *OH* and *AY* are shortened to single vowels in *rotating, chaotic*.

Final vowels and those followed by voiced consonants will take longer, more gradually falling inflexions; vowels followed by voiceless consonants will have shorter, swifter-falling inflexions.

(5) Consonants

The Alveolars—T, D, N, L, S, Z, etc.

Begin your study of consonants as indicated in Section 6 of Chapter Nine by paying special attention to the explanations of the *Alveolars*, T, D, N, L, S, Z, etc.

The alveolar or upper gum ridge is the focal point for the articulation of English. When we fail to place the tongue there properly, the entire structure of our speech pattern is distorted.

In Fig. 18, the short distance between the teeth and the alveolar ridge may suggest that the difference is not important. But this is a serious mistake. Lifting the tongue to the upper gum for *T, D, N, L* will poise the tongue habitually higher for many other sounds, including the vowels; whereas dentalized articulation permits the tongue to lie, relatively inert, on the lower jaw. In your practice emphasize the exercise for stretching your tongue up to the gum for these alveolar consonants.

The Linguo-Dentals

Next study the linguo-dentals, the *TH*'s. These are included in Fig. 18 for purposes of contrast. You will improve your articulation of these consonants most if you practise *prolonging* them, and then practise sliding the tongue *easily* and *lightly* into position without any sudden, sharp contact. In fact, instead of thinking of touching the tongue to the edge of the teeth, think of keeping the tongue just *away* from the teeth.

The 'R' sound

In studying *R*, remember that you are trying to produce a sound which is probably quite different from your native sound. Avoid trilling

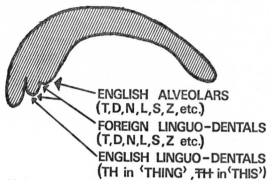

ENGLISH ALVEOLARS
(T,D,N,L,S,Z,etc.)
FOREIGN LINGUO-DENTALS
(T,D,N,L,S,Z etc.)
ENGLISH LINGUO-DENTALS
(TH in 'THING' , TH in 'THIS')

Fig. 18. Tongue positions relative to the alveolar ridge

it. Follow the directions given in Section 6 of Chapter Nine and use these special aids:

Say *TR-* words, such as *trip*, *tree*, lifting the tongue-tip somewhat higher than usual on the gum for the *T*, and then curling it up and back still higher for the *R*. Prolong the *R*, trying for a vowel-like and forward sound.

While prolonging *ZH*, drop the jaw slightly, then raise the point of the tongue towards the roof of the mouth. The resulting sound should be an *R*.

The foreigner must realize that learning to use an English *R* in conversation will take long practice. Begin your study of it early and come back to it from time to time as you go through the remaining consonants here and in Chapter Nine.

The 'W' and 'V' Sounds

The initial sounds of *will* (W) and *veal* (V) should be carefully distinguished. *V* is a friction-sound. The lower lip is raised to the upper teeth, and the voice is sent audibly between the lip and the edges of the teeth.

W is a glide or semi-vowel. To make it, quickly say the vowel *OO* with rounded, protruded lips, and then as quickly move into the following vowel. Practise:

W	V	V	W
way	vain	vote	woe
word	verb	voodoo	woo
wick	Vic	veal	wheel
why	vie	vigour	wig
was	vase	vim	whim

The 'Y' and 'J' Sounds

Some foreigners confuse these sounds. The initial sound of *yes* (*Y*) is a glide or semi-vowel. For *Y*, quickly say the vowel *EE*, the tongue being arched high and front, and then as quickly move into the following vowel.

The initial sound of *jam* and *gem* is thought of as a *J* by English-speaking people, but foreigners will do better to think of it as a *D* plus a *ZH*, the two being said in very quick succession. (See Section 6 of Chapter Nine.)

Practise the following:

Y	DZH	DZH	Y
yam	jam	juice	use
yard	jarred	jeer	year
your	jaw	gyp	yip
yoke	joke	Joe-Joe	yo-yo
yarn	jar	Japan	yap

(6) Cognate Confusion

Most English consonants occur in pairs: the two consonants are identical in articulation except that one is made with the *voice* and the other with the *breath*. Such pairs are called **cognates.** The cognates *T* and *D*, *S* and *Z*, *SH* and *ZH*, the *TH* in *thing* and the *TH* in *the*, and *TSH* and *DZH* (*TCH* and *J*) are discussed in Chapter Nine. Other cognates are *P* and *B*, *K* and *G*, and *F* and *V*.

The foreigner probably has these cognates in his native tongue, but the difference between 'voiced' and 'voiceless' sounds may not be as important there as in English, or the rules for using them may be different. Again, the foreigner may tend to use only voiceless consonants at the ends of words. There is always, moreover, the problem of English spelling.

As a result, the foreigner frequently confuses cognates. Most often his error is to use voiceless consonants for sounds which should be voiced. Thus, in the sentence, *He has no keys*, the foreigner may say, *He haSS no KeySS*, instead of *He haZ no keyZ*. Or in *The dog begs*, he may say, *The doK beKS*, instead of *The doG beGZ*. But he may also do the opposite. In the phrase, *The price of something*, he may say the *pryZZ of ZZomething* instead of *the prySS of SSomething*.

Although cognate confusions are among the most conspicuous traits of foreign accent, they are also among the easiest to correct. Time spent on the following special exercises will bring quick improvement.

First, fix in mind the difference between sounds made with the voice and those made with the breath. Place your fingers on your Adam's apple and say the vowel *EE* very loudly. Prolong it and feel the vibration. Your vocal cords are vibrating: the sound is *voiced*. Still holding your fingers on your Adam's apple, *whisper* an *EE* and prolong the whisper. You will feel no vibration, because the vocal cords are not operating. A whisper is made with breath, and the sound is *voiceless*.

Now say a strong, prolonged *ZZZ*. You should feel as much vibration in your Adam's apple as when saying the *EE*. Keep on saying the *ZZZ* until the vibration-feeling *is* as strong. Now say a prolonged *SSS*. You should feel the same *lack of vibration* as when you whispered the *EE*. Keep on saying the *SSS* until you feel no vibration whatever. You will then have established the difference between voiced sounds, such as *Z*, and voiceless sounds, such as *S*.

Holding a finger in each ear while you say *ZZZ* and *SSS* will emphasize the difference between voiced and voiceless sounds.

Use the same techniques to bring out the difference between the other cognates. Be sure to use the sound *itself*, however, not the *name* of the sound. Use *FFF*, not *EF*; use *VVV*, not *VEE*.

EXERCISE NO. 114

(*a*) Practise the following words, preceding each *S* word with a prolonged *SSS* and each *Z* word with a fully-voiced, strong *ZZZ*.

S	Z	Z	S
ice	eyes	maze	mace
bus	buzz	phase	face
loose	lose	bays	base
cease	seize (SEEZ)	Lee's	lease
hearse	hers	lies	lice
hiss	his	cause	course

Note that these very common words are all said with *Z*: *as, was, has, these, those*.

Remember that vowels are shorter before the voiceless *S*, held longer before the voiced *Z*. When you are sure that you have learned to say the above list with *S* and *Z*, go over it again several times for proper vowel lengths as well as careful differentiation between the cognates.

(*b*) Explode a *T* (the *sound*, not the *name TEE*) with a puff of breath. Say a strongly voiced *D*. Say three such aspirated *T*'s before each of the *T* words below, and three such strongly voiced *D*'s before each of the *D* words. Practise the words in pairs to emphasize their difference.

T	D	D	T
at	add	bowed	bout
height	hide	bud	but
cot	cod	bed	bet
cut	cud	heed	heat
heart	hard	ladder	latter
ate	aid	madder	matter

Note that these very common words have *T*: *it, that, what, not, sit, set, put, shut, first*.

Note that these very common words have *D*: *and, had, would, should, could, hand, second, third*.

(*c*) Similarly practise:

TCH (TSH)	J (DZH)	J (DZH)	TCH (TSH)
batch	badge	ridge	rich
larch	large	urging	urchin
'H'	age	edging	etching
much	smudge	badger	catcher
etch	edge	margin	march in

(*d*) Similarly practise:

F	V	V	F
half	have	believe	belief
safe	save	love	luff
life	alive	believes	beliefs
waif	wave	waves	waifs
leaf	leave	loaves	loafs

The P, T, K, B, D and G Sounds

The consonants *P, T, K, B, D, G* are called **stops**. In making them the voice or breath is momentarily stopped and then released in any one of a variety of ways. *P* and *B* are stopped at the lips; *T* and *D* are stopped by the tongue on the upper gum ridge; *K* and *G* are stopped by the back of the tongue pressing against the soft palate. (*K* is stopped farther forward before front vowels.)

The following pointers should be of special help:

At the beginning of words or stressed syllables, as in *tea, attempt, pie, appear, key, recall*, the stops *P, T* and *K* are released or exploded with a *puff of breath*. The sounds have an '*H*' quality and are called *aspirated*.

But foreigners frequently explode these sounds in these positions *without aspirating* them. To English ears the *P* then sounds like a *B*, the *T* like a *D*, the *K* like a *G*. Though the foreigner is not actually confusing cognates, he *seems* to be doing so.

Practise *P, T* and *K* by allowing air pressure to build up strongly behind the lips, tongue and gum, back of tongue and soft palate, respectively, and then releasing or exploding the air with a strong puffing out of the breath. Practise exploding *B, D* and *G*, with strong voice (feel your Adam's apple), but with *no* puff of breath.

Practise these techniques in the following:

P	B	T	D	K	G
pea	bee	to	do	call	gall
pie	by	tame	dame	coal	goal
pen	Ben	ten	den	come	gum
impose	imbue	attune	produce	recall	against
repute	rebuke	attain	disdain	placate	regain
upon	abuse	return	redo	recur	ago

The above does not apply to *sp-*, *st-* and *sk*-words. In these the *P, T* and *K* are exploded but unaspirated, and have something of the quality of *B, D* and *G*.

Distinguish between the aspirated and unaspirated stops in:

pill	spill	till	still	kill	skill
pie	spy	tie	sty	cane	skein
peak	speak	tier	steer	kin	skin

When two stops occur together in the same or consecutive words, the first is not exploded, but is held very briefly and then the second is exploded: *back door, big day, cup-cake, rub down, sit down, bed-clothes.*

The same is true for double stops: *hot tea, mid-day, book case, big gun, stop payment, tub bath.*

Foreigners should be especially careful to observe this rule where two stops occur together in the same syllable. Say the following words by not exploding the first stop, allowing a moment of silence, then exploding the second: *act, fact, licked, nagged, lugged, apt, rapt, inept.*

When a stop occurs before *L, M* or *N*, it is not exploded, and the air is released on the *L, M* or *N*: *sudden, mitten, little, ladle, at night, midnight, at last, odd lot, Buckley, Bagley, rack man, ragman, acknowledge, ignoble.*

Distinguish carefully between the voiced and unvoiced stops in the above words, even though they are not exploded.

Final stops, if they follow a consonant, are exploded only very lightly: *crisp, bulb, mist, Lent, mind.*

The foreigner with an acute ear will have noticed that final stops which follow a vowel are frequently not exploded at all: *lap, lit, leak, lob, lid, leg.* Whether these stops are exploded or not is of little importance to the foreigner. In any case he should refrain from trying this method of articulation until he has learned extremely well how to explode aspirated initial stops.

Words ending in -d and -ed

The endings *-d* and *-ed* of the past tense and past participle of regular verbs are pronounced:

T if the verb ends in a voiceless sound: *seeped* (SEEPT), *lacked, coughed* (KOFT), *missed.*

D if the verb ends in a voiced sound: *seemed* (SEEMD), *failed, loved.*

ID if the verb ends in a *d* or *t: fainted* (FAYN-tid), *raided* (RAYD-id).

Words ending in -s and -es

The endings *-s* and *-es* of the regular plurals and possessives of nouns, and of the third person singular of the present indicative of verbs are pronounced:

S if the preceding sound is voiceless: *lights* (*LYTS*), *makes, sips, laughs, Kate's.*

Z if the preceding sound is voiced: *needs* (NEEDZ), *John's, calls, seems, goes, legs, cabs.*

IZ if the preceding sound is an *S, Z, SH, ZH: mazes* (MAYZ-iz), *faces, losses, wishes, pitches, colleges.*

(7) 'NG' Clicks and Confusion

The words *finger* and *singer* look as if they should rhyme. Yet the first is said FING-Ger, and the second SING-er. Similarly *linger* and *flinger* are pronounced LING-Ger, FLING-er.

To avoid confusion in pronouncing these and similar words, the foreigner should memorize the following simple rule for the pronunciation of the spelling 'ng':

The spelling 'ng' is pronounced NG-G when it occurs in the middle of a root. Otherwise it is pronounced NG.

The **root** is that basic part of a word from which all related words are formed. Thus, the roots of *singer* and *flinger* above are *sing* and *fling*. A *singer* is 'one who sings' and a *flinger* is 'one who flings'. But a *finger* is not 'something that fings', nor does *linger* mean 'one who lings'. The roots of the latter two are the entire words. The *ng* occurs in the middle of each and so, by the above rule, is pronounced NG-G.

The only important exceptions to this rule are the words *younger, youngest, stronger, strongest, longer* and *longest*. These are pronounced YUNG-Ger, STRONG-Gest, etc.

Learning this rule will help the foreigner to avoid confusion in pronouncing *ng* words. But he may also have to improve his *articulation of the NG sound*. For his native language either may not have the *NG* sound at all, or it may always have the *NG* followed by *G* or *K*.

In the first case he will tend to substitute a sort of *N* for *NG*. *Coming* will sound like *KUMM-in* or *KUMM-een*.

In the second, he will tend to add a *G* or *K* to *NG*. *Going out on Long Island* will be said as *GOH-ing GOWT on long GY-land* or *GOH-ing KOWT on long KY-land*. This is called an **'NG click'**. It is an unmistakable trait of a foreign accent, and the student should work hard to correct it.

Correcting the Substitution of N for NG

With the mouth slightly open, close the mouth cavity by lifting the tongue to the gum ridge, and let your voice resonate in the nose. This is an *N*.

With the mouth open, close the mouth cavity by raising the back of the tongue against the soft palate as if to make a *G*. Allow the voice to resonate in the nose. This is the *NG* sound.

EXERCISE NO. 115

Say several strong *N's* before saying each *N* word below, several strong *NG's* before saying each *NG* word. First read down each column, then read the words in pairs.

N	NG	NG	N
sin	sing	singer	sinner
win	wing	winging	winning
pin	ping	pinging	pinning
thin	thing	thinggumabob	thinner
kin	king	kingly	kinship
hand	hang	hanger	Hannah
tan	tang	tang-y	tanner
Lon	long	longing	clonic
Hun	hung	hung out	Hunnish

Correcting the NG Click

To eliminate the *NG* click *at the ends of words:*
Prolong an *NG*, beginning very loudly and gradually letting the sound die away. Do not move tongue or jaw until the sound has died away completely. Then slowly relax the tongue to a rest position, being careful to avoid even the smallest clicking noise.

Gradually shorten the time spent in letting the sound die away. Then apply the same method to the words in the first *NG* column in the list above. Prolong the *NG* in these words, letting it die away gradually; shorten the time spent in letting it die away; relax from the *NG* position gently and without any click.

To eliminate the *NG* click *in the middle of words:*
(*a*) Emphasize or sharpen the distinction between *NG* and *NG-G*. Say *FING-GER* loudly, stressing *both* syllables, and even saying the second syllable with more stress than the first. Use a strong, voiced *G* to begin the second syllable.

Now say *SING-er* (or *SING-ing*, if you have eliminated the click at the end of words). Say the first syllable loudly and strongly; say the second lightly and weakly, 'tossing it away' so that it is almost unheard.

Using the above technique, say *SINGerSINGerSINGerSINGer* very rapidly, hardly moving the back of the tongue at all.

Contrast *longer* and *hanger* in the same way, 'LONG-GER' and 'HANG-er', 'HANGerHANGerHANGerHANGer'. Feel as well as hear the difference between *NG* and *NG-G*.

Read the words in the second *NG* column above, saying them as you said *singer* and *hanger*.

In *NG* words, say the syllable which follows the *NG* fairly lightly; in *NG-G* words, say the syllable which begins with *G* fairly heavily.

(*b*) Notice that the nasal *M* and the stops *B* and *P* are made with the lips; that the nasal *N* and the stops *D* and *T* are made with the tongue and upper gum; that the nasal *NG* and the stops *K* and *G* are made with the back of tongue and the soft palate.

If, in some foreign language, *M* were always followed by *B* or *P*, and *N* were always followed by *D* or *T*, anyone who used that language as his native tongue would tend to say the English sentences *Jim came home, John ran in*, as:

JimB camB homB	Or:	JimP camP homP
JohnD ranD inD	Or:	JohnT ranT inT

This may seem fantastic, yet the *NG* click is precisely the same sort of articulation effect. And the foreigner can learn to say *NG* properly by comparing it with the way he says *M* and *N*. Consider the words:

simmer	SIM-er	(*Not:* SIM-Ber)
sinner	SIN-er	(*Not:* SIN-Der)
singer	SING-er	(*Not:* SING-Ger)

In *simmer*, the lips part gradually from the closed position for *M*. In *sinner*, the tip of the tongue is released gradually from its contact with the gum ridge as one moves from the *N* to the vowel. If, in either case, the release is sudden or abrupt, like a learner-driver letting out the clutch, the articulation result is an unintended stop-sound, *B* or *D*.

Likewise with *NG*. The back of the tongue must be released *gradually* from its contact with the soft palate, as in the proper operation of a motor-car clutch. Otherwise, just as the car will jolt, so will an unintended *G* or *K* be interjected.

Exercise No. 116

(*a*) Establish the muscular feeling of easy, gradual release of the tongue from the *NG* sound. Practise the words below, prolonging the nasals as follows: DIMM . . ., DIMM . . . er; DINNN . . ., DINNN . . . er; DINNNG . . ., DINNNG . . . er.

dim	dimmer	Sim	simmer
din	dinner	sin	sinner
ding	dinger	sing	singer
whim	shimmer	ham	hammer
win	winner	Han	Hannah
wing	winger	hang	hanger
clam	clammer	Tam	Tammer
clan	clanner	tan	tanner
clang	clanger	tang	tang-y

(*b*) Practise the following for the avoidance of *N* substitutions and for eliminating *NG* click.

Coming and going.
Eating and drinking.
Working and playing.
Coming in and going out.
Climbing up and falling off.
Swinging along.
Singing a song of longing.

(*c*) Practise the following for a strong *NG-G*.

English language.
Anglican Englishman.
Single angler.
Singular angle.
Strongest finger.
Younger wrangler.
Longest tango.

(*d*) Consolidate by practising the following sentences with their mixed *NG* and *NG-G* sounds:

The youngest of the English singers was fingering his song book longingly. The seemingly longer was stronger and the seemingly stronger was longer. The youngish angler lingered along with the angry stranger.

Key (only exploded *g*'s are capitalized):

The young-Gest of the Eng-Glish singers was fing-Gering his song book longingly.

The seemingly long-Ger was strong-Ger and the seemingly strong-Ger was long-Ger.

The youngish ang-Gler ling-Gered along with the ang-Gry stranger (STRAYN-dzher).

Note that words like *stranger* do not come under the above rule or discussion because the *n* in such words has a true *N* sound made with the tip of the tongue. *Range* is said RAYNDZH, and *astringent*, a-STRINN-dzhent. Other words of this type are: *singe, mange, strange, danger, manger, dingy, flange, longevity, harbinger, laryngeal, laryngitis, pharyngeal, pharyngitis.*

Having learned to make *NG* without an *NG* click, be careful not to introduce this sound into words which take *NG-G*. If you find this happening, revise the rule for pronouncing *ng* and practise the last two exercises above.

(8) Consonant Combinations

When two consonants occur together in the same syllable in English, as in *play*, some foreigners will say these consonants as distinctly separate sounds. It is good English, however, to run the sounds together more. The second sound follows the first, of course, but the succession is a very rapid one.

The foreigner will be helped if he adopts the concept that he should preparing for the second consonant while saying the first.

In saying *play*, have the tongue in position for *L* before actually saying the *P*. Use the same technique for *blow, clay, glow*, and other words with the same consonant combinations.

In *crawl, green, pray, brown, free* and similar words, have the tongue in position for *R* before saying the initial consonants.

In *play, clay, crawl, pray, free* and similar words, the puff of air from the initial consonant carries over into the second so that the *L* and *R* are half voiceless, half voiced.

In *tree, draw*, etc., the *T* and *D* are made somewhat higher than usual on the gum ridge to ease the upward movement of the tongue-tip for *R*. In *width, breadth, eighth* (AYTTH), the *D* and *T* are made somewhat lower than usual to ease the movement of the tongue downward for the *TH*.

When three or four consonants occur together, as in *fists, sixths* (SIKSTHS), careless speakers eliminate sounds, using for these words a prolonged *SSS* (FISSS, SIKSSS). Careful speakers will split the combination up into two parts, pausing slightly between the parts (FIS-TS, SIKS-THS). Foreigners, of course, will want to follow the example of careful speakers of English.

(Practice material will be found in the sections entitled *Linguo-Dentals* and *Omissions* in Chapter Nine.)

ANSWERS

EXERCISE No. 28

Question	Answer
(a)	Reports, Treasurer's
(b)	New Business
(c)	Reports, Committee
(d)	Unfinished Business
(e)	Reports, Officers'
(f)	Minutes, Correction of
(g)	New Business
(h)	Reports, Committee
(i)	General Orders

CHAPTER SEVEN

EXERCISE No. 61

In (a) emphasize *bury, praise.*
In (b) emphasize *cowards, many, valiant, once.*
In (c) emphasize *sleep, forgetting.*
In (d) emphasize the words italicized below:

He who *knows,* and *knows* he knows,
He is *wise—follow* him.
He who *knows,* and knows *not* he knows,
He is *asleep—wake* him.
He who knows *not,* and knows *not* he knows not,
He is a *fool—shun* him.
He who knows *not,* and *knows* he knows not,
He is a *child—teach* him.

CHAPTER EIGHT

EXERCISE No. 82

The pronunciations in the first column are the acceptable ones.

EXERCISE No. 83

1, 3, 6, 8, 10 are right in the first column;
2, 4, 5, 7, 9, 11, 12 are right in the second column.

EXERCISE No. 84

1, 5, 10 are right in the first column;
2, 3, 4, 7, 9 are right in the second column;
for 6 and 8, both columns are correct.

Exercise No. 85

4, 5, 7, 8, are right in the first column;
1, 2, 3, 6, are right in the second column;
9, 10, are right in both columns.

Exercise No. 86

1, 3, 7, 9, 10 are right in the first column;
5, 6 are right in the second column;
2, 4, 8 are right in both columns.

Exercise No. 87

1, 2, 3, 4, 10 are right in the first column;
5, 7, 8 are right in the second column;
6, 9, 11 are right in both columns.

CHAPTER NINE

Exercise No. 89

Single Vowels: 1, 3, 7, 11, 12, 13, 14.
Diphthongs: 2, 4, 5, 6, 8, 9, 10, 14.

(The last word, *poet*, has two syllables. The first contains a diphthong, the second a single vowel, thus: POH-et.)

Exercise No. 90

(*a*) keyed, kid, Ked, cad, cud, cod, cawed, code, could, cooed, cued, cared, curd, etc.
(*b*) kit, cat, Kate, kite, cot, cut, caught, coat, cute, coot, curt, etc.
(*c*) mean, Min, main, men, man, mine, moan, moon, Marne, mourn, etc.
(*d*) teen, tin, Taine, ten, tan, Tyne, ton, town, tone, tune, torn, turn, etc.

SUGGESTED FURTHER READING

Acting and Speech for Actors

Actor's Handbook, an, Constantin Stanislavski. Theatre Arts Books: New York, 1963.
Amateur Actor, the, Frances Mackenzie. J. Garnet Miller: London, 1966.
Life of Acting, the, Bertie Scott. Bertie Scott Foundation: London, 1967.
Voice and Speech in the Theatre, Clifford Turner. Pitman: London, 1956.

Anecdotes, Published Speeches, Reference Material for Talks and Speeches

Annual Register of World Events, the, Longmans, Green: London.
Anthology of Oratory, an, A. N. Gilkes and R. H. Ellingworth. E. J. Arnold: London, 1955.
British Humanities Index, the, The Library Association: London, published quarterly.
Classic Speeches, Richard Crossup (Ed.). Vision Press: London, 1965.
Oxford Dictionary of Quotations, the, Oxford University Press: London, 1965.
Public Speaker's Treasure Chest, the, Herbert V. Prochnow. A. Thomas: London, 1965.
Quotable Anecdotes, compiled by Leslie Missen. George Allen & Unwin: London, 1966.
Spoken Word, the, a selection from 'The Listener' chosen by Richard Church. Collins: London, 1955.
Spoken Word, the, an anthology of broadcast talks edited by A. F. Scott. Macmillan: London, 1961.
Stories for Speakers, compiled by Geoffrey J. Matson. Foulsham: London, 1965.
Times Index, the, Times Newspapers: London, published bi-monthly.
Toptable Talk, compiled by Leslie Missen. George Allen & Unwin: London, 1968.
Whitaker's Almanack, Whitaker: London, published annually.

Conversation

Art of Conversation, the, M. Wright. McGraw-Hill: New York, 1936.
Conversation and You, Hitch and Sorenson. Van Nostrand: London, 1964.
How to Win Friends and Influence People, Dale Carnegie. Cedar Press: New York, 1953.

Discussion and Debate

On Speaking Terms, Keith Dadds. E. J. Arnold: London, 1966. (This book is particularly suitable for work with children and students. It also contains sections on argument, reading aloud and lecturing.)

Pros and Cons, a Guide to the Leading Controversies of the Day, Anne Robinson. Routledge & Kegan Paul: London, 1963.

Etiquette and Social Procedure

Complete Etiquette for Ladies and Gentlemen, Ann Page. Ward Lock: London, 1964.
Etiquette Handbook, Barbara Cartland. Paul Hamlyn: London, 1962.

Forms of Address

Complete Etiquette for Ladies and Gentlemen, Ann Page. Ward Lock: London, 1964.
Written and Spoken Guide to Titles, and Forms of Address, L. G. Pine. Elliot's Right Way Books: London, 1959.

Logic and Clear Thinking

Clear Thinking, R. W. Jepson. Longmans: London, 1962.
Clear Thinking for All, Alex Russell. Pergamon: London, 1967.
Elementary Logic, Benson Mates. Oxford University Press: London, 1965.
Logic, W. C. Salmon. Prentice Hall: London, 1968.
Straight and Crooked Thinking, Robert H. Thoules. Hodder & Stoughton: London, 1930.
Teach Yourself Logic, A. A. Luce. English Universities Press: London, 1958.
Thinking to Some Purpose, Susan Stebbing. Pelican: London, 1959.
Use of Reason, the, E. R. Emmet. Longmans: London, 1960.

Parliamentary Procedure and Procedure for Meetings

A.B.C. of Chairmanship, Lord Citrine. N.C.L.C. Publishing Society Ltd.: London, 1952.
Chairman's Handbook, the, Sir Reginald F. D. Palgrave. Dent: London, 1949.

Pronunciation of Standard English

English Pronunciation, Peter MacCarthy. Heffer: Cambridge, 1944.
Everyman's English Pronouncing Dictionary, Daniel Jones Dent: London, 1964.
Pronunciation of English, the, Daniel Jones. Cambridge University Press: London, 1966.

Public Speaking

How to Say a Few Words, David Guy Powers. Dolphin: London, 1953.
Public Speaking, Dale Carnegie. Cedar Press: New York, 1957.
Public Speaker's Pocket Book, the, Carlton Wallace. Evans: London, 1961.
Speaking is Your Business, Vera Gough. English Speaking Board: London, 1963.
Successful Public Speaking, H. G. Garrett, Newnes: London, 1964.

Salesmanship

Manual of Sales Management, a, Institute of Marketing and Sales Management. Pitman: London, 1961.

Toasts

Complete Toastmaster, the, Frederick Berman. Blandford Press: London, 1953.

Speeches and Toasts, and Chairman's Guide, Leslie F. Stemp and Frank Shackleton. Ward Lock: London, 1964.

The Use of Words

English Made Simple, Waldhorn, Zeiger and South. W. H. Allen: London, 1967.

Living Words, D. Butt and J. Merrick. Pergamon: London, 1966.

Voice Production and Speech Training

Improve Your Speech, Audrey M. Bullard. Anthony Blond: London, 1960.

Practical Speech Training, Harry Johnson. Herbert Jenkins: London, 1958.

Speaking With a Purpose, Christabel Burniston. English Speaking Board: London, 1961.

Training the Speaking Voice, Virgil A. Anderson. Oxford University Press: London, 1961.

Voice Production and Speech, Greta Colson. Pitman: London, 1963.

Year's Course in Speech Training, a, Anne H. McAllister. University of London Press: London, 1938.

Speech and Drama, Rose Bruford. Methuen: London, 1948.

INDEX

Accent, 180–81, 184–88, 232–33
Acoustics, 230
Acting, 36
Action groups, organization of, 125–131
Acton, Lord, quoted, 11
'Adam's apple', *see* Larynx
Added sounds, 183, 229–30
Adenoids, enlarged, 172
Adjectives, 178, 186, 188, 234
Adjournment, parliamentary,
    as an order of business, 96
    motion for, 100, 101, 108, 117
Adverbs, 175, 188, 234, 235
Aesop, cited, 73
Affectations, 19, 186–87
Agendas, 90, 91, 96, 141–46
Alveolar ridge, 201–202, 218, 220–25, 240–41, 244–49
Alveolars, 218–26, 240, 241
Amendments, parliamentary, 98–104, 106, 115, 123, 124, 129–31
Archaic pronunciations, 186
Arguments, 2, 8, 11, 51–53, 78–84, 133–36
Articles, 175, 234
Articulation,
    artificial, 230–31
    as muscular habit, 199–201
    foreign influence on, 200, 231
    general faults of, 228–31
    importance of, 199
    of consonants, 218–28, 240–49
    of vowels, 203–18, 238–40
    social influences on, 199–200
Assimilation nasality, 172
Authorities, citing of, 84
Authority to interrupt, parliamentary, 97, 99, 100
Auxiliary verbs, 234

Betjeman, John, quoted, 65
Breathiness, 157–58, 159
Breathing,
    controlled, 159, 160–62
    mechanism, 154
Business interviews, *see* Interviews

Business, parliamentary,
    new, 95–96, 117
    order of, 90–96, 101, 109–10, 112, 114, 132
    unfinished, 94–95
By-laws, 94, 114, 131–33

Chair, the,
    appeal from decision of, 98, 100, 111–12, 123
    rules concerning, 87–89
Churchill, Sir Winston, cited, 45–46
Cognate confusion, 242–45
Colloquialisms, 179
Conjunctions, 234
Consonant sounds,
    alveolar, 218–26, 240, 241
    cognate, 242–45
    combinations, 249
    definition of, 218
    linguo-dental, 218, 226–27, 240, 241
    NG, 245–49
    R, 227–28, 240–41
    stop, 244–45, 247
    voiced and voiceless, 239–40, 242–43
    W and *V*, 241
    Y and *J*, 241–42
Constitutions, 91, 94, 114, 129–33
Conversation,
    definition of, 1–2
    faults in, 11–12, 18–21
    good attitudes in, 9–11
    in business interviews, 1, 2, 22
    stimulation of, 6–8, 12–17
    telephone, 17–18
    topics for, 3–6, 12, 14–17, 21
    with children, 8–9
    with the elderly, 8
    with V.I.P.s, 9
Co-operative discussions, requirements for, 139–41

Deafness, 203
Debates, platform, 133–36
Demagogues, 78
Demosthenes, cited, 37
Denasalization, 172

255

Dialects, 232
Diaphragm, the, 154, 160, 161
Dictionaries, use of, 177–79
Diphthongs, 203–204, 210–14, 216, 217, 238–40
Disagreements, 11, 15
Discord, 4
Discussion,
    informal group, 137–46
    parliamentary, 121–33
    platform, 136–37
    see also Debates *and* Forums
Dogmatism, 2, 10, 11

Ear, training of, 148–49, 162, 168, 202–203
Einstein, Albert, cited, 76
Eisenhower, Dwight D., quoted, 66–67
Enunciation, 29
Exhalation, 160, 161
'Extemporaneous' speeches, 44, 46–47

Fad words, 19
Falling inflections, 236–38, 240
Faux pas, 17
Foreign accents, 177, 200, 231, 232–49
Foreign place names, 197
Foreign words and phrases, 19, 190–95
Forgetfulness, 2, 20–21
Forums, 136–37
Fosdick, the Rev. H. E., quoted, 67
French words and phrases, 19, 192–94

Generalizations, 11
German words and phrases, 194
Gestures, 43
Glottal shock, 157, 158–59
Glottis, the, 153, 157
Grammar, 175
Group dynamics theory, 138–39
Gum ridge, *see* Alveolar ridge

'Having the floor', 90, 91
Health, influence on voice of, 147
Hitler, Adolf, cited, 78–80
Hoarseness, 157, 159
Humming, 163
Humour,
    in conversation, 12
    in interviews, 27
    in public speaking, 40, 50, 65–66
Huskiness, 157, 159

Impromptu speeches, 44–45
Inflexions, 13, 163, 166–68, 236–38, 240
Inhalation, 160, 161
Interpolations, 175
Interviews,
    nature of, 22
    preparations for, 1, 2, 23–26, 28–29
    sales, 31–35

the applicant in, 22–28
the employer in, 28–31
Intonation, 163, 165–66
Introductions,
    at formal functions, 55
    development of, 14–15
    importance of, 7–8, 20–21
    on the telephone, 17–18
    principles of, 12–14
Irony, 140
Italian words and phrases, 194

Jargon, 41, 75
Job interviews, *see* Interviews
Johnson, Dr. Samuel, quoted, 11
Jokes, 12, 65, 66
Jones, Daniel, cited, 178, 196

Lallation, 222
Laryngitis, 159
Larynx, 153, 154, 155, 159, 202
Lateral emission, 224
Latin words and phrases, 190–92
Lincoln, Abraham, quoted, 80
Linguo-dentals, 218, 226–27, 240, 241
Lisping, 200, 224, 225, 226
Lloyd George, Lady Megan, quoted, 65
Logic, 80–81, 135, 190
Lungs, the, 154, 159, 161

Memorized speeches, 45, 46
Memory, 21
Microphones, use of, 57–59
Minutes of meetings,
    additions and corrections to, 90, 92–93
    reading and approval of, 92–93, 130
    taken after adjournments, 96
Monologues, 2, 11, 31
Motions,
    appendage, 103
    classes of, 102, 110
    considered by parts, 115–16, 129, 130
    debatable, 98, 100–101, 104–108
    incidental, 100, 102, 110–18
    leave to withdraw, 116–17
    main, 95–96, 100, 102, 103, 106, 117–19
    making of, 90–91, 94–96, 98–101
    objections to considering, 115, 123, 124
    precedence of, 90–91, 97, 100–101, 103, 106–109, 113–14, 117–20
    privileged, 100–102, 107–10, 117, 118
    reconsideration of, 118–19, 120, 123
    renewable, 99–101, 120
    repeal of, 119–20
    required votes for, 98–100
    review, 100, 102, 118–20
    seconding of, 90–91, 94–96, 98–101
    strategic, 104, 106–107, 123–25
    subsidiary, 100, 102–107, 110, 117, 118
    Table of, 100–101

Names, remembering of, 20–21
Names of persons and places, 195–98
Nasal resonance, 171–72
'Nasal twang', 172
Nasality, 171, 172
   see also Assimilation nasality
NG clicks and confusion, 245–49
Nouns, 175, 188, 234, 245

Omitted sounds, 183–84, 228–29
Oral resonance, 172–73
Orations, 16
Order, parliamentary,
   call to, 92, 96
   motions in, 90, 97
   motions to suspend rules of, 114–15, 132
   points of, 100, 110–12, 123, 125
   rules of, 87–88, 97, 124–25
   standing rules of, 131–33
Orders, parliamentary,
   general, 94, 105
   of the day, 100, 109–11
   special, 94, 105
Organs, speech, 201–202
Over-articulation, 230–31

Palate, the, 153, 171–72, 192, 201–202,
   244, 246–48
Palgrave, Sir Reginald, cited, 87
Panting, 160
Parliamentary procedure,
   definition of, 87
   formal and informal, 121–23
   inquiries concerning, 111, 125
   points of, 97–99, 110–11
   strategy of, 106–107, 123–25
Parties, 1, 7, 12
Pedantry, 177
Personal privilege, questions of, 97, 100,
   106, 109
Personal questions, 8
Personality, 147, 163
Persons, names of, 195–96
Pet words, 18–19, 22
Pharyngeal resonance, 172, 173
Pharynx, the, 173, 202
Phonation,
   breathing and, 160–62
   definition of, 153–54
   faulty, 157–60
   good, 154–57, 168
Phrasing, 148, 175–76
Physical fitness, importance of, 147
Pinched tone, *see* Stridency
Pitch,
   definition of, 148
   huskiness and, 159
   movement of vocal cords and, 154, 162
   training in pitch-level, 159, 162–68, 173
Pitch-level,
   habitual, 163

   optimum, 163–64
   varied, 164–65
Places, names of, 196–97
Platitudes, 66
Posture, 42, 155
Prejudices, 4, 53, 79
Prepositions, 175, 234
Privilege, questions of, 108–10, 117
   see also Personal privileges, questions
   of
Pronouns, 234, 235
Pronunciation,
   acceptable, 177
   aids to better, 188–90, 200
   choice of, 189–90
   common mistakes in, 181–87
   key, 179–81
   see also Foreign words and phrases
Public speaking,
   audience analysis, 50–54, 80–83
   basic concepts of, 38–40
   beginner's faults in, 40–41
   choosing a subject, 47–49
   'extemporaneous' speeches, 46–47
   feeling at ease in, 36–38
   impromptu speeches, 44–46
   memorized speeches, 45, 46
   reading speeches, 45–46
   visual factors in, 41–44
   see also Speeches, composition of

Quality of voice, 148, 154, 168, 170–73
Quibbling, 142
Quorum, definition of, 131
Quotations, use of, 44

Radio, talking on the,
   preparation for, 59
   problems involved in, 57
   speed of (rate), 174
   Standard English used on, 178, 203
   techniques of, 57–59
   use of written speeches on, 45
Rate of talking,
   and phrasing, 175–76
   definition of, 148
   personal, 149, 150, 174
   used on the radio, 174
Reading aloud, 151
Recess, parliamentary, 96, 100, 101, 108,
   130
Regional accents, 177, 178, 201, 232
Regional words, 181
Relaxation, 10, 156, 159
Reports, committee, 93–94
Resonance,
   in foreign pronunciation, 192
   methods of achieving, 154
   nasal, 171–72, 246
   oral, 172
   pharyngeal, 173

Reversing order of sounds, 183
Ribs, the, 161
Rising inflexions, 236–38
Roosevelt, Franklin D., cited, 37

Sales interviews, *see* Interviews
Shouting, 159
Sibilants, 223–26
Sigmatism, 224
Singing, 165
Slang, 2, 19, 22, 27
Sophistry, 78, 80
Speech impediments, 200
Speeches, composition of,
    all-over structure, 84–85
    argument, 78–84
    conclusion, 68–69
    exposition, 74–78
    introduction, 64–68
    main body, 60–64
    narration, 69–74
Spelling pronunciations, 181–82, 184
'Stage fright', 36–37, 45
'Standard English', 178
Stevenson, Adlai, quoted, 65–66, 69
Stevenson, Robert Louis, quoted, 11
Stop consonants, 244–45, 247
Stress, 178, 192, 231, 232–35, 244, 247
Stridency, 157, 159–60, 173
Substitution of sounds, 184–85
Summarizing,
    a group discussion, 145–46
    a speech, 68–69

Taboos in conversation, 2–6, 12, 14–17, 21
Tact, 10, 22, 27
'Talking shop', 5
Tape-recordings, 149
Telephone conversations, 17–18, 32
Television, talking on,
    and use of written speeches, 45
    rate of speech in, 59
    'Standard English' used in, 178, 203
    techniques of, 59
Temperament, 147
Tennyson, Alfred, Lord, quoted, 139

Throat resonance, 173
Timbre, 148
Toasts, proposing of, 54–57
Toning sluggish muscles, 147, 156–57

Uvula, 201, 202, 227

Verbs, 175, 178, 188, 234, 245
Vocabulary, 177
Vocal cords, 153–55, 157–60, 162, 202, 242
Vocal habits, formed in childhood, 147, 150, 199
Voice, developing of,
    basic concepts of, 150–52
    pitch, 148, 154, 159, 162–68, 173, 232
    principles of practice, 147–48
    quality, 148, 154, 168, 170–73
    rate, 148, 150, 174–76
    volume, 148, 154, 159, 168–70, 232
Voice-box, *see* Larynx
Voice mechanism, 152–54, 163
Volume,
    and huskiness, 159
    and resonance, 154, 168
    definition of, 148
    training in, 168–70
Voting procedures, parliamentary, 87, 94, 98–101, 104–105, 107, 112–19, 131
Vowel sounds,
    and diphthongs, 203–204, 210–14, 216, 217, 238–40
    back, 212–13
    central, 213–16
    definition of, 203
    distortions of, 216–18
    extreme, 205–10
    front, 210–11, 244
    low, 211–12
    production of, 205–18, 238
    special role of, in speech, 204

Wilde, Oscar, cited, 12
Wilson, Charles E., cited, 77
Witticisms, 7, 11, 12, 19, 50, 66, 140, 141
Written speeches, 44–46